THE
QUEST

GEORGE GARRISON
THE
QUEST

A CITY BOY'S QUEST AT FULFILLING A LIFE-LONG
DREAM OF BECOMING A GREAT ALASKAN HUNTER

TATE PUBLISHING
AND ENTERPRISES, LLC

The Quest
Copyright © 2015 by George Garrison. All rights reserved.

No part of this publication may be reproduced, stored in a retrieval system or transmitted in any way by any means, electronic, mechanical, photocopy, recording or otherwise without the prior permission of the author except as provided by USA copyright law.

This book is designed to provide accurate and authoritative information with regard to the subject matter covered. This information is given with the understanding that neither the author nor Tate Publishing, LLC is engaged in rendering legal, professional advice. Since the details of your situation are fact dependent, you should additionally seek the services of a competent professional.

The opinions expressed by the author are not necessarily those of Tate Publishing, LLC.

Published by Tate Publishing & Enterprises, LLC
127 E. Trade Center Terrace | Mustang, Oklahoma 73064 USA
1.888.361.9473 | www.tatepublishing.com

Tate Publishing is committed to excellence in the publishing industry. The company reflects the philosophy established by the founders, based on Psalm 68:11,
"The Lord gave the word and great was the company of those who published it."

Book design copyright © 2015 by Tate Publishing, LLC. All rights reserved.
Cover design by Rtor Maghuyop
Interior design by Jomar Ouano

Published in the United States of America

ISBN: 978-1-63449-945-3
1. Nature / Animals / Bears
2. Nature / Animals / Fish
15.05.07

This book is dedicated to the hunters and non-hunters alike. And to everyone and anyone who has, will be or is still sharing the passion to hunt. It goes without saying that in this day and age, the art of this skill and passion is unfortunately becoming extinct. My only hope for the future is that somewhere in all of the mess that is this debate, that reason will prevail and preserve the very thing that allowed for our species to flourish in the first place: hunting!

ACKNOWLEDGMENTS

In preparation of writing this dedication, I compiled a list of worthy credits that have helped and nurtured me along the way. What I thought would be a few names quickly grew to several pages and then some. Then I thought, if I start trying to list everyone, I know that somewhere along the way, I'm going to miss someone, and that would not be good. So to alleviate that from happening, I will just say that if you know me or know of me, thank you, for without all of you, all of this would never have been possible. My inspiration and motivation for writing these stories came from an endless and continuing source of friends, family, and of course, the Last Frontier itself. Most of all, though, my sole inspiration came from my daughter, Olivia, who every day inspires me to become a better man. She is and always has been the most precious thing in my life, and without her wisdom, sarcasm, and just plain goofiness, I'm not sure any of this would have ever been possible. I can't even count the number of times when things got rough that I would think of her and push on through. She is my life, my love, and the heart and soul of why I write these stories. I only hope that someday when I'm long gone that she'll be able to look back and remember how much I love her, hunting, and this incredible country we call home.

Liv and I

CONTENTS

Introduction 11
About the Author 13

1   Forty Below 15
2   911 51
3   DM-426 79
4   DS-138 91
5   Fish On 101
6   Hey, Boo Boo 109
7   The How-To Guide for Hunting Kodiak Brown Bears 121
8   Hunting the Hunter 139
9   It's Not Your Turn! 157
10 The Kings of Kodiak 185
11 Shit Hook 223
12 The Gimme 261
13 The Other Guide to Hunting Black Bears
     in Prince William Sound 285
14 The Real Deal 307
15 Luck of the Draw 319
16 The Hunter 341
17 The Annual 353

Appendix 367

INTRODUCTION

This is an education like no other about hunting, fishing, life in Alaska, and more. An exclusive and real-life journey of what it's like to live in the Last Frontier from a person who was fortunate enough to be given the opportunity to realize how incredibly beautiful Alaska really is. A window into some of the craziest and wildest experiences that can only happen in Alaska. True and honest tales of bravery, courage, stupidity, and more. I hope you will find these stories fascinating as well as educating and entertaining. Hope you enjoy.

ABOUT THE AUTHOR

George F. Garrison III was born and raised in Miami, Florida. In 1978 he followed his father to Seattle where he later joined the air force at age seventeen and spent the next twenty years serving his country. George, an Alaskan resident and hunter since 1995, retired from the air force in 1998 and has been with the FAA ever since. His last trip to Africa in 2008 yielded him two red hartebeest, A Kudu, Gemsbok, springbok, common blesbok, white blesbok, warthog and a Zebra. He has taken or helped take every species of animal in Alaska, except for the elusive wolverine and mountain goat and currently holds two Boone and Crocket records for a Kodiak brown bear and dall sheep. He has been hunting Prince William Sound for the last ten years and has taken or helped take more than thirty bears from that area.

1

FORTY BELOW

When I opened the case, all I could see was the outline of a bow, covered in snow and ice! I knocked the ice off best I could and made my way back over to James, who was glassing the lead bull.

"Crawl up to them slowly, and they probably won't charge," James said, smirking the whole time. "If they charge, stand up fast and shoot if you can!"

"Thanks, James, that's good information," I said as I started my belly crawl on top of the frozen tundra toward the herd.

Between 1935 and 1936, thirty-one musk ox (*Ovibos moschatus*) were transplanted from Greenland to Nunivak Island to reestablish musk ox in their former range—the northern slope of Alaska. Since then, the herd has flourished and almost outnumbered the small community of the island. In the past, commercial fishing was the only source of income and food for the people of Nunivak. Today, however, musk ox hunting has offset the decline in fishing and has become a major source of income and food for many there.

Each year, the Alaska Department of Fish and Game opens the drawing hunt to both residents as well as nonresident hunters. Besides being able to hunt one of the rarest animals on the planet, the best part about the hunt perhaps is that you can do it using a rifle or a bow. If you're like me and become one of the lucky few who draw a tag, the options on how to hunt it are limited. You can either go with a local and experienced guide or hope for the best and do it yourself. Because the hunting months are January through March, the extreme weather conditions make it an incredibly tough hunt. With an average temperature of ten below and wind speeds that can reach more than one hundred knots, you better be prepared for everything on this one. I personally suggest hiring one because they know the island, have all of the equipment, and know how to find the herds. I have talked with several individuals who did the DIY (do-it-yourself) hunt and ended up either broke, empty-handed, or both; one even had to be rescued.

They had to ship in all their gear to include snow machines, food, water, equipment, and then pitch a tent in the middle of nowhere and try not to freeze to death for the duration of the hunt. My plan was to fly from Anchorage to Bethel, a small town and major air hub for all traffic coming in and out of what's known as the Kuskokwim Delta. Encompassing most of the southwest side of Alaska, the Kuskokwim Delta is home to hundreds of villages and thousands of people. Because no major air carriers fly to Nunivak Island itself, I would need to charter a smaller bush plane in Bethel to fly into Mekoryuk, the main village on Nunivak Island. After hearing all of the war stories of previous hunts, I opted for hiring a local master guide by the name of James Whitman. He was born, raised, and lived in Mekoryuk, so it was kind of a no-brainer. From there we would use his house as a base camp for the hunt and use snow machines and pack sleds for transportation around the Island. I had arranged everything months in advance, so all I needed to do now was practice shooting my bow. I would be bringing a rifle just in case; however, I really wanted to do this one with my bow. I practiced for weeks before the hunt, gearing up in the huge RefrigiWear parka and pants, gloves, baklava, and ski mask. My first shot with the parka was nothing short of a disaster as the string ripped through the sleeve and sent the arrow sailing into oblivion. I lost four arrows that day but learned a lot about what duct tape could fix. By the end of the third week, I was shooting pretty well and was more than ready to go. Between the 110-grain slick-trick broad-heads and my blue Diamond Atomic compound bow pushing just over three hundred feet per second), all I needed now was a nice, big bull in front of me.

I arrived in Bethel about midnight on February 17 only to be greeted by one of the largest snowstorms of the winter. The pilot of the 737 had to go around twice because the wind had blown us off the centerline the first time, and he couldn't see the runway on the second. All I could think about was getting on the ground when the plane finally slammed down on the runway and slid to a stop.

"Ladies and gentlemen, welcome to Bethel," the pilot said in a nervously shaken tone. "The outside temperature is a balmy thirty-five below, so don't forget your sunscreen!"

Everyone was yelling and whistling as we taxied up to the terminal. This was my first time here, so after picking up my gear, I headed for the taxis. I knew it was blowing pretty bad outside but didn't realize how bad until the ice-covered automatic doors popped open and the wind about blew me over. I was wearing a parka designed for temperatures of minus fifty, but the cold ripped through it like I was wearing a T-shirt!

Holy mother of, I remember thinking as I struggled to stop shivering. The air felt like I was inhaling pepper as it was now burning the back of my throat. I had never felt cold like this, and it was terrifying to think that I would soon be hunting in it. The cab pulled up, I grabbed my gear, and off we went into the cold, dark night. In the distance I could see the rest of Bethel through the occasional snow drift. To my surprise, I thought it would be bigger, but it wasn't. We had just passed what appeared to be a body in the snow when I asked the driver if he had seen that.

He cocked his head back a bit and said in a deep Russian accent, "Dat is Thomas. He's always like dat!" I kept looking back as the driver headed toward town. Then he said, "I vill come back lader to get heem."

"Later?" I asked. *He'll probably be dead later*, I thought as the car just then started to slow down. I thought at first that he was going to go back when I realized he was stopping to pick up more people along the side of the road. There were two men and two ladies who all piled in, and we were off again.

Unfortunately, the way the cab was positioned when we stopped allowed the snow to blow straight into the cab when the door was opened, and we were all now covered in the fresh, frosty white stuff.

Awesome, I thought as we again made our way toward the town. Next thing I know, the cab was slowing down again, and to my surprise, we picked up two more people who were going to a bingo game. With seven snow-covered people in a 1970 Caprice Classic, we were now hobbling down the snow-packed road toward the town. There were people sitting on top of people who were sitting on top of people, who were sitting on me! Moments later we arrived at the bingo hall and dropped the one couple off.

Thank God, I thought as I scooted back over to where I was originally sitting. Then, out of the bingo hall came four more people who were all now eyeing up the cab.

Oh no, I thought, *no way all of these folks are getting in here.*

Fifteen minutes and a lot shoving later, we had five people in the back, four in the front, and one guy in the trunk, who was holding on to all of the luggage. We were already in town, and I thought I would be the next to be dropped off; however, the four that we had just picked up needed to get to the airport or they would miss their flight; so back to the airport we went. We passed Thomas again, who looked to me as if he were dead, but Alex (the cabby) said he was fine. We dropped the folks at the airport, went back, and dug Thomas out of the snow, threw him in the backseat, and made it to the hotel about 3:00 a.m. What a night!

The morning came way too early; however, the storm had broken overnight, so the weather would be perfect for getting into Nunivak. About an hour airtime from Bethel, Nunivak was due west over some of the most barren, desolate, and inhospitable terrain in Alaska. In the summer, most of it was water-covered tundra; however, in the winter, it was nothing but a sea of snow and ice that stretched forever. Bethel airport was nothing more than a small cluster of old hangars, which, funny enough, had a really popular pizza joint: Brother's Pizza & Subs. With a runway surface of just over 3,818 feet, about 3,000 in the winter, it's a general aviation mecca. I was flying out with a locally owned and operated outfit with a good history in this region, Grant Aviation. They operated a small fleet of four Cessna 208 Caravans, two Piper Chieftains, and a Cessna 207 Skywagon. With the hangar located almost on the runway, they had a small waiting area, which had restrooms, vending machines, and even heat! With a maximum capacity of about fifty people, it was small, cozy, and quaint.

We got the preboarding call about eight thirty, so about six others and myself lined up at the small steel door that led out to the ice-blown tarmac. It was about 9:00 a.m. when we all started to cram ourselves into what a lot of people out here call the "bush taxi," a single-engine turbo-prop airplane known to all in Alaska as the "van." Nothing more than a stretched-out Cessna 210 with a huge cargo hold on the belly, the Cessna Grand Caravan is the workhorse of the Alaskan bush. With a seating capacity of about twelve normal-sized people, it was a formidable and stable aircraft with good range and a proven history of service and safety. I checked the one fifty-pound duffel bag, my bow, and a small daypack—which came to a total of seventy-eight pounds.

The girl behind the counter said something in Yupik to her friend, then looked back, at me and said, "We'll be boarding in just a minute, Mr. Garrison. Please make sure you have *all* your cold-weather gear on when you get on the plane."

It didn't hit me until I was walking away from the counter; however, it was then that I realized why she had said what she had just said. If we crashed, the chances of survival were slim to none to begin with. If we survived the crash, though, our chances were higher if we were suited up for the weather. Made sense to me. Suiting up, I watched the pilot do a short walk around, throw some more bags in the back, and then wave to the people inside to send the passengers out. It was about twenty-five below with a wind chill of about forty, so after an extended engine warm-up run, we taxied out to the end of the runway. A few more radio calls to the tower and a quick check out the fogged-up windows for other aircraft and we were blasting down the ice- and snow-covered runway, lifting off just short of the fence at the end. I could still see my breath, which was now fogging up the window, and as I looked down along a frozen river, I spotted a couple of moose running along. We were finally on our way, and as I sank back into the cold, torn fabric of the seat, I started drifting off to sleep. I was just about out when I heard the pilot throttle back. The plane was banking to the right, and after scraping the ice off the window, I could see what seemed to be a road in the distance. The pilot leveled off, hit the flaps, and next thing I know, we were rolling down the middle of the road, which was now the runway. There were a bunch of people on snow machines all towing sleds to meet us, and after the pilot killed the engine, we off-loaded and uploaded a bunch of gear and picked up two more people. No sooner than the doors were closed when the pilot cranked the engine, and we began taxiing down the road. The road/runway was nothing but ice, and when we got to the end, the pilot struggled to maintain control as we slowly slid toward the end. He spun the nose around and crammed the throttle full forward, and we were once again bouncing and jumping down the road. We lifted off and caught a gust of wind that almost pushed us into a small microwave tower, but the pilot leveled out real quick and recovered it.

Funny part was the look on his face when he looked back to see if any of us had noticed it. I could see the sweat on his brow as he pulled the stick back a little more. We had one more stop, and then we would be in Nunivak. A few minutes later, we again landed in the middle of nowhere, and again were greeted by people on snow machines.

Where were the buildings and houses? I thought as I struggled to look out the iced-up windows. No sooner than we had landed when we were in the air again and heading over the last piece of land on the west coast of the Alaskan peninsula. I could see the water now as I peered through a small hole in the icy window. We were over the strait of Etolin, the last bit of water between the mainland of Alaska and the island of Nunivak. There was nothing but large chunks of broken ice surrounded by an endless amount of ocean. The pilot had made sure to gain altitude before crossing the strait, for it would be fatal if we had an engine fail and were too low to glide to land. In the unfortunate event that you did go down out here, the mere fact that you probably wouldn't survive the crash was bad enough. Then factor in that the water is just above freezing and that there weren't any rescue crews for hours, and you basically have a recipe for death. The best a person could do if they survived the crash would be to say a prayer before expiring completely.

A few minutes later, the pilot pulled the throttle back and pointed out the front window. I could hear he was saying, "That's Nunivak," but still I couldn't see anything. We circled over the spot we would be landing and made a tactical assent that was nothing short of horrifying. We landed and slid the rest of the way down the ice-covered road.

I couldn't see anything out the iced-up windows but as soon as the pilot killed the engine, I could hear the voices of people and could see their silhouettes. Next thing I know, the doors were all flying open, and there must be twenty people on the ground, all grabbing whatever they could.

The pilot looked back and said, "Birds!"

There was a whole flock of ravens at the end of the runway, so I had to bank her hard. "Sorry about that!" I pried my hand from the flimsy plastic handle by the door and made my way to the back of the plane. I had just about made it to the end of the wing when I heard "Clear," a signal that the pilot was going to be starting the engine.

I turned back to look at the pilot when something in a really large parka grabbed me and pulled me away from the wingtip. He cranked her up, turned her around, and blasted back into the sky. In all of the confusion, I didn't realize that I was the only person left on the airstrip. All I could see now was the plane lifting into the air, the back of a few snow machines, and what appeared to be a small village about a mile away. Not sure what I was thinking, but I tried calling James on my cell, which gave me the dreaded "extended service area, no coverage" message. Only thing that would work out here was a sat phone (satellite phone), and I didn't have one. I grabbed all my gear and started heading down the ice road where the snow machines had just gone down. It was probably twenty below; however, with the sun being out and no wind, it didn't feel too bad, especially while carrying about sixty-five pounds of gear.

After about ten minutes I decided to make a sled out of my bow case and with a piece of 550 nylon cord and started dragging my gear down the road. I could make out the town now and could hear the sound of snow machines but still couldn't see them. Off in the distance I spotted a fox that seemed to be following me. It was huge, and at first glance, I thought it may be a wolf. Then another popped up, followed by another. I stopped to take a picture when I realized that they were everywhere. There must have been twenty of them all around me. Then it hit me, can foxes kill a human? Has that ever happened? This was weird I thought as I started looking for something to throw at them. They were starting to get really close when I snapped open the latches on my bow case.

Any closer and I'm bringing back some fox hides, I thought. I had seen foxes before, but not this aggressive. They were coming in and coming fast. Next thing I know, it was like someone dropped a bomb as they scattered into the snow. The snow machines I had heard a few minutes earlier had arrived to pick me up and scared the foxes away. It was my guide James Whitman and his cousin Theo. He thought I was coming in tomorrow until a friend of his said he had seen me at the airstrip.

"Did you see those foxes?" I asked?

James and Theo just looked at me like I was a tourist or something.

James smiled and said, "Those are our pets. They're everywhere!"

We loaded up on the snow machines and blasted down the road to the house, which would be our base camp for the next five days.

Contrary to popular belief, the natives don't really live in igloos, although I have seen them build some pretty nice ones. James's house was a regular three-bedroom, one-bath, single-family house located on the edge of town. With an incredible view of the ocean from the front porch and rolling tundra from the back porch, it was a welcomed site. It was about 1,400 square feet with a nice living room, dining room, and kitchen. With hot and cold running water (in the summer), it had all the comforts of home to include an oil-burning stove and even TV, which unfortunately only had one channel but worked.

After a short tour of the house which actually had an inside toilet, we decided to take a run through town on the snow machine's. In Alaska, people call snow machine's sleds, and an actual sled, which is normally towed behind a sled (snow machine), is called a pack sled, so everyone knows what you mean. James had a few lying around the yard, so we fired one up and rode into town. We stopped by his other cousin's house, which was right on a bluff and looked as though the waves had washed up over it. Then we stopped by the post office, general store, and gym. The whole time we were riding around, I couldn't help notice the number of dog tracks that covered every inch of snow in town. They were everywhere and blanketed every inch imaginable.

"Do you guys breed dogs here?" I asked.

James looked back at me like the *chechako* (new guy) I was and said, "Damn foxes! We have a small fox problem here. They're like rats!"

Wow, I thought as we rode back to the house, *that's a lot of foxes!*

It was midafternoon when we got back to the cozy confines of the house, and after a quick warm-up, James asked if I'd like to go shooting.

"Does a bear poop in the woods?" I replied.

We suited up and fired off the machines. It was about forty below, so after half an hour of gearing up, I was trying to figure out how I was going to shoot a rifle. I tried shouldering his marlin, but it kept getting stuck in the folds of my parka. Between the face mask, muffs, hat, and parka hood, I could barely move yet shoot a rifle; this was going to be interesting, I thought as I slung the rifle over my shoulder and rode off into the white!

No sooner did we come around the first snowbank when I saw two foxes running. The wind was blowing pretty good, and when I finally shot, the rounds went everywhere. The foxes just looked back as if they had done this before and disappeared into the snow. A few minutes later, we were riding along the coast and spotted a few more. They were a long way out, and as I laid the rifle across the seat of the snow machine, I struggled to find the fox in the sights. Seconds later I had him in the crosshairs and let one rip.

Snap!

The round toppled him like a Mack Truck. I put the sights on the second one and pulled the trigger once more. Again the fox rolled up into a ball and was down. We rode up on them, shut the sleds down, and I picked up two of the biggest foxes I had ever seen. They were as large as most wolves I had seen and absolutely beautiful. Thick, furry red tails with amazing red and black coats.

James looked over at me with a weird kind of smile and said, "Not bad, now we just need to take another 998 to even the herd out!"

We got back to the house just before dark and just in time to have some home-cooked musk ox stew. To my surprise, it was awesome, and as I went back for a second and third, I couldn't help thinking that the only thing missing was a nice, cold beer. Unfortunately, like many bush towns in Alaska, Mekoryuk was dry—bone dry!

It was about 10:00 a.m. when I heard the knock at the door. At first, I had forgotten where I was, which is always scary until James said, "Hey, do you want to go hunting?"

The sun was just coming up, and as I rolled out of the bed and made my way into the living room, Theo greeted me with a hot cup of freshly brewed coffee.

This is the life, I thought as I sank into the warm, toasty couch sipping the hot, robust brew.

"It's warmed up," James said as he listened to the CB for the weather report. "It's only twenty-five below, good time to go!"

"Awesome, James, that's awesome," I said, wondering what the hell I was doing out here. "I'm ready, James, let's gear up and giddy up," I said in my usual sarcastic tone.

The whole time I was thinking about just finishing the coffee and crawling back into my nice, warm bunk. But, as fate would have it, we finished off an amazing breakfast of eggs, bacon, toast, and a lot more coffee and began the arduous task of getting ready for the long ride. According to James, who was a master guide, we could be gone a few hours or a few days, depending on where the herd was. On the average, we were looking at least a twenty-mile ride, so we would need to be prepared—really prepared. It was at least twenty-five below with a wind-chill factor of about forty below, so dying out here was more than a real possibility; it was a reality!

It was about 11:00 a.m. when we rode out of town into the endless expanse of barren white wilderness. The terrain was as white and flat as flat could get, surrounded by more white and flatness. We picked up a small, frozen river just outside town and followed through a maze of switchbacks until it finally dumped out into a clearing just shy of the steep cliffs that dropped off into the open frozen sea. We chased foxes it seemed the whole way out; then they just disappeared. James stood up on his machine and glassed the coastline looking for sign of tracks and animals as I snapped pictures of the incredibly frozen coastline.

"We need to get up on that hill," he said, pointing to a small hill about five miles away and inland. He took off as I followed playing in the fresh powder and snow berms. I took advantage of the small snow drifts and did some jumps here and there as we made our way farther into the blinding white of the tundra. We made it to the base of the hill pretty quick and had just rounded the western side of the hill when James stood up and gave me the stop signal. I hit the brakes and almost flew over the front when I realized what he was looking at. He signaled for me to come up slowly so I throttled up to where his sled was and shut it down. As I peeked over the edge of the berm, I spotted a small herd of about twenty animals. I think in all of my hunting days, it was the coolest thing I had ever seen. Here in front of me were remnants of an ancient animal species matched only by the bison itself. A living breathing specimen in its own element untouched by man, machine or time. Raw, pure, and about thirty yards in front of me now, I was staring down the nose of the biggest bull musk ox I had ever seen! James was pointing to the one I was already looking at and gave me the thumbs-up. Unfortunately, when I returned to the pack sled to open the bow case, one of the latches was halfway open, allowing snow to be shot into it by the track on the sled. When I opened the case, all I could see was the outline of a bow covered in snow and ice! I knocked the ice off best I could and made my way back over to James, who was glassing the lead bull.

"Crawl up slowly to them, and they probably won't charge," he said kind of smirking the whole time. "If they charge, stand up fast and shoot—if you can!"

"Thanks, James, that's good information," I said as I started my belly crawl toward the herd. I used a really small snow drift that paralleled the herd to hide behind and slowly inched my way toward the herd on my belly. I was in shooting range now and finally realized why they call them musk ox; the stench was overwhelming. The good news I guess was that I was definitely downwind! I peeked up over the berm to try and spot the lead bull when a bull on the end busted me.

Like herd animals do, they immediately surrounded the alpha male, forming an impenetrable wall of meat! To my amazement though, the herd just stayed there and wasn't moving at all. The moments clicked by as my body grew tired and cold lying in the snow.

I needed to do something, or this could go on forever, I thought.

I looked back to where I had left James but couldn't see him. Then, just like that a lone bull started walking my way. I was lying there motionless when he got to me in an arm's length. I was looking right at him as he snorted and clawed at the ground. We were eye to eye, but I was pretty sure he still didn't know what I was, or he would have stomped me by now. Regardless, it was too late to stand up now, or I would probably be going for a musk ox ride, so I lay there with an arrow knocked, awaiting his next move. He grunted and stomped at the snow a few more times and then backed up into the herd.

Whew, that was close, I remember thinking as my now-frozen body began to shiver. All I knew at that moment was that I needed to get up, or I was going to freeze to death. I rose from the berm, raised my bow, and struggled to get to my feet. You could hear the ice cracking off of me as I now stood ready to draw. I could now see the bull I was after, which unfortunately was smack-dab in the middle. I thought that if I could just get around this one bull, I might have a shot, so I began walking to the right of the herd. They were all pretty nervous and started to spook and turn.

I was losing the main bull now, and just like that, the whole herd broke into a run and was gone. I stood there completely iced up with at least a twenty miles per hour wind freezing every hair on my face, thinking, *This is going to be a tough hunt.* I watched them run until they disappeared into what almost looked like a mirage. James called it temperature inversion; I called it a lot of other things!

After cracking open a bunch of hand warmers and stuffing them in my shirt, we were off again, chasing the herd we had just lost.

A few hours later, we spotted another herd and made our way toward them. James thought he spotted a monster and was anxious to get a closer look. Problem was, we were in wide, open country with nothing but snow to hide behind. I was wearing a white parka, which helped, but it was still going to be tough. We got up to about one hundred yards from the herd when they took off running. We followed them about another mile and again got to within one hundred yards, but this time, they just herded up and encircled the lead bull.

James said I should try again but this time just walk real slow until I get into shooting range, and then take a shot. I grabbed my bow and started for the herd, while James stayed back. I was only about seventy-five yards out at first, but it took almost an hour for me to get within fifty yards when the herd spooked again. Bad part was, the herd and I were now playing a game of really cold cat and mouse! I would move a little, and they would move a little. After about an hour of this, I finally threw in the towel and started running straight for the lead bull. I think they were probably as frustrated and surprised as I was, for I closed the fifty-yard gap pretty darned fast. Before I realized how fast, I had passed two animals and now was looking at the main bull right in the eye! At full draw, I was running as fast as I could while trying to keep the bull I was after in my sights—not an easy task standing still no less on the run.

Out of the corners of my eyes I could smell and see animals fleeing in all directions as I made my way into the mass of the herd. He was right in front of me now, and as my finger began to squeeze the trigger on my release, I stopped, put him in my sights, and let the arrow fly! At just over forty yards, I watched as the bull turned, and the arrow sailed along his left side and vanished into the snow. As if someone out here was going to hear me, I screamed as loud as I could in disgust as I watched that behemoth animal just walk away with the rest of the herd. He ran a little, turned back toward me, and shook his mane as if to say, "Ha! You missed!" It was as if he knew how close I came to taking him and was now taunting me. I knocked another arrow, put the fifty-yard pin on his chest, and sent it whistling through the thick, frozen air.

As if in slow motion, I watched as the arrow left the rest flying straight and true toward the now-broadside bull. The shot felt good, and I was feeling pretty confident it would connect as I watched the arrow's neon-green fletchings disappear in front of me. Then as if the arrow was powered by a rocket that just ran out of fuel, it dropped straight down and went right under his chest. It was so close that he bucked as if being hit but then ran off with the rest of the herd. I had missed again, and the herd was gone. James said he thought that I had hit him good and watched the bull buck, but he never dropped. We scoured the area for blood and my arrow but never found anything so decided to start heading back. I was cold, tired, and frustrated, but in all, it had turned out to be a fairly good day. After all, we had found two herds of oxen, which was hard enough, then had made several stalks, so not a bad day of hunting by anyone's standard. And besides, we still had four days to hunt, and the weather was supposed to get better, or at least warmer.

We huddled up for a quick cup of hot cocoa before starting back where James told me about how arrows reach a drop-off point when they're cold. The colder it is, the higher the drop-off ratio. Who knew! I had practiced a lot in Anchorage before coming, but the temperatures here were more extreme. In full gear and on an outdoor range, I was flinging at least thirty arrows a day for the last two weeks in temperatures averaging ten to fifteen above. I had made a few sight adjustments to compensate for the cold, however, not for the cold we were in on Nunivak. The difference between fifteen above and thirty below makes a huge difference, and I was finding out the hard way!

It was starting to get late, so we fired up the sleds again and started riding back. James was towing a pack sled for the ox to go in if we got one, but my sled was clean, and I couldn't stand the opportunity to carve some pow (play in the snow) at every chance I got. The snow was perfect, and as I gunned the throttle, the power of the Ski-Doo Summit 700 surprised even me. I was having a blast and tearing it up when out of nowhere I hit a hidden berm that launched the nose straight up. All I could see was sky as the sled just kept going. In an attempt to hold on, my throttle hand and finger jammed the throttle, and it rocketed straight up and over the berm and into the air. I don't remember much after that except the sled and I coming down pretty hard and me eating a lot of white stuff. I picked myself up, dusted the snow off, and stumbled over to where the sled was now lying on its side.

Holy crap, did that just happen? I thought, standing now over the battered sled. I was straining to right it when I realized that James was nowhere to be found. The horror of the moment hit me like a ton of bricks when I realized that I was now completely alone on an ice-covered island and had no idea which way to go. I righted the sled and tried to pull start it, but it wouldn't fire off. I pulled and pulled until breaking into a sweat. I ripped my hat and parka off and pulled the start cord over and over until I couldn't breathe anymore. My sweat was freezing as fast as I could produce it, and after a few moments, I couldn't even see, for the sweat was freezing my eyelids shut. I scraped my face clean and tried cranking the sled again. This time it fired off and slowly sputtered like it was going to quit. The seconds seem to stand still as I listened to it sputter and spit until it finally kicked in. I threw on my hat and parka again and tried following the tracks that James had left. It was my only chance on finding him, so if I lost them, I lost him, and if I lost him, I was pretty much dead! The wind had unfortunately picked up again and was blowing pretty good as I now struggled to find James's tracks. Forced to go slow now, I was loosing his tracks at an alarming rate.

I tried not thinking about dying out here, but as the wind picked up, I lost all visual references and was now in the middle of a total whiteout. I was completely iced up and could barely see out from my ice-covered glasses. The wind and snow were now blowing sideways, and as I continuously wiped the snow from my glasses, I realized that if I didn't find James real soon, I would probably be dead in a few hours. Not sure why, but a weird sense of calm came over me as I sat there pondering which way to go.

Then I thought about how they always find hypothermia victims: naked and frozen. That would be pretty embarrassing I thought, sitting out in the middle of the frozen tundra. Bad enough dying, but I don't want to be found naked. I guess the last thing that happens to you is you get really hot like you're on fire and start stripping off clothes.

That would suck, I thought as I tried warming my hands on the sled's exhaust.

Then another fun fact hit me. Holding my hands over the exhaust, my eye caught the reading on the fuel tank, which was showing less than one fourth tank of gas.

Perfect, I thought as the smell of my burning glove now made its way to my frozen nostril, *that's just perfect*. I was staring the end pretty much in the face, contemplating my last few options when in the distance I saw a flickering light. At first it looked like someone with a flashlight; then I realized it's somebody on a sled! I gunned the throttle and shot over to where the light was only to find James now sitting and looking at me like I was crazy.

"Where in the heck did you go?" he asked in a puzzled and slightly angry tone.

"Yeah, well, James, I had a little mishap back there. Let's get back to the house, and I'll tell you all about it."

To my surprise, the village was only about five miles away, and as we rode in along the coast in the dark, the foxes were again out in full force. They were shooting in and out of every nook and cranny, and at one point, I was pretty sure I had run one over. We pulled up to the front of the house, shut the sleds down, and crawled up the snow-packed stairs and into the house's entry foyer. I was completely frozen and could barely see as I tried to unzip my parka. The zipper was frozen and covered in ice. I picked up an old knife on the cutting table and, not thinking straight, stabbed at it to chip the ice. With everything I had, I tugged at the zipper splitting ice the whole way down. Where I wasn't covered in ice, I was covered in sweat, and as I made my way into the hot living room in my sweat-soaked long johns, I thought I was going to pass out. It felt as though I had run a one-thousand-mile marathon in one of those rubber sumo-wrestling suits. Every inch of my body, including my brain, was numb. I shuffled my way over to the small-oil burning stove and lay down next to it. Next thing I know, James's dog Kaka is sitting on my chest looking at me much like James was when he found me. A mutt by birth, Kaka was a little white-and-brown ball of furry love and James's constant companion. I lay there for almost two hours while my body thawed, thinking to myself, *It's good to be alive; it's good to be alive.*

The next day we awoke to clear blue skies and temperatures in the thirties—thirty below! The sunrise was spectacular as I watched the sky turn blue and white, then orange and red, then yellow, and then blue again. As soon as the sun was full up, it started warming up quick, so after a quick breakfast, lots of coffee, and another gearing up session, we fired the sleds off again and made our way back onto the cold, icy tundra. We shot up the road toward the airstrip and past the corral where they harvest reindeer in the spring. We made our way along the shore again then straight out into the endless, flat white terrain.

It was a beautiful day, and as we zigzagged across the soft, powdery snow looking for a herd or sign, I couldn't help but ponder the events of the previous day. I almost died out here, and as we made our way farther and farther back into it, I couldn't shake the idea of going through that again—ever again! We had been riding about an hour now when I spotted a small herd on top of a small hill. Because we were upwind, we would have to ride around and come at them from the opposite side, which, according to James, was a lot steeper. From where I was sitting, the hill looked pretty small, but James knew better. In minutes we were sidehilling on the back side of the hill. James's was right: The hill was steep. I was hanging off the right side of the sled trying not to roll over when the herd came around the hill. I hit the kill button and coasted to a stop about seventy yards from the herd. James was right in back of me and quickly crawled up to where I now was lying in the snow.

"Looks like there's a good bull right there," he said, pointing to one of the big brown things in front of us.

"Which one, James?" I asked.

"See the one with the horns?"

And not thinking, I asked, "Where?" As I turned to see which one he was talking about, he was lying there with the biggest grin on his face I had ever seen, trying his best not to bust out completely. "Good one, James," I said. "Good one!"

He then pointed to really nice bull who was just stepping out past the back of the herd. "That's him," he whispered. "That's a good one!"

I pulled my bow out of the case again, knocked an arrow (attached it to the string), and slowly crawled through the waist-high snow on the steepest hill on Nunivak Island. He was a big, old bull and now standing just shy of forty yards straight in front of me. As I slowly pulled my legs up to get into a kneeling position, the bull spooked, and the whole herd started to slowly walk away. I stood up, came to full draw, and put my forty pin of my sight dead on his chest. I could see nothing but his silhouette and was a nanosecond from releasing when another bull stepped in front of him. I pulled my finger off the trigger as the whole herd started moving again. The bow wrenched my shoulder as I let off of draw.

Dammit, I thought as I followed the herd around the hill. They stopped again about another forty yards out, and I again slowly and painstakingly made my way toward them. Moments later, I found the bull again and went to full draw. This time, he was about thirty yards out and seemed to be looking straight at me. They have the strangest eye's I've ever seen, and you can't really tell if they're looking at you or something else entirely. As soon as I came to full draw and put the thirty pin on him, he turned straight at me and just stood there staring. I thought for sure this was the quiet before the storm, but he wasn't charging. He just stood there for what seemed like forever when I started shaking. My breath was now starting to ice up my peep sight, and as I stood there waiting for a shot, he dropped his head and started coming at me. I released the arrow just above his head as my feet took flight. The snap of the string followed by the sound of stampeding animals followed by the taste of fresh snow affirmed that again I was not dead. As I staggered to my feet, I realized I had missed, and the herd had run off again. Guess my feet were in deeper than I thought, for when I started running, I had forgotten that I was in four feet of snow!

For some reason, the herd liked this hill and had only run around to the other side and stopped again. This was getting kind of old, I thought as I made my through the deep, wet snow. Again I was within thirty yards of the bull who was now unfortunately hiding in the middle. I was starting to get tired and cold, so I just started walking toward the herd to see if I could separate them. I came around the bottom side and walked straight up to a bull that was hiding the one I wanted when he got mad and did a false charge.

I was starting to figure these guys out and just threw my arms up and scared him back. The bull I was after was now in sight again, and as I drew back again, I put his big, brown ice-covered chest in my thirty-yard pin. I let the arrow go and watched as the green fletchings of the arrow disappeared right over his back. Completely in shock as to what just happened, I hesitated for a split second as the herd again made its way farther around the hill. We were on the windy side again, and as I struggled to knock another arrow, the herd started down the hill. I gave chase and within moments was again looking my bull dead in the eyes. I put the forty-yard pin on him and let it fly. This time I failed to account for the fifty-knot crosswind and watched as the arrow left the rest at a forty-five-degree angle and vanished into oblivion.

This time the bull didn't even flinch and just looked at me as if to say, "You suck!" The whole herd was just standing there as I now contemplated running after the bull and just sticking one in him! The funny thing was, I had now chased the herd completely around the hill, and as I looked at my back, I saw James just looking at me again, like I was crazy. I made my way up to where he was, threw my frozen bow in his pack sled, pulled out my Marlin .457 Magnum, chambered a round, and made my way back down the hill and toward the herd. This time I was loaded for bear and not playing around.

As if they knew I was now packing a rifle, they herded up hiding the bull and then just sat there. It was a standoff now, and as the wind blew straight into my parka and down the back of my neck, I put the big guy in my sights. He was about one hundred yards out and downhill a bit, but this HSM 450 grain Magnum bear-bonded slug didn't care where he was. The only thing I was sure of at this point was one way or another, this slug was going to find him. The only way this bull was getting off this hill was in the back of James's sled. I pulled the trigger back, took it off safety, and put him in the crosshairs of my Leupold 1× scope. All I needed now was for the one right in front and back of him to move. I sat in the snow with just the muzzle sticking out of the top when a bull on the end started moving.

This is it, I thought as I put my frozen gloved finger onto the trigger. The one in front had moved away but was followed by another. Then the back was clear, but front was not. What seemed like forever was now turning into a long, cold waiting game. And then just like that, he was in the open. I squeezed off the round, which blew snow up and all over me because of the muzzle break. I couldn't see anything for a minute and could hear the herd running when I stood up. I quickly cycled another round, stood up, but didn't see anything on the ground and was now unsure of which bull was which. I raised the rifle again and tried finding the lead bull when the herd took off running. They were running pretty good now and had disappeared around the other side of the hill when I realized there was one kind of straggling behind.

That's weird, I thought as I raised my rifle to get a better look. He was just standing there like a statue when I realized he was the bull I was after. I put my finger on the trigger again and started to squeeze off another shot when I watched his back end drop out from under him. I watched through the scope as the rest of his massive body fell, sending a plume of snow into the air. It made the same sound Grandma used to make when smacking the living room rug with a broom—just ten times louder!

From in back of me now, I could hear I heard James yelling something in Yupik. Then in English, I could hear him saying, "You got him, you got him!"

I had made an incredible shot on the bull and had hit him square in the heart and lungs; he was dead upon impact but just didn't know it.

We grabbed the sleds and ran down the hill to where he lay to find the biggest, hairiest animal I had ever seen. He was a massive bull with beautiful cylindrical horns that turned white at the tips. The smile on James's face pretty much said it all, I think. He was more excited than me, I think, and couldn't stop talking about how big it was. After a bunch of pictures and a hot cocoa toast later, we decided to load the bull into his pack sled and take it over to the leeward side of the hill to cut it up. The wind was picking up now and blowing snow right in our faces. Using the slope of the hill, we positioned the pack sled so we could roll the beast into it. Even then, I couldn't believe how hard it was. I had sliced and diced moose on numerous occasions, but this was by far a lot harder. We got him into the sled, and James started pulling away when the sled overturned and dumped the bull right back into the snow. We positioned the sled again and rolled him back in but couldn't get his legs all the way in. James was yelling and pointing to the other side of the hill, but with the wind and all the gear I had on, I couldn't hear him. I just shook my head and followed him on my sled. It was like someone had turned the wind switch off when we got on the other side. It was still cold but not as cold as it was out in that darned wind. We rolled the beast off the sled, broke out a lot of tools, and began the arduous task of butchering the beast. It had only taken us about thirty minutes to get to where we were on the hill; however, as I began making my first cut, I was startled to find that the flesh was already frozen. There was no blood, guts, nothing. Everything was as hard as a rock, and it was like cutting up a really tough steak. It took us almost three hours of nonstop

cutting, but the beast was finally done and in the back of James's pack sled.

The good news was we had a fairly short ride back to the house, so after we gathered up the rest of the knives, saws, and hatchets, we fired up the sleds once more and headed back into the freezing wind. I had forgotten how hard it was blowing until we cleared the protection of the hill and got hit by the fifty-knot ice wind. It was like someone was poking at my face with thousands of freezing needles. In minutes my right side was completely iced up, and every so often, I had to make a deliberate movement to crack the chunks off. I was dead on James's tail and moving pretty good when I saw something fly off the pack sled and shoot off into the snow. All I saw was that it was long and white, and as I watched it disappear into the spray coming from James's machine, I flipped my high beams on and off to get his attention. Like me, he had one thing in mind, and that was getting back home. I throttled up to try and catch him when I noticed the sled leaning to one side; it was a skid that had come off, and now the sled was just dragging. I throttled up and came alongside James, pointing to the back. He hesitantly throttled down and came to a stop.

"What's the matter?" James asked.

"I think we lost a skid back there, James," I yelled through my ice-covered baklava.

We made our way back to the sled where James took a quick look, waved his hand as if to say "no big deal," and we were off again. The wind was really blowing now, and as I started to get back on my sled, a gust came up and knocked me right over the seat. Now I was completely iced up and covered in snow as I watched James start to disappear in the distance. I jumped on my sled, hit the throttle, and shot out like a bullet, for this time, I was not going to lose him.

I guess I stayed on the throttle a little longer than needed, for within seconds I had passed him up like he was going backward. I slowed down and waited for him to catch up knowing the whole time that he was just sitting there thinking, *What is this dummy doing now?*

As we made our way across the frozen tundra, I thought about the people like me who never get the opportunity to get to know the real Alaskan people, the people of this Last Frontier. I had been in Alaska almost fifteen years and before this trip had never personally known or spent any real time with the locals. For me, this was more than just a musk ox hunt. This was a virtual window into a culture like no other, and I was honored to be privileged and lucky enough to be experiencing it. Then I began thinking about how it must have been out here before the airplane and the iron dog (the snow machine). Unless the ice was completely frozen, they would have been completely cut off from the mainland. If lucky and the ice was thick, they might be able to make it to another village or Bethel in about a week. I thought about the box of fruit and vegetables I had brought in after hearing how hard they were to come by out here. A few locals at the airstrip who had helped me unload my gear had seen the box, and within minutes of arriving at James's house, one person after another was showing up to share in the bounty. Before I knew it, the whole house was full of people holding heads of lettuce, tomatoes, and other assorted fruits and vegetables. The best part of all was watching how happy and grateful they were to just have one tomato or a head of lettuce. It was both humbling and scary to watch as they all shared in what I took for granted every day. I was overwhelmed at the realization of just how secluded and cut off from the rest of civilization they actually were out here. These were the descendants of probably the most resilient people I had ever met. My throttle finger had iced up completely now, which made riding a lot easier; unfortunately, I was stuck at one speed, which left more time for my mind to wander.

I thought about James's family whom I had met and how all of them were always smiling—except for maybe his stepbrother who had missed shooting a bunch of foxes on his ride over. They were an incredible people dedicated completely to their culture, family, and nature. These people were a close-knit group of villagers living and flourishing in one of the harshest environments and places in Alaska. We were getting close now, and as we rode on, I couldn't help but think of how easy my life was compared to what these people had to endure every day.

We rode for what seemed like hours until coming to the coastline where I could now see the lights of the village. It was dark, cold, and I could barely see out of the glasses that were now frozen to my face. At one point, I started pulling them off to scrape the ice off, but my skin started coming with them. I used a heat pack to melt the ice, then wiped them the best I could with a dirty rag I had stuffed in my shirt to keep from freezing. My gloves were frozen solid to the grips now, and there was about an inch of ice covering everything. I could tell from the sound the sled was making that the weight of the ice was bogging it down, but I wasn't stopping now. There was no way in hell I was going to stop for anything unless James did.

We pulled up in front of the house, and I couldn't take my thumb off the throttle, for my glove was frozen solid to it. I pulled my wet, cold, and now-frozen hand from inside the glove and hit the kill button on the sled. It took just about everything I had to just stand up, and as I did, layer after layer of ice fell to the ground. I felt and looked like the abominable snowman escaping the confines of the glacier he had been frozen in for the last thousand years.

Wanting nothing but to get inside, James said we better get everything in or the foxes would get it. With the help of Theo, who was wearing nothing but his skivvies and some snow boots, we dragged the beast into the storeroom and shut the door.

Tomorrow would be here soon enough, and we would have plenty of time to deal with it then. It was time to get inside, and as I made my way into the living room foyer, my glasses started making a popping sound from being warmed too fast. It felt like it was a thousand degrees, and the heat ripped at my frozen face like a rabid cat in heat! I stepped back outside, hoping the cold air would stop the pain but didn't. I made my way back into the storeroom, stripped off all of my gear, and then walked back in the door.

Much better, I thought as I lay down once again next to the stove.

A few hours later, I woke up to the snoring of James, who had passed out on the couch next to me. I was still on the floor where I had started out; guess I really was tired. I grabbed the blanket that someone had thrown over me, fluffed the pillow back up, and drifted happily back to sleep.

I thought I was dreaming when I awoke to the smell of bacon and coffee. Theo had come in early and started cooking up a storm. I thought I had heard the clanking of pots and pans but blew it off as something stupid in my dream.

"Morning, Mr. George," he said.

"Morning, Theo, how are you?" I replied.

"Good," he said, the whole time whisking the eggs. Next thing I know, he was handing me a fresh cup of coffee in the biggest mug I'd ever seen.

"Theo, if you weren't so damn ugly, I'd kiss you," I said.

He laughed and walked back over to stir up the eggs. "Why you on the floor?" he asked curiously.

"I have no idea," I said. "This is where I passed out last night I guess."

He just cocked his head a little, gave me a weird look, and then returned to stirring the eggs. We finished breakfast around 10:00 a.m. and got to work cutting the skull out of the hide. James got a call on the UHF radio about ten thirty saying they had another plane coming in to drop a few folks off.

"Did you want to try and get out on that one going back to Bethel?" he asked.

"Do you think we can make it?"

He looked around for a second, then paused, and said, "Probably."

We made quick work of the hide, packed up all my gear, and threw it in the back of his broken pack-sled and headed down the road to the airstrip. We had no sooner left the confines of the village when I saw the plane fly over. It circled back around, did a real low pass over the strip, then circled back, and landed right as we were getting there. The pilot taxied in but was having problems with the starter, so he couldn't shut it down. Standing now in the middle of the prop wash, I was having flashbacks of the last two days of battling the wind. I shook hands with James, loaded all the gear and meat, and once again blasted down the frozen runway and into the air.

It was just me and the pilot going back, so I took right seat in the cockpit.

Pretty cool, I thought as we made our way over the Etolin Strait.

"We need to make a few stops on the way back. Hope you don't mind," he asked like I had a choice or something.

I looked over at him with the most serious face I could hold and said, "I can't stop. I have a flight I have to be on, and they won't wait."

For what seemed like forever, all you could hear was the sound of the engine when he looked over at me and started to say something. I was now looking back smiling when he realized I was joking.

"Good one, that was good," he said as he shook his head and smiled. "I thought you were serious and was trying to figure out how to tell you to stick it, nicely."

We were both laughing now as he pointed out the windscreen at what looked to be a village. "That's Tanunak. We need to pick up a few people and some cargo there before heading back to Bethel."

We flew right over the road and banked hard left. I could see some people on machines coming across the tundra, and then the nose leveled out.

The plane was bucking and jumping all around when the pilot said, "Looks like we got a little wind."

I tightened my belt and grabbed the "oh crap" handle again. Next thing I know, we are on the ground and rolling toward the people at the end who seem to be sitting in the middle of the runway/road. He feathered the prop, pulled the throttle all the way back, and was pulling back as hard as he could on the stick to keep the nose in the air and slow our speed. I couldn't see anything in front of us but knew we were getting close to the end. Then just like that the nose dropped, and we skidded to a stop about fifty feet from the end. Funny thing was, those people had all moved in the few seconds it took for us to get from one end to the other. We loaded the plane to the hilt with cargo and two more people, and then we realized we couldn't turn around so the people on the ground all sat on the stabs to lift the nose wheel and pointed the plane back down the runway.

The pilot looked over at me and said, "Buckle up—this is going to be a fun one."

We were heading downwind now, and the strip was short—really short. We throttled up, went to full flaps, and just clearing a snow berm at the end.

"Wow, that was really close," I said as we made our way just above the tundra—100 feet, then 150, then 200 feet, then 300. I watched as the pilot struggled to maintain altitude and at the same time turn the plane into the wind. Too much bank and we would stall and crash. He meticulously worked the controls and as we circled into the wind; I watched the altimeter needle jump up. Before I could exhale the breath I had been holding since we lifted off, we were passing 500 feet and climbing at just over 500 feet per minute.

"Tell me that wasn't fun," the pilot said, smiling the whole time. We had just leveled off at 1,000 feet when the pilot pointed out the window again and said, "Crap!" I knew exactly what he meant as soon as I looked out.

There was a solid wall of "crap" about a mile out, and we either needed to fly in, over, or through it or turn around and try to land somewhere else. I knew what the pilot was thinking, and as we started our descent to 500 feet, it didn't take a rocket scientist to figure out that this was not going to be a lot of fun. We were about a quarter mile out and doing about 170 knots when I realized how bad this was going to be. The pilot yelled to the passengers in the back to buckle up, and I watched as he cinched the straps on himself. It was a solid-black-and-gray wall of crud that stretched for miles on each side of us; it reminded me of the sandstorm walls we used to see when I was working in Saudi Arabia. It would be sunny and warm one minute there, and then the next thing you knew, you could hear and see the wall of sand coming for miles. Only thing you could do there was get inside and wait it out. The weather report from Bethel said to expect mild turbulence, but I had a feeling it was going to be more than mild. We went from clear skies and five miles visual to complete whiteout in less than a second. It was so thick I could hardly see the propeller, and as I looked over at the pilot, I could see the concern in his face. I think we were both surprised to find that the air was actually smooth and in fact calmer than it was on the other side. We were flying on nothing but instruments now, and I watched our ground track on the GPS screen as we made our way toward Bethel.

We were about seventy-five miles out now, and with the exception of not being able to see anything, things were going great when all of a sudden, it felt like we had hit a brick wall. The plane dropped like a rock, and I watched as debris from the floor momentarily rose and dropped again. I looked to the back for a second to see one of the passenger's legs touching the roof, and then they dropped and slammed to the floor.

"Holy crap," the pilot said in a nervous and shocked tone.

The plane was being tossed around like a little kid's toy, and all we could do was hang on and pray. At one point the left wing was pulled down hard and in an attempt to recover it, the pilot countered hard right and then the right wing dropped about 50 degrees. I remember being able to see the ground for a second and thinking it was really close when we recovered and were flying straight again. What seemed like an eternity of being tossed around in a blender was only about thirty minutes when the pilot radioed Bethel as we approached to get clearance to land. They were reporting heavy fog with zero visibility, which meant we would be doing a full-instrument approach and landing. I could see on the GPS screen that we were close but still couldn't see anything except the cowling and a little of the prop. We were still getting bounced around a bit, but nothing like before. The pilot pulled the throttle back, and we started descending.

Bethel had strobe lights that even Ray Charles could see, so I was busy looking for those when I noticed our altitude. We were just passing three hundred feet, and I still couldn't see anything. I looked over at the pilot, who now had his head up high looking over the nose for the runway. With only a mile indicated on the screen and at just 250 feet, I knew we were close but still couldn't see anything. I pulled on my belt straps as hard as I could and grabbed the "oh crap" handles one more time.

I called out to the pilot that we were at 100 feet when he said in a really calm voice, "Hang on!" He chopped the throttle, and the plane dropped out of the sky!

"Holy crap," I yelled as our wheels impacted the ice-covered runway. "Did you see the runway?" I asked the pilot.

"Nope, I couldn't see anything but knew it was down there somewhere," he said as he taxied down the runway. The people in the back all had smiles on their faces except for the one who was still doing Hail Marys. We taxied up the hangar, shut it down, and made our way across the icy, wind-blown tarmac and into the hangar.

I would lay over in Bethel one more night and head back to Anchorage in the morning, so after another exciting cab ride, I arrived at the Long House in Bethel once more. Having not bathed in four days, I used every ounce of hot water they had and must have spent at least an hour in there. I was beat and, after that plane ride, was just glad to be alive and in one piece. I grabbed a hot meal in the little restaurant downstairs, then watched the news, and that was about it.

I awoke the next morning, jumped into another taxi, and made my way to the airport. I was back in Anchorage by noon and dropped the beast off at Knights Taxidermy. They are without a doubt the best taxidermists in Alaska and really good friends too. Having had work done in other places, I learned from them what true artists' work really looks like. So after hanging out there for a while and telling big lies, I headed for home. I drove down the street looking at all of the stores, houses, fast-food restaurants, shopping malls, traffic, and people. I began feeling like the time when I was in the air force and had just moved from Okinawa, Japan, to a place called Soesterberg in the country of Holland. The two cultures were so different that I had a really hard time adjusting to the differences. Once again, I was caught in the middle of two completely different cultures even though they were just hours away from each other. I tried to wrap my brain around all that I had experienced and done in the four short days in Nunivak. but it was too much. I turned the key to my midtown condo, walked upstairs, and fell into my bed.

Two days and a lot of sleep later, I rolled out of bed feeling like it was all a dream—a really good dream that I will never forget.

2

911

If you were to ask me where I was a few hours ago,
I probably couldn't tell you.
If you were to ask me where I was on 911,
though, I could and will tell you everything about that day.
The day that changed our world and lives, forever!

The sun was just starting to rise when I looked out the iced-up window of the house. The original plan was to blast out of Anchorage on Friday after work, hit Fairbanks for some G&G (gas and grub), then shoot up the haul road to hunt for moose, caribou, and bear. Unfortunately, the road conditions were less than the usual crappy, so we didn't get in till late and decided to overnight at one of Troy's friend's house.

Sam had been working on the house trying to get it ready to sell but unfortunately hadn't spent much time on the heating system. As I lay there blowing smoke in the middle of the framed-out living room, I saw something big and brown walk in front of the window.

"What in the hell was that?" I asked Troy, who was just waking up.

"What was what?" he asked still half-asleep.

"Dude, I think there's a moose right there," I said as I tried to remember where my rifle was.

Troy popped up and crept over to the window to get a better look when I realized that all of our rifles were still in the truck. Brushing up and along the side of the house now was a nice two-by-three bull moose. At the time, anything fifty inches or more or a moose with three brow tines was legal. We were outside the city limit and totally legal; all we needed now was something to shoot him with. Troy crept upstairs to wake up Sam to get a gun, but by the time they got back downstairs, the bull was gone.

"Did you see the size of that thing?" I asked.

He looked over at me, shivered a bit, and crawled back into his bag. "Wake me when there's one on the ground," he said. "Wake me when it's on the ground."

A few hours later we loaded the truck back up and made our way back into town (Fairbanks). We were listening to the only AM station talking about the time the World Trade Center was bombed when we finally pulled in for gas. No sooner than we cut the motor when this old sourdough (Alaskan veteran) pulled up and skidded to a stop. He was trying to get out of the truck, but the bungee cord that was holding his door shut got hung up.

He finally loosened it up and jumped out, yelling, "They did it, man. They finally did it!"

Troy and I were just about to write it off as just another "Fairbankian" when we heard the public address system warning tone. "We interrupt this program for the following message." In a noticeably shaken and wavering tone, the reporter said, "We are getting word from our affiliates in New York that the north tower of the World Trade Center has been struck by an aircraft! Again, the north tower of the World Trade Center in New York City appears to have been struck by a commercial aircraft."

We both sat there pinned in our seats waiting for more information when the reporter began repeating the previous statement. "For those of you who missed our previous broadcast, the north tower of the World Trade Center has just been struck by a commercial airliner!"

The old sourdough grabbed my window, which was halfway down, stuck his face in mine, and said, "I told you, man—it's going down!"

Aside from scaring the hell out of me, all I could think about was that he must have been the guy who invented the toothbrush, for if it had been anyone else, they would have called it a teeth brush.

"You guys got any fifty-five-gallon drums I could bum?" he said. "I'm getting all I can now, that's all I can tell ya," he said, shouting profanities about terrorists and Arabs as he stomped away in his half-laced combat boots.

I think both Troy and I were in shock as I remember just sitting there motionless and unsure of what to do or when to do it.

We just sat there staring at the radio like it was going to do something when the next thing we hear is "We are getting word now that a second plane that appears to have also been a commercial airliner has just struck the Pentagon!" I remember looking up at Troy who, probably like me, was completely white.

"What in the hell, Troy?" I remember saying. "Is this for real? What do we do? Where do we go? What in the hell is happening? All I could think about was getting back to Anchorage and my wife, Kristin, who was now three months pregnant. I needed to call her but had no cell reception, so I ran into Fred Myers, a local grocer, to use the phone."

We were probably as far as you could possibly get in the United States from ground zero, but people in the store were going crazy. They were buying everything they could get and then some. I only had a dollar's worth of quarters and wasn't getting in line to get more, so I dropped in the dollar and ten cents and spun the numbers into the rotary dialer of the oldest phone I had ever seen.

"Kristin, are you okay? Have you heard what's going on yet? What are you hearing down there? Are we at war?" To my amazement, she was quite calm and said that the local news was telling people not to panic and standby for more information and updates. I had just asked Kristin to call Troy's girlfriend and my family to let them know we were okay when the phone went dead—damn pay phones. When I turned and looked back, there was a line of people a mile long, all waiting to use the phone.

Holy crap, is this really happening? I thought.

I made my way through the maze of rude people and the lines of cars and jumped back in the truck. "Troy, we need to get the hell out of here and quick."

He looked over and just shook his head. We got back on the highway and pulled off to listen to the radio and decide what we were going to do. That's when we heard, "We interrupt this program for the following messages: We are getting reports now that a second airplane has struck the south tower of the World Trade Center. I repeat, a second airplane appears to have struck the south tower of the World Trade Center. At this time we are unaware of any terrorist attack and no groups have claimed responsibility. Please stay tuned for more information."

All I could hear was the sound of the hissing from the radio as we sat there baffled at the events unfolding in front of us. "What do we do?" I asked. "What can we do?"

Moments later, a local radio station broke in with an update, which stated "By official proclamation of the president of the United States, all air traffic in the United States has hereby been cancelled and grounded until further notice."

"Troy, do you know what that means?" He had the deer in the headlight look when I began to explain. It was the middle of hunting season, which meant all of those people who were out hunting and had gotten there by aircraft were now stuck there until they reinstated the use of aircraft.

I'm not sure how long we sat there, but the longer we listened to the details coming in on what was going on, the more we both realized that there was absolutely nothing we could do, nothing. Then another report came in: "We interrupt this program to... We are unsure at this time of the association of this aircraft with the other three; however, we are now getting word that a fourth commercial aircraft, United flight 93, has crashed just outside the town of Shanksville, Pennsylvania. The information we are getting from rescue crews on scene is that there are no survivors! Standby for more information."

My mind flashed back to 1969 when I remember sitting in my nice, air-conditioned living room in Miami watching our boys in Vietnam get their asses shot off. Day after day the news would fill the room with nothing but horror, death, and despair. We had a neighbor across the street (the Neelys) who had lost a son over there and had the flag with the star in the window. I didn't realize until years later how Mrs. Neely would always come outside whenever I was playing in the front yard. She would always watch us kids play and try to strike up a conversation with us. Maybe I reminded her of her son, I don't know. I was almost ten at the time and could only think about being there to help out. I remember thinking about sneaking on a plane somehow and just getting into the country. They'd never notice I was just a kid with everyone else running around. I mean, I had played army for what seemed like my whole life and had gotten really good at it. How hard could it actually be? I just wanted to help, to do something useful, and I couldn't and never did. Maybe that's why I joined the air force when I was just seventeen—who knows. All of those feelings were now coming back as I again just sat there waiting for more news.

We decided to drive north to the town of Fox where they had a small general store with a TV in it. Maybe we could get more information on what was going on. The parking lot was packed when we pulled up; people were everywhere buying up gas and just about everything else that wasn't tied down. We made our way through the crowd and into the back of the store where we could now see the TV. It was probably the most shocking and unbelievable thing I had ever seen. Both towers were completely engulfed in flames and people were throwing themselves off to end their horror. It was beyond belief as we all watched person after person crash into the ground. The sound of their bodies exploding as they hit was overwhelming. The next thing we knew, the north tower just folded up and collapsed to the ground! There were no words that could describe the horror of watching that tower and the thousands of people inside disintegrate before our eyes. The reporter was trying to narrate what was happening but was struggling with every word. People in the store kept looking around at everyone else as if looking for a reason or answers to what was happening. The next thing we knew, the south tower blew fire and smoke out of its middle and collapsed on top of the north tower. All you could see on the screen was smoke and ash.

People were running for their lives as they were engulfed in the dust of what was once two of the most iconic structures of the twentieth century and thousands of human lives. The news panned over to what was happening at the Pentagon, which was just as horrific. Another aircraft had come in low and went straight through the side of the West Wing. They were unsure of the death toll, but when the first images appeared, you could tell it was going to be devastating. There was a huge, round hole where the fuselage tore through, and there were cuts on each side where the wings had followed. The entire plane had disintegrated upon impact, and all on board were instantly killed. Reports were coming in saying that there were over two hundred people in the wing at the time of impact, but nobody was really sure.

They panned back to the now-smoldering five-mile-long and two-mile-high dust cloud that was once the World Trade Center. There was nothing left to see; all of it was completely gone. There was no narration for what seemed like forever—just live footage of the huge dust cloud now engulfing the rest of the city. Inside the store, you could have heard a pin drop as we all just stood there in disbelief. The lady standing next to me was now holding my arm and sobbing uncontrollably.

By the time the attack was over, three aircraft had found their targets; the fourth had crashed in a field for unknown reason. The good news was, the onslaught of carnage and destruction seemed to be over. We stood in the store for about another hour waiting for more news of more attacks, but thankfully there were none. It was over for now, and our country's first attack by a group of terrorists known now as Al-Qaeda was finally over. Little did we know at the time how commonplace the words *terrorist* and *Al-Qaeda* would become in our lives.

Kristin was about three months pregnant, and I couldn't help but think of how much of our baby's life had just changed. In just a blink of an eye, our country and way of life had changed forever; we had been attacked and dealt a catastrophic blow by a small group of Muslim extremists. After standing in line for an hour to use the phone, I was finally talking with Kristin again. To my disbelief, she was handling it quite well and said there wasn't a whole lot anyone could do. She again confirmed that there were no new attacks, and it looked like it was finally over. We both sat there for what seemed like forever saying nothing as I continued to dump quarter after quarter into the slot.

"Are you okay?" I asked.

"I'm fine," she said in a somber, sad, and exhausted tone.

"Troy and I are going to head back in a little while, probably be in late, so don't wait up."

That's when she told me that she had heard the highways were completely blocked due to the initial panic and that we might be better off just waiting it out. I told her we would try it anyhow and that I loved her, when my quarters ran out again. After a few hours we decide to head back to Anchorage; maybe there would be something for us to do there. We got back on the highway and started heading south when we ran into the largest traffic jam I had ever seen. We weren't even in Fairbanks when all we could see was a huge snake of red lights for at least ten miles. Seemed that everybody and their brother had the same idea and were now heading for Anchorage. It was complete chaos as we sat in the middle of the highway creeping along at less than a mile an hour.

"This is stupid," I said to Troy as I sipped on my now-cold coffee. "We should just go hunting!" As sad as that may have seemed, it was really all we could do.

"Let's just hit Coldfoot and see what it looks like, and we'll turn around from there," I said to Troy. He was looking at me like I was crazy until I threw out the fact that nobody was going north; everybody was heading south.

His eyebrows stood up a bit; then he said, "Okay, but just to Coldfoot."

Our original plan was to blast up to Deadhorse and hunt our way back, but Coldfoot would do. That and they had the biggest cinnamon rolls south or the Brooks Range! Troy spun the truck around and put the pedal to the metal; we were hunting now, baby! We stopped into Fox's general store again to top off and make another call to Kristin to let her know what was going on and headed north into the Last Frontier.

We lost the radio about ten miles outside Fox, so now had nothing but road noise to listen to. The pavement runs out about forty miles north of Fox and ends. From there until Deadhorse, it's seven hundred miles of some of the worst gravel, ruts, and washboards you'll ever see. As we made our way down the lonely, winding road through rolling hills of spruce, we talked about the events we had just witnessed. How unbelievable the whole day had been.

Then to Troy's amazement, I began telling him about how Al-Qaeda operates and what they stood for. Having spent the last three years in Saudi Arabia working for the Royal Saudi Air Force on their F-15 program, I knew a little about the Arab world and Islam. I had gotten lucky over there and made a good Saudi friend who helped me learn Arabic and taught me about Islam.

Tequel Al Harbi was a good man and a devout Muslim. He taught and showed me that the Koran was originally written as a survival guide—how to live, how to pray, how to treat people, and your responsibilities in life as a man and a woman. Much like the Bible, the Koran was a book of peace; but like anything else, there are those who always have to take it to the next level—

the extremists. We had many of conversations about terrorism and what it meant to a Muslim to die during a holy war (Jihad). When called upon, a Muslim must fulfill whatever it is that is asked of them or face disgrace in the eyes of Allah (PBUH), peace be upon him.

The other Saudis that I also came to know, including Tequel, were nothing but kind. They were some of the most hospitable, gentle, and family-oriented people I had ever met or known. Unfortunately, Tequel had a son who had some psychological issues and decided one night to stab his father seventeen times while he slept. As barbaric as this may seem, the Saudis look at people with mental issues as demons and therefore treat them as such. To the best of my knowledge, his son was thrown in a Saudi prison, which in itself was a death sentence. You are thrown in a cell and left there to rot. If the family doesn't bring food, water, or medicine, the person will simply starve and die. They have a saying for everything in Saudi: "En shallah." It basically means that "everything is in God's hands and God's will."

So how could there be so much hate for another nation that is equally peaceful and life bearing? We talked for hours as we drove deeper into the darkness. We got to Stevens Bridge about midnight and pulled into the vehicle-packed parking lot. They had a small café and a gas station that we now needed but was unfortunately closed for the evening. We would have to sleep in the truck and head out in the morning.

The bridge was a major starting point for hunting on the mighty Yukon River, and therefore the parking lot was full of nothing but trucks with empty trailers. We counted at least one hundred rigs, which meant there were at least three hundred people on the river in boats.

Then add about another two hundred that used planes out of Fairbanks and Coldfoot to fly in, and you have a lot of people that were now stranded. We hunkered in the best we could among the gear and trash-filled truck and drifted off to sleep.

I awoke the next morning to the sound of people yelling. We had parked next to the gas pumps so we could be first in line and were now unfortunately in someone's way.

"Hey, are you guys getting gas or just sit there all day?" I heard from the back of the truck.

"Uh yeah, are they open yet?" I asked.

"Yeah, they've been open since eight."

"Troy, Troy, wake up, we need to move."

Not a good morning person, Troy flew up in a rage like a rat had gotten in his bag. "What's happening? What are we doing?"

"They're open," I said. "We need to pull up and get some gas." Little did we know, but during the night, a line had formed, and we were holding up about ten angry hunters. We filled up, parked in the south 40, and made our way across the expanse of ankle-high mud that was now the parking lot. It took me five-minutes to scrape off all the muck on my boots before going inside. We were about in the middle of our breakfast when a couple of truckers came in and were talking about shutting down the road. Unlike other places to hunt in the world, Alaska doesn't have a huge road system. There's a road going south (the Seward Highway) and a road that goes north (the Dalton) or what locals refer to as the Haul Road. We were on the Haul Road, and they were now talking about shutting it down. Things were going from really bad to really worse really quick!

Problem was, along this road sits one of the longest most expansive oil pipelines in the world. Just because the attacks had been thousands of miles away and seemed to be over didn't mean they were. If a terrorist were to just put a hole in the line, the whole thing would have to be shut down and repaired. In fact, just a few years prior, two inebriated brothers decided to do just that—and did. With a .338 rifle they shot time after time until one penetrated the pipe and sprayed thousands of gallons of oil onto the tundra. It took months to repair and leaked an ungodly amount of oil onto the protected environment. If someone were to blow it up, it would completely devastate our economic infrastructure and cost billions of dollars each day. Easiest way to protect it would be to shut down the only two ways to access it: air and road. Because the president had already shut down all air travel, the only thing left to do now was to shut down the road.

We finished our breakfast and shot back up the road in hopes of making it to at least Coldfoot. We rolled past the thousands of fish-filled streams, purple-and-red alpine meadows of fireweed, and spruce-covered hills. It was beautiful up there, a place connected to civilization only by a single stretch of barren gravel road. It was just amazing to be in the middle of nowhere and one of the largest pieces of wilderness in the world. There were no fences, no boundaries, and no people—just miles and miles of endless wilderness.

Why couldn't the rest of the world just get along like all the animals out here? I thought. Then I remembered watching a bear mauling a deer one time, and that killed that thought completely. It was hard to believe there was so much chaos going on when it was so peaceful out here.

I'm not a religious person, but I think if there actually is a God, things like this would not be happening. Religious people say that this is not God's will, but the devil's. Personally, I could care less whose will it is; all I know is that it's wrong.

Tequel taught me about how a Muslim, any Muslim, could be called on at any time to perform a Jihad (act of violence for a holy cause) in honor of Allah (PBUH). He explained time after time how this in itself was an extremist misinterpretation of what the

Koran was actually trying to say. Unfortunately, the extremists only care about their cause and ignore the real meaning of the words altogether. I remember having numerous conversations with the Saudis about their insatiable hate for Israel. I always think about this because when I would ask them if they had ever met a Jew, the answer would always be a resounding no.

Then I would ask, "How can you hate someone you have never seen or met?"

They would usually just walk away; however, I asked one of the Saudis I was working with how he knew that I wasn't a Jew. He stomped off in a bitter rage yelling something in Arabic and waving his hands in the air. I didn't think anything of it until a few days later when I was called into the boss's office where the Saudi base commander and a Boeing representative were waiting.

They reinitiated my background check and stated that if it came back and they found out that I was a Jew or had any ties to Israel, I would need to pack my bags and immediately leave the country. So unfortunately, I understood firsthand how the hate for a nation, its people, and ideals could force people to act irrational, but it didn't make matters any better. We rolled past the quiet, peaceful countryside and farther into the dark abyss that was night. It was about 1:00 a.m. when we pulled off at a small rest stop. Wasn't really sure it was a rest stop but was pulling over nonetheless. Troy was still asleep, so I dropped my seat back as far as it would go (which wasn't far due to the trash and gear) and closed my exhausted and dust-filled eyes.

The next morning I awoke to the splendor and beauty that is Alaska. We had parked in a small rest stop that actually had a public toilet. It was on the edge of a small pristine lake surrounded by beautiful green, yellow, orange, and red brush-covered mountains. It was a picture straight of a postcard, and as I stepped out of the nice, warm truck, I was greeted by the reality of the season. It was freezing out, and dressed only in a pair of jeans and a light jacket, I was now freezing to death. Troy was wandering around the lake to see what he could see, so after rummaging around in the back of the truck, I pulled out one of the largest jackets I could find. I grabbed my glasses and made my way over to where Troy was standing and noticed him glassing a spot on the side of this hill.

"What are you looking at?"

"A moose," he said in a whisper. "He's way up in that clearing, but he's a moose."

I focused in and got a look at our first moose. Couldn't tell how big he was but appeared to have a nice rack. No matter, he was miles away, and we'd never get him unless we called him in, and it was kind of early to be calling yet. I fired up the cookstove and made some camp coffee to take the edge off the cold. Troy didn't drink coffee, but I was an addict, so after a few cups, I was wired and ready to go. A few years back I had made the mistake of giving Troy a cup of coffee and learned too late what a mistake that was. I have seen kids do better after drinking a twenty-ounce Red Bull than he did on that coffee. It was like watching a monkey in heat that was trapped in a room by himself!

After a few more cups of coffee, we cracked open some granola bars, fired up the truck, and headed back up the highway. Didn't realize it until Troy brought it up, but we hadn't heard or seen a single vehicle all night.

Did they close the road? I thought. *It doesn't matter at this point; we were only a couple hundred miles from Coldfoot, and until someone stopped us, that's where we were heading.*

We were on the road for no more than about thirty minutes when we spotted a couple of moose on the edge of a field. I pulled over as far as I could get off the road so we could glass them from the truck. Turned out to just be a cow and a calf, but we were seeing moose. We got back on the road and made our way around to the other side of the field to get a better look. You could spot them a hundred miles away from the steam rising off of their bodies. It almost looked like they were on fire as they made their way through the branches of the small but thick spruce. After a few minutes, we couldn't see them anymore but could see where they were from the steam flumes rising from the trees.

We made our way into Coldfoot just in time for lunch and call me surprised but the parking lot was again full; this time with nothing but eighteen-wheelers. Seemed that somewhere in the night they had all been instructed to stand down and stay put until further notice. Probably it was why we hadn't seen anyone on the road for the last twelve hours. We made our way into the smoke-filled dining area that was packed to the hilt with big, burly, hairy guys—and gals! It didn't take long for us to see another image of the burning towers and bloody people running for their lives. Everyone was glued to the TV like flies on the stuff flies stick to. I ordered a large coffee, paid for some gas, and made my way back outside to fill up the truck. Up to this point, the whereabouts of the president had been unknown; however, the kid who came out to unlock the pumps updated me on that and just about everything else. The president and first family were all safe, and the attacks were over. Al-Qaeda under the leadership of Osama bin Laden had claimed responsibility and was celebrating the success of the attacks. In one single blow, he had taken the lives of over two thousand Americans, many of them just women and children.

This was cause to celebrate? Killing innocent people because they chose to live in a society that was different than theirs? Up to about forty-eight hours ago, the words *Osama Bin Laden*, *terrorist*, and *Al-Qaeda* were known by none; now, they were known by all and would become a staple in our vocabulary and unfortunately heard daily. I remember when I first flew into Jeddah and was picked up by my sponsor Jerry Rushing. He had been in Saudi for almost twenty years and had been a millionaire a few times over working for Boeing and a sister company called Al Salam. Our compound was high in the mountains by a town called Taif, which unfortunately was directly on the other side of Mecca. What would normally have taken about an hour if allowed to go through Mecca now took about four because we weren't Muslims. Only Muslims were allowed into Mecca, which meant we had to take the "Christian bypass," which detoured you around and out into the middle of the desert. Unfortunately, the only way to get to the highway was straight through the middle of town. I was still in shock from the plane ride that was a little different than anything I had ever experienced. I got on the cram-packed 747 in Germany, and by the time we landed in Jeddah, we could not see the floor.

It was littered with everything from soda bottles, diapers, incense burners, clothes, towels, toilet paper, and then some. I even saw a used can of Sterno fuel rolling around! I knew something was wrong when all of the men began lining up for the restrooms holding towels. After a few hours, I was sitting next to and in a plane with hundreds of grown men wearing nothing but white bath towels! It was Ramadan, the holiest of holy months, and these folks were on the pilgrimage to Mecca! It is written in the Koran that somewhere in a Muslim's life, if able, they must make the pilgrimage to Mecca to fulfill their commitment to Allah (PBUH).

After a few minutes of driving through town, there was no doubt in my mind that I had made one of the worst decisions of my life by going there. It was barbarism at its finest. Millions of people packed into a tiny port town surrounded by desert. People were everywhere and littered the streets like trash. People intermingled with cars in the middle of the road, and at every stoplight and round-about were people missing arms and legs could be seen begging for money. Besides football (soccer), the national sport here was shopping. There were millions of gold souks (stores) filled with people bartering for gold and jewelry. Because Ford Motor Company had a Jewish owner somewhere in its past, the only cars allowed into the country were primarily Chevys and any other piece of rolling junk. Most were lucky to be rolling; however, rest assured that the horns all worked. Didn't matter when the light turned green or if there was even someone in front of you to honk at, you had to honk your horn at every light or stop. The only thing that was going through my mind now was how in the hell can I get back on that plane and get out of here.

Osama had made the news a few years before in another terrorist incident; however, it was overshadowed by other events and quickly disappeared into the mess that is our media.

We had just passed another legless person when Jerry pointed out the window and said, "That's the Bin Laden compound; you need to stay away from there."

It looked like a small military base with its twenty-foot high Constantine wire–covered walls, stadium lighting, and uniformed guards with machine guns every fifty feet. I couldn't see anything except walls and guards but could occasionally sneak a peek through one of the many massive wrought-iron gates. Jerry said that Osama doesn't live there, but the rest of his family does, and he visits from time to time. He joked that you could tell when he was visiting because there would be two guards every fifty feet then.

All I could think about is, *Here is the residence of a well known terrorist, and we know about it. Why would our government just sit there and do nothing about it?* It took almost ten minutes to get to the other end of the compound wall, which had a small watchtower in it. You could see the guard in it watching us as we passed, almost as if waiting for us to stop. It was creepy, really creepy, and as we got to the top of a small hill that overlooked the compound, you could see the whole palace. Lavishly adorned in real twenty-four-karat gold and sterling silver trim, they had two helicopters, twenty-seven vehicles, four pools, and a house for every family member; the Bin Ladens were obviously doing well.

I finished pumping the gas, parked the truck, and went in to find Troy. He was deep in conversation with a bunch of angry truckers ready to kick Bin Laden's ass when I sat down and ordered another cup of coffee. Seems that the fourth plane that crashed into the field was heading for the White House and somehow crashed. Like the others, there were no survivors. We grabbed some grub, threw back another pot of coffee, and piled back into the mud-covered truck. We pulled up to the edge of the highway when Troy looked over at me and said, "Which way do you want to go?"

Left went south and back to Anchorage, and right went north to Deadhorse. I was just about to tell him I really didn't care when he turned the wheel to the right, and we headed for Deadhorse.

We had stopped a few times throughout the day to glass and stretch and had burned up a lot of daylight in doing so. It was starting to get dark now, so we decided to get off the road and try to find somewhere to set up a tent and do some real hunting. We were somewhere between Deadhorse and Coldfoot when I spotted a small dirt road that looked pretty good. We kicked her into four-wheel drive and made our way through and down the overgrown trail that dead-ended about three miles back. It was getting dark fast, so we made quick work of setting up the tent. We were close to either a stream or river, for we could hear it but couldn't see it through the dense spruce and alders. I gathered what I could find for wood and got a nice, toasty fire going. After a few mountain house meals and their blueberry ice cream in a pouch, we stoked the fire with more wood and decided it was time to crack open some beers. On my walk over to the cooler was when I noticed the indisputable odor of something dead.

"You smell that, Troy?"

"Smell what?" he said as he poked at the fire.

"Smells like something dead and close. I didn't smell it till now. Maybe that's why we're the only ones back here."

He looked across the fire at me and said, "Thanks for that, now I'm really going to get some sleep tonight." Then he said, "Yep, I smell it now."

We both got up and used our headlamps to see if we could find what it was. It seemed to be coming from the alders, and we were not going in there now. If it wasn't grunting or charging us, we were leaving it alone. I cracked open a couple of beers, and we both slammed them pretty quick. It was colder than I thought it would be, and every time my face was pointing away from the fire, my face would freeze up and remind me how cold it really was. We went through two sixes reliving the events of the last two days. By the time we crawled into the tent, I could hardly find the zipper; we were hunting now!

It was still dark out when something woke me up. I thought it was Troy, but as usual, he was fast asleep. I could hear something moving outside and started digging through my daypack for my .44 when it brushed up along the side of the tent again. My first thought was a bear, but then I heard it peep and realized it was nothing more than a porcupine. An almost-ventilated porcupine but a porcupine nonetheless. Troy rolled over and mumbled something, but I couldn't tell what he'd said. I turned my headlamp on and listened to it scamper away. I rolled over and tucked the .44 under my pillow and tried to go back to sleep. All I could think about was that I was glad it wasn't a bear, for I really liked this tent; it would have been a shame to put a bunch of holes in it!

A Dalton Highway Icon, the Arctic Circle Sign

Morning rolled around way to soon, and once more, I awoke to the sight of my breath in front of me. We had forgotten to bring a thermometer, but it didn't matter much at this point. It was cold, really cold, which was good for moose hunting but bad for everything else. Troy was already out stoking the fire when I crawled out of the ice-covered tent.

"Holy crap, it's cold out here," I said.

"Yeah, that and it's cold too," he said with a smirk on his face.

Good news was, we were in the thick of it now, and we're finally moose hunting. I made my way back through the alders we couldn't see through last night and down to a small stream for a nature break. Figured I'd gather some wood on the way back and maybe cook up some hot dogs over the fire—always a good hunting breakfast. I was just standing there in the middle of my nature break when I noticed that smell again and saw something black off in the distance.

I had my .44 but it still scared the bejesus out of me when I realized it could be a black bear watching me. I pulled my zipper and my .44 out of its holster at the same time. Troy and the camp was about seventy-five yards away; by the time I could get back there to tell him what was going on, whatever it was would probably be gone. I slowly made my way along the creek and around to where it was lying. A few more feet and I'd be right on top of it. I drew back the trigger on the .44 Magnum and made my way around a small alder plant only to realize that it was a black bear. Fortunately for me, a really dead black bear. There was no wondering where the smell was coming from now. Apparently, someone had poached the bear and took only the organs and its paws. I couldn't believe what I was looking at. I had heard of people doing this but still couldn't believe my eyes. They would poach these animals and sell or use the organs and claws to cure illnesses and even as aphrodisiacs. Although highly illegal, people will pay thousands of dollars for these items making it worthy of the risks. This was a sad sight, and as I called for Troy to come down and look, he spotted another one not more than fifty yards from the one I had found.

After another mountain house breakfast of sausage and eggs, we spent the rest of the morning glassing for moose on a small hill just outside camp. The only thing we spotted was a bunch of ground hogs and a coyote, but we were hunting. Somewhere in it all I guess we both started to feel guilty and decided to pack it up and head for home. By now the traffic had probably settled down and back to normal—hopefully. We got back out on the highway around noon and headed back toward Coldfoot. My emotions were flip-flopping everywhere as we made our way farther south. The trees and hills were covered with frost turning everything a beautiful frosty white. My mind wandered as we passed stream after frozen stream where ice had started to form; winter was here, I thought. The good news was, the water in the billions of potholes was frozen now, making the long ride a little smoother.

I flashbacked to a time when I was just a kid and my family was still together. People always say things were much simpler then, but I had always wondered about that. Were they better and easier then, or did they just appear that way? Was the world more peaceful then, or did we just think it was? Then I remembered the Cuban missile crisis when Fidel Castro of Cuba was ready to launch every nuclear weapon he had on America. I was just a kid then and remember it like it was yesterday. We were practicing for an all-out nuclear war at the elementary school I was in. We would practice drills at least two times a day and sometimes three.

I remember the news suggesting the things to buy like gas masks, food, and water for a year or more. It was crazy, and as we hid under our tiny wooden desks to shield ourselves from the five-megaton bursts, I couldn't help to think about how everything I knew and loved could be taken from me in a split second. The world was no different then than it was now; we just had different players and tactics now. Humans always have and always will be consumers and destroyers of things. It is unfortunately the way of the world and surely will be a determining factor in the ultimate demise of the human race.

I was just starting to delve into a deeper chapter of my mind, when out of nowhere a huge bull moose stepped into the middle of the road! I think it took a minute to register with Troy, but he locked up the brakes and skidded past the bull. It shot across the road like a small hundred-pound deer and disappeared into the dense thicket of spruce. I jumped out to get my bow from the backseat, while Troy checked the hunting regs.

"Are we legal, Troy?" I asked while knocking an arrow.

"I can't find it. What area is this?" he asked while frantically turning pages.

"I think were still in 22," I said as I stood, trying to find the bull in the spruce. I could see a big patch of gray in the middle of two spruce trees, but it wasn't moving. That had to be him, for you could see the tracks that he had made in the dew.

The seconds ticked by as I stood there waiting for whether or not we could shoot. Most areas past Fairbanks were any bull areas, however, not all. We would need to make sure before we shot, and as Troy fumbled through the pages, I saw the bull move. He was off the road about fifty yards and unfortunately in some really thick spruce. I would need to get in really close and get a good opening, or the arrow would deflect and end up wherever.

I was just about to yell at Troy again when he said, "We're good, shoot that bastard."

I made my way into the thick and noisy brush where I had last seen the bull and stopped. He was in here somewhere and close, for I could actually smell him. Standing there with my release in the string and arrow knocked, the branches just twenty yards away began to snap. My adrenalin shot through the roof as my mind now realized that this bull was just a few trees away. I could hear him grunting and the sound of his hooves pounding the ground. I could hear him breathing and smell the pungent odor of the sweat on his back.

I knelt down below the spruce branches to see is I could see him and, to my surprise, did. He had his head down too, and we were both now looking dead into each other's eyes. He popped his head back up when my eye's met his and stomped the ground once more. If I could just get down low enough, I could possibly have a shot. Problem was, I just had a regular rest and not the type where you could turn your bow at any angle and shoot. I got on my belly and crawled across the frozen ground like a snake in the grass. I was within twenty yards now but still had no shot. I tried peeking around the frozen tree limbs and between the twigs but could only see what looked to be his hind quarter. Every time I moved, he would move, and we were now playing a game of really cold hide-and-seek; unfortunately, he was winning.

I stood back up to see if I could see him over the spruce when our eyes connected again. He was staring right at me and didn't look real happy. I didn't realize how close I had gotten until I stood back up and then realized that if he charged, I'd be toast. He could easily get me now as I looked down at my flimsy twenty-four-inch arrow with the tiny 110-grain broad head on it. I usually packed my .44 when bow hunting just for circumstances like this, but in all of the excitement, I had left it in the truck. My heart was beating fast now, and even though it was freezing out, I was burning up.

The steam was coming off my jacket like I was on fire. Next thing I know, he started moving and moving pretty good. With every step he took, I took two and was soon running through the maze of spruce. Seconds later, I dumped out of the brush and into a small clearing only to find no moose. I quickly scanned the ground for sign but didn't see anything. My glasses were fogging up now, and as I went to wipe them clean, I saw the top of a tree shake about twenty yards away. I ran straight at him and came to full draw at the same time. I had him dead in my sights now and was ready to let loose the twenty-four inches of primitive fury when I spotted a small calf just in back of him.

The arrow flew fast and true cutting its way through the thick, cold air as it shot straight past and between the two moose! I stood there for a second waiting for the bull's reply and expected charge when he just turned, looked straight back at me, and disappeared into the bush with the calf in tow. It took me another half hour to recover my arrow, but at twenty-five bucks a pop, you have to at least try. I made my way back through the spruce and up to the road where Troy was waiting in anticipation.

"Did you get him?" he asked. I guess the look on my face told the story for his next words were, "What happened?"

I don't know why, but I told him that I couldn't get a good shot and decided not to shoot. I spent the next couple of hours contemplating why I let that bull go; I mean I was completely legal, and it wasn't like shooting a sow with cubs! I kept thinking about the look in that bull's eye's as my finger began squeezing the trigger on my release. I think with everything we had seen and heard over the last couple of days—the killing and destruction of life consuming our every thought—that I had just had enough. Besides, the calf was really cute.

We got to Coldfoot again about 4:00 p.m. and decided to grab some more G&G (grub and gas) before heading for Fairbanks. The only thing on TV was footage of the attacks, and as before, all we could do is just sit there and watch. It was humiliating to say the least to watch time after time as the towers and Pentagon were hit by commercial airliners filled with innocent people. Women and children, fathers and mothers, sisters and brothers, husbands and wives. It was more than I could handle and was tugging at every ounce of emotion I had.

We hit the road again and made it to Fairbanks around 11:00 p.m. We had turned the radio off and forgot to turn it on after leaving Coldfoot, but it was nice. Not listening to anything but the endless amount of road noise was just fine with me. We stopped into a small diner to top off on coffee and were once again bombarded by visual images and reports of the horror. It was as if someone was following us around and constantly tapping you on the shoulder to say, "Look, do you see what's happening?"

We got back into Anchorage in the early hours of the morning, and as I made my way up the stairs to see my wife and unborn child (Olivia), I just remember feeling like something was different. What I didn't realize at the time was that everything was different. What I didn't realize is that I was different. Our way of life, the way we think, live, act, who we were as a nation—everything was different now and would never be the same. For the first time since I was a child, there was instability and uncertainty in what being an American meant.

As I slipped into the clean, soft, and warm covers of my bed and put my hand on my wife's round, warm stomach, I prayed to God that my daughter would never know this type of horror and would live a long and peaceful life.

To this day, that was by far the strangest and most memorable hunt I had ever done. What began as another ordinary day turned into everything but that: a hunt filled with twists and turns of emotions and life-changing events. The scenario of me at full draw looking into that bull's eyes still haunts my dreams to this day. Only difference is, in my dream, there are no more wars or hate. The world is a peaceful orb of equal and respectful nations divided only by distance.

3

DM-426

It was blowing sleet and snow sideways, and then it started to rain. Before we knew it, we were sliding back down the road we had just walked up. I couldn't see but thirty feet out when I looked over at Joe who was not there anymore! "Joe, Joe, where in the hell are you?" I called out. The temp had dropped to minus five, and with over a mile to cover in two feet of snow, I needed to find Joe and find him quick. What started out as a moose hunt just a few hours before had now turned into a search-and-rescue mission!

It was late October when I started reconning for the upcoming winter moose bow hunt on Fort Rich. Months earlier and to my complete surprise, I had drawn the prized tag for DM-426, an area on Fort Rich used only by the military for training and prohibited from hunting unless you have a tag. Because the hunt was on military property and close to Anchorage, you had to attend a mandatory hunting seminar and shooting tests. Here was a team of fish and wildlife experts along with field biologist and enforcement officials with a ton of information. Over the years, I have attended more hunting courses than I care to remember; however, this one really hit home. These folks were incredible and really knew their stuff. Because of the complexity of the training areas associated with the military, you needed to be on your game, and these guys were definitely on theirs.

It was about 7:00 p.m. when my daughter, Olivia, and I pulled up to what looked like an old, abandoned munitions bunker. I thought for sure I was in the wrong place until I saw a guy with a bow in his hand walking around a revetment. We made our way through the labyrinth of concrete walls and finally into a small briefing room where a small crowd was seated.

"Is this the hunting seminar?" I asked like it would be anything else.

A tall, thin guy dressed in camo answered, "Yep, just sign in there if you would."

About an hour later, Livvy and I gathered all of the pamphlets, maps, and diagrams we could and made our way out of the bunker.

"That was pretty cool, wasn't it, Livvy?" I said.

"That was awesome Dada! Can we hunt now?" she asked.

"No, baby, not yet, I still have to prove to them that I can shoot." Because of the proximity of the city to Fort Rich, they had in past hunts unfortunately experienced several wounded moose running across roads, highways, and even dropping dead in someone's backyard. Therefore, to ensure hunters were making the right shots, they set up a 3-D shooting skills range. I had been practicing in the last few weeks and was tuned in pretty good, so I wasn't too worried about qualifying.

I arrived a few minutes early that day and threw a couple downrange at a block they had set up at twenty yards. Moments later we were in the thick stuff, and to my surprise, they had set up one of the coolest 3-D ranges I had ever seen. There were eight different stations that made you shoot through and around varying objects and terrain. Uphill, downhill, standing, sitting, and kneeling shots and then some. With full-size moose targets in varying positions, it was a lot harder than I envisioned but still a lot of fun and learning experience. After eight arrows and an hour later, I got the go card and was on my way. All I needed to do now was to keep practicing and wait for opening day in December.

It was December 15 and opening day when I rolled out of the nice, warm garage and into a cloud of fog, snow, and ice. This was just great, I thought as I rode through the condo complex looking at the two feet of snow we got last night. I swung by to pick up Joe, who had partaken in a few of the spirits last night and wasn't too thrilled with me at the moment. After a brief stop at his favorite coffee shop, we headed to a trail that skirted the east side of the city and Fort Rich property. Even though it was almost 9:00 a.m., it was still dark, and as we sat there watching the snow blowing sideways, we contemplated doing this another day. The snow finally stopped about an hour later, and as we emerged from the truck, the cold hit me like a ton of bricks. It was a balmy 5 degrees, and as we began gearing up, I questioned whether this would be better on another day.

"What do you think Joe?" I asked. "Want to try this another time?"

"Hell no," he said. "I didn't get all dressed up for nothing. Let's hit it!"

About a half-hour later we were on top of a ridge that I had previous reconned when the weather was nice and would have been a good place to glass if it wasn't for the fog. Unfortunately, we couldn't see past our noses and as I tried to wiggle my toes to keep the blood flowing, I realized that I couldn't feel my fingers.

Joe was standing next to me when I turned and asked, "How you doing?" His ski mask was completely caked with snow and ice, and I could barely see his eyes when he gave me a thumbs up. I could tell he was ready to bag this, and when I turned to him again, he was gone.

"Joe, Joe, where in the hell are you!" I called out. The temp had dropped to minus five and with over a mile to cover in two feet of snow, I needed to find Joe and find him quick. What started as a moose hunt just a few hours before was now search-and-rescue mission! The fog was thick, and as I now yelled for Joe, I got no response.

Where in the hell did he go? He was just standing here a minute ago, how far could he have gone? For a moment I thought maybe he was playing a joke, but after a few minutes, the joke was over. It was deathly quiet, and as I stood there freezing to death, I wondered if I should call in help or wait awhile.

"Joe, Joe, Joe," I screamed over and over until I lost my voice. Then out of nowhere, there he was.

"Where in the hell were you?" I frantically asked.

"Dude, that doughnut was killing me," he said, chuckling the whole time.

"Whatever you do, man, don't go over that way—whew!"

We made it back to the truck about an hour later, and as I squished my frozen body into the cab and cranked up the heater, I couldn't help but think that this was going to be a really tough hunt. We sat there for another half hour defrosting into the now-soaked seats. The temperature had gone back up to zero, and the snow and wind started to blow again.

"The hell with this," I said as I put the truck in drive and headed back home.

Due to work, weather, and everything else, Joe and I didn't get back to hunt until December 21. We tried another area of the fort that was known for having a lot of moose but some really rough terrain.

Couldn't be any worse than the last time out, I thought as we headed for the access road. After an hour or so, we were knee-deep in cold and snow; however, unlike our previous outing, the weather was clear, and we could at least see now. We hiked for almost four hours through some of the thickest brush and snow I had ever seen, and although we saw a lot of moose sign, we never saw a moose. It was my turn to buy now, so after the trek back to the truck, we hit the Village Inn for some welcomed pie and piping hot coffee.

It was December 22, and because Joe had to work (yeah right!), my other bud Sam decided to partake in the festivity. It had warmed up to about ten above, and there wasn't a cloud in the sky—a perfect day for hunting! We drove to an entirely different area on the Post and arrived just shy of 10:00 a.m. Still dark out, we suited up, grabbed our gear, and headed down an old access road that dead-ended about seven miles back. Although the

gauge in my truck read 8 degrees, it felt a lot cooler as we shuffled along on the snow-packed road. The sun was up now, melting the clumps of snow off the branches of the trees. Every time a clump would hit the ground, it sounded like something coming through the woods, so we spent a lot of time freaking out. Sam spotted a couple of hovering eagles in the distance, which usually means something is dead, so we decided to check it out. A few minutes later, we were on top of a previous moose kill.

Lucky bastard, I thought as I walked and slid down the hill it was on. We had covered a lot of terrain and were almost at the truck, when we picked up some really fresh tracks. We followed them down the road until they just disappeared as if the moose had flown away.

"That's really weird," Sam said.

We walked down a little farther in hopes of picking them back up but didn't find anything. We were just starting back when I noticed a single set of tracks across the road that seemed to cross where we were standing.

"That's different," I said to Sam. "Were those tracks there when we came this way?"

Sam just shrugged and said, "I didn't see them."

I walked back and forth along the road trying to figure out what direction he was going, but it looked as though the moose had come out onto the road, then danced around a bit, and headed back in! That's the goofiest thing I'd ever seen, a dancing moose, imagine that.

"Must have been cold," Sam said as if he felt like doing the same thing.

I scanned the tracks over and over, and the more I looked, the more I got the feeling like this moose was really close. There were a lot of open woods on the east side of the road, but the west side went in about one hundred yards and then was walled up by a small ridgeline. The best I could tell is that he had maybe gone into the small patch of spruce right in front of the ridge. It was a long shot to say the least, but the curiosity was killing me, and I knew that I needed to go in.

Because noise amplifies even more when it's cold, Sam decided to stay out on the road while I went in. That and I think he just didn't want to get back into the cold, deep snow again. I knocked an arrow, slid down an embankment, and slowly started making my way into the thick, snow-covered canopy of thicket and spruce. The snow was, deep and it seemed to get deeper the farther I got from the road. I lost sight of Sam about one hundred yards in, and as I pulled my boots from the deep snow, crisscrossed with fallen logs and alders, I picked up a fresh set of tracks.

That moose is close, I remember thinking as I fastened my release to the loop on my string. With bow ready to draw, I slowly pushed farther into the darkness of the forest.

Every step now was a struggle in itself as the snow-covered hidden maze of roots and tussocks tripped and grabbed at my boots. Despite the cold, I was sweating now, and I could feel it freezing on my uncovered neck as it dripped slowly off my head. I had just made my way around a thick cottonwood when in the distance I spotted what looked like the top of a moose paddle. The snow was almost up to the base of the spruce, which gave me less than a foot to see through. I tried moving to confirm what I was seeing; however, I couldn't because of the noise. I would need to close the gap, and unfortunately, the gap was really big. I was less than thirty yards away now slowly moving along when before I knew it, I was on my knees crawling in the waist-high snow. I made my way to the base of a spruce tree surrounded by alders and slowly rose up to take a look. In front of me now and less than twenty yards out was what I had envisioned in all of my dreams: a huge bull moose just lying there. He had his back toward me and appeared to be sleeping. All I could see was the top of his head and what appeared at the time to be a huge rack. I could hardly contain myself and the adrenalin flowing through me as I sunk back down in the snow.

This was it, I thought as I now shook uncontrollably with anticipation. I rose back up to take another peek, this time taking my time to assess the situation. He was so close I could have probably ran up and stuck one in him before he got to his feet. As I sat watching him through the tiny window of spruce and alders, I realized that unless he stood up, I had no shot. To make things worse, unless I moved again, the shot would have to go through the tiny opening I was now staring at him through—an area of about twelve square inches. I would need to change one of these dynamics in this situation but wasn't sure which. If I hit just one of the million twigs or branches between him and me, the chances of the shot connecting would probably not be good. I was just sitting there for what seemed like forever, contemplating the options when the bull turned his head around and looked me dead in the eye.

Dammit, I thought, *he busted me*. It took him less than a nanosecond to go from a full prone to a full standing position, and as I watched the snow fly off its back, I went to full draw. He was standing there with his head down in front of his chest looking dead into my eyes. I thought for sure he was going to charge and almost let an arrow fly but held fast. As I struggled to hold the twenty pin on his chest, I waited for the charge, but it didn't come.

"Come on, you big bastard, turn broadside for me," I remember saying to myself. The moments clicked by as the standoff continued. I had been at full draw now for what seemed like eternity, but the bull was not backing down at all. I was shaking pretty good now, but the bull was still content on just waiting it out.

This is really stupid, I thought as I could now feel my leg start to spasm from the cramping. He was still facing me with his head down as if he knew I had no shot, when I went to adjust my now-sleeping leg.

The bull picked his head up and reared up a bit giving me the shot I had been waiting for.

Fuuuuwunk!

I let the arrow fly, and to my surprise, it never touched anything before slamming into its chest. Little did I know at the time that the arrow had sunk deep into the bull's chest splitting its sternum and severing the upper aorta of its heart; it was dead and neither it nor I knew it at the time. I tried jumping up but fell on my sleeping leg. I struggled to get on my feet while knocking another arrow at the same time. Cutting my way through the snow and brush, I ran up just ten yards from the bull, which was wavering from the first hit and sent another deep into its lungs. Blood sprayed profusely from his chest and lungs as it struggled to stay on its feet. Seconds later his hind quarter dropped, and he folded up and fell onto his side. The bull was down, and as I walked up to the first moose I had ever taken with a bow, I couldn't help but to yell, "BBD baby, big bull down!"

My first moose with a bow!

Moments later Sam made it in, and after a BBD victory dance and a lot of knuckling, we both looked at each other like, "What now?" The best part about hunting on military property be it Fort Rich or Elmendorf is the fact that there are a lot of access roads. After making our way back to the truck, we decided to call the game management folks and see if we could get the key to the gate to the road where our moose was down. They had to come out anyhow to record the kill, so why not accompany them to the site? As it all worked out, we were able to drive my truck right up to the road where the moose was and get him out from there. Because of the temperature, we decided to just cut the big guy in half and use a sled to drag him to the truck. We could then butcher him up later at Sam's house.

BBD! Big bull down!
Note my first arrow sticking out his chest!

A few hours and a lot of back-breaking drags with the sled later, we were sipping on beers while cutting up the biggest moose I had ever shot. Although not a monster by any means, the moose measured in at thirty-seven and a half inches, the second-largest moose taken that season on Fort Rich.

Unlike a lot of other moose hunts I had been on and done, I had never taken a moose myself, so this one meant a lot to me. To just draw the tag was lucky enough, then to fill it was even better—especially in light of the weather and conditions. Then to take the moose with a bow was the icing on the cake. Call it what you want, but unfortunately there are moments in my life that I can't recall at all. I seriously doubt, however, that I will ever forget the day I took that moose. The day that I sat just twenty yards away from a behemoth bull moose at full draw freezing my butt off. The day I locked horns in a full-out stare-down or the day I made two of the best shots ever and filled my tag for DM-426.

A special thanks to both Sam and Joe for sticking with me through some of the harshest hunting conditions ever. Thanks, guys.

4

DS-138

As much as I hate to say it, I'm not a religious man by any means; however, sometimes you have to wonder if there actually is a hunting god who oversees everything and decides when and where it's your turn—regardless of whether you're ready for it or not!

It was finally November, and anyone who knows about hunting in Alaska knows that this is the month you need to apply for the seasonal drawing hunts. As with every year, I put in my picks in for the usual moose, caribou, bear, and of course the ever-so-coveted Dall sheep.

Well, to my disbelief, I pulled what's known as the DS-138 (dall sheep) tag. Unlike most other tags, this one was unique, for the area it encompassed was right in my backyard—the foothills of the Chugach Mountains, an alpine area encompassing about one hundred square miles that skirted the beautiful city of Anchorage on three sides and a highway on the other. Now you're probably thinking, how hard could that be?

Well, the tag comes with one small stipulation: the use of any motorized vehicle is prohibited. You can't fly in, parachute, hang glide, or use any other mode of motorized vehicle to get in, out, or anywhere in between. So what would seem like a great tag to draw is, in reality, a really hard tag to fill. The good news was, there's only a total of seven permits, which means the chances of you seeing another hunter back there is probably slim to none. That, plus the fact that most of it is high-country meadows surrounded by endless jagged, snowcapped peaks almost guarantees you low hunting pressure. It goes without saying, though, that no matter how you hunt sheep or mountain goat, it's never easy. This one, though, would be even tougher, for I would be doing this hunt alone. Call me crazy, but it's kind of hard trying to find someone who wants to hike up some of the tallest, most inhospitable mountains in North America on a chance of helping you carry down a dead sheep!

Given the hunt area and limited ways to access it, I spent the next few months doing a lot of "recon" in hopes of finding a place that would prove both easy to access and had an abundance of sheep. Finally, I decided on taking a route through a valley used frequently by hikers and bicyclists to access the southern base of the hunting zone. A valley where I had spotted sheep on many occasions but never had the tag to get one. A valley that would later have significant meaning to me, for just one week before hunting it, I would spread my Mother's ashes among the meadows there and say my final good-byes. She had passed suddenly in June, and one of her final wishes was to have her ashes spread along the hills of the Chugach Mountains. It was a beautiful valley and popular with hikers, cyclists, outdoor enthusiast, and a very small percentage of fortunate hunters like myself.

My original plan was to hunt at least five days: one in, one out, and three to seal the deal! Everything was going according to plan when in July I received word from the boss that because of personnel shortages, all leave was cancelled until further notice. The one time I pulled a tag like this, spent months planning and preparing for it, and just like that, it's over. I was now left with only two weekends between the dates of my tag that I could hunt; however, because of other commitments, I was now only left with just one: Labor Day weekend.

It was finally here, and because I knew the chances of taking a sheep over a weekend were pretty much slim to none, my plan was to bike in on the trail and see what I could see; after all, it was an incredibly beautiful day. If I spotted something, which I really didn't think I would, I could work out a plan then. I loaded my day pack with some jerky, ammo, water, binocs, knife, and of course my rifle. And off I went.

I drove to the trail head parking lot at the base of the mountains; however, because it was Labor Day weekend, the lot was packed with people, cars, dogs, and even a German Oompah band, so I ended up parking about a mile below it. I strapped my rifle, day pack, and everything else to my bicycle, and up the hill I went.

By the time I got to the actual parking lot, I was exhausted and thinking to myself, *Maybe I should have just stayed home.* I mean seriously, what were the chances of taking a sheep over a weekend anyhow? And what were the chances of seeing any wildlife with all these people running everywhere?

As fate would have it, I pressed on and was soon on a well-traveled trail, which after about five miles would put me at the base of the hunting zone. The trail itself was a well-maintained path, which winds its way through the valley like a long gravel snake. For the most part, it was a pretty mild grade; however, what you don't realize is that going into the valley is all uphill. It's so gradual that you really don't notice it until you're coming back down and are on the brakes the whole time. After two hours of some serious pedaling and dodging bear scat, I finally arrived at the base of the mountain and hunting zone. It was pushing seventy-something degrees and blistering hot for Alaska.

After a short break, I broke out the binoculars and started glassing. I had seen tons of bear scat on the trail coming in and figured I would see more bears than anything else when out of nowhere I spotted three huge sheep on top of a ridge.

I had left my spotting scope at home thinking, "I won't need that," and as usual, the sheep were just at the point where I did! My tag was for a full-curl ram, which one of them definitely was. The other two, however, I couldn't tell for sure. As I struggled to focus, I knew that I needed to make a decision and make it now! I dropped my pack, threw my bike in the bushes, grabbed my rifle, and was off. Looking at the hill from the base of the valley, I estimated two to three hours to get into shooting range; however, thanks to adrenaline (not the drink), I made the trek in just over an hour. When I reached the top, all three rams were lying down behind a false ridge, and as I tried making my way along the back side of it, I started a shale-slide, which spooked them. The lead ram stood up quickly followed by the other two, and in less than a second, they were gone.

I thought, *Well, I'm here now. I might as well see what's on the other side.*

A few minutes later I crested the ridge, and to my surprise, all three rams had bedded down about seventy yards from the top. I was sweating profusely and was soaked from head to toe, glasses were all fogged up, and I could hardly breathe. I needed one last look to make sure the "big guy" was legal, and then I would need to shoot.

Panting like a dog that just ran a million-mile marathon, I was sliding my rifle into position and cranking the power up to get a better look when the smallest of the three stood up and looked right at me. I was anticipating him to bolt when the other two lying next to him slowly stood and started looking too. Then the big guy turned broadside and raised his head to get a better look.

It took less than a microsecond to realize that this was a huge and legal ram, and as I put the crosshairs on his chest, the resounding beating of my heart was all I could hear. Not having time now to adjust the power back down, all I could see before I shot was the outline of a shoulder and a lot of white hair! The sound of rocks slamming together in the background was not the sound I was hoping for when I shot, but when the smoke cleared, the big guy was still standing there looking in my direction. I had missed and shot right over his back. I cycled another round and put him in my sights again.

Ka-wam!

He flinched when I shot; however, unlike the first round, this time you could hear the *whap* as the bullet smacked him in the left hind quarter. I struggled to chamber another round, but by the time I was ready to shoot again, he was nowhere to be found! I jumped to my feet to get a better look thinking maybe he rolled down the hill but found nothing. He was gone. I traversed the ridge over and over and did not see anything—no blood trail, nothing.

How could an all-white animal disappear among black and gray rocks? I thought as I helplessly slid on the unstable shale.

I traversed the ridge for what seemed like forever and was just about to give up when I made my way around an outcropping of small boulders; there he was! He had wedged himself up under a small boulder where I couldn't see him, at least that's what he thought. As I made my way around the hill to get a better shot, he limped out and just stood there looking at me as if almost to say, "You lucky bastard!" I put the crosshairs on his chest and dropped him in his tracks! Now the real fun would begin!

Funny sometimes how things work out, but somewhere between the time I rolled out of bed that morning to the time I dropped that sheep, I had completely lost my mind. As I stood there on top of that mountain, next to the biggest ram I had ever seen, I realized that all of my gear was still at the base of the mountain! All I had with me was my rifle and binoculars. My knife along with everything else was all the way down at the base of the mountain! If there ever was a "you dummy" moment, this was one of them.

I had two options now: First, I could go down, get the gear, then come all the way back up; or second, I could try dragging him down. Problem with the latter was the fact that this was a really big ram and weighed a ton; I would need to gut him first. I tried sifting through the abundance of shale rock, but nothing seemed to be sharp enough. I was just about ready to start the trek down the hill to get my gear when I remembered that I had my car keys! With my newly cut house key, I ripped a hole from one end to another and rolled the largest gut pile I had ever seen. It looked like a huge bag of lawn mower clippings mixed with rocks, blood, and bile. It was getting late, and as I scraped and pulled the rest of its insides out, I knew the hard part was just getting started. I had about a fifty-yard pull straight up; then it would be pretty much all downhill from there.

If I could just get it to the top, I thought, *I might have a chance of getting this done today.*

After about an hour, I crested the top of the ridge and could now see the trail. Even gutted, the sheep was a behemoth, and with every drag, I was only gaining a few feet at a time. I sat on top of that mountain until my sweat-soaked body began to shake; then with the last ounce of energy I had, I began the long drag down.

To my surprise, it was a lot easier than I anticipated, especially seeing how well the carcass slid on top of the shale portions. Once in the meadows, I just stayed on top of the berry bushes, and he slid right down the hill. After about an hour, I had gotten to a point where I couldn't drag him any more but was close enough now to make the hike to my bike and pick up the rest of my gear. For the next two hours, I sliced and diced and packed what I could of the meat into my pack and made my way back to the parking lot. I buried the hide and horns under a boulder to keep the bears from getting it, but I would need to be quick in getting back in. It took me about two hours of hard riding with almost two hundred pounds of meat on my back, but I got back in town in time to unload the meat, grab some food, and head back up the hill to get the rest.

I made the ride in just under two hours and started up the hill when I noticed the eagles. There were at least five of them, and some were ravens circling what I knew was the carcass. As I made my way closer toward the site, all I could think about was that a bear had found it and the birds were cleaning up what was left. As I crested the last ridge, I could finally see the boulder and what looked to be a portion of hide with an eagle on top of it.

He was sitting on top of the rear portion of the hide picking off what he could, and it must have been tasty, for I had to actually swat at him with the butt of my rifle before he took off. I had gotten lucky again, for it was just the birds that had found it and not the bears.

My plan had worked, and as I dug the hide and horns out from under the rock, I could only think about how lucky this whole thing had been. In retrospect, what were the chances of pulling the tag in the first place? Then, what were the chances of actually filling it in one weekend, nonetheless one day, then filling it with a beautiful trophy-class ram in an area I accessed with my bicycle?

My bike with the hide and horns waiting to be rolled up on the crossbar.

As I said before, I've never been a religious man, but as I sat there on top of that mountain holding the horns of that majestic animal, looking out across the fall colors of the sun-drenched Chugach Mountains, I couldn't help but to feel like the luckiest man in the world; and I thanked God!

5

FISH ON

"Fish on, fish on" was all I heard when out of nowhere flew a fishing pole past my head. The guy standing next to me sucking on a cigar just chuckled a bit and without even skipping a cast said, "Wow, besides being a nice pole, it looked like it had a fish on it too." Lines and poles were flying everywhere when the next thing I know, someone else is yelling, "Fish on, fish on!" People everywhere had fish on their lines, and I was smack-dab in the middle of it now. With hooks, lines, and one-ounce sinkers flying all around my head, I backed up toward the shore and out of the chaotic mess unfolding in front of me. This was Alaskan combat fishing at its finest, and I was going to savor every moment of it!

People lining the banks

Before getting to Alaska in 1995, my visions of fishing here were of surreal and vast landscapes where only I and the fish existed. Thousands of streams and rivers untouched by human hands. The dream of me standing alone in a salmon and trout-packed river, casting my hand-tied fly with my four-pound fly rod, hooking into fish after fish until my heart was content. Yeah, whatever!

What I found was just the opposite, however, equally as much fun. Before you get discouraged, though, read on. There are basically two schools of thought when it comes to fishing in this great state of ours. Whether you're a serious sport fisher or just a killing machine with a meat hook, Alaska has some fishing for you. The first theory is to kill and catch everything with a gill! The other is to venture away from the norm where you can actually cast a fly rod without wounding someone around you.

THE QUEST

More people lining the banks

If you've never been fishing up here and are thinking "How hard can it be?" well read on, and maybe you'll find out. If you're coming up to do some sport fishing for grayling, trout, dollies, or even pike, your chances of seeing a lot of people are slim to none depending on the time of year and the water you choose to fish in. There are millions of rivers, streams, creeks, and tributaries all offering an abundance and variety of these species.

If you're like me, though, and aren't into catch and release, then strap on a helmet son and grab a rod because you're in for a hoot! Because some of our best salmon fishing spots are accessible by road, the odds of seeing other people increase exponentially. The most popular of salmon fishing rivers located within reasonable driving distances are the Kenai, Russian, Kasilof, and the Big and Little Susitna Rivers. The most popular of course would have to be the Kenai, famous for its ninety-seven-pound king salmon record, followed by the Russian, which hosts more fishermen in a square mile than any other river in the world.

Tom (second from the right) trying to hook one up.

The reason is that you can only fish in certain areas at certain times, and when the fish are in, so are the people; and I mean all of them! There is currently almost four hundred thousand people in Anchorage itself. When the fish are in, the population decreases to around one hundred thousand, and that's during the week! If you plan it right, you'll hit it during the week when the fish are in and crowds are not; however, if not, then, strap in, hang on, and get ready for the ride!

Aaron (second from the left)
trying his luck

First thing you need to know is unless you're looking at spending the money to do a fly out, you're going to get there by driving, hiking, biking, or all of the above. Problem there lies in the fact that others can do the same, so no matter how you cut it, you're probably not going to be completely alone on that beautiful, pristine river. Trust me when I say that if you see a road-accessible body of water in Alaska that's not inundated with fishermen, there aren't any fish in it! This, however, is not a problem if you know where to go and know what to expect. The following are some rules, gear, and styles of fishing universal for almost all salmon fishing in Alaska with a few exceptions. Because the Kenai and the Russian Rivers are the most popular and only about a two-hour drive from Anchorage, I'll start with them first.

In June 1995, a buddy of mine called me up and told me to meet him at the Russian River campground to do some fishing. I showed up the next day with an old saltwater rod and a spool of cord that I've had since a kid. My friend Bill was an Alaskan through and through, and after taking one look at my gear, he walked over to the big green dumpster by the campsite and began smacking it furiously against the bin!

"Ain't gonna be needin' that no more," he said, chuckling the whole time. He walked to the back of his truck and pulled out the biggest Ugly Stik ever made with a reel that could have pulled in Moby Dick and handed it to me. "Eer, this is what you're gonna use ya damn Chechako!"

It was a nine-foot, ten-weight rod with the largest reel I'd ever seen. The line was nothing shy of steel cable.

"Are we fishing for salmon?" I asked in a curious kind of tone.

"Yep, and ya better not lose that damn thing, or you're gonna be goin' swimmin'!"

Being fairly new to Alaska, I had never seen an actual salmon aside from the ones you see in the markets, and all I could think of now was, *Holy crap, what have I got myself into!*

Long story short, if you are thinking about bringing that special hand-made rod or family heirloom that your great-great-grandfather fished with in the '40s up here, don't! Whether you're partial to a fly rod, bait caster, or spinning rig, go and get yourself the biggest damn pole, reel, and line you can find and gear up! Unless you took the first ferry across to where you can fish on the Russian and there aren't that many people around, when you hook up, you need to reel in. Ain't going to be none of that fighting him for an hour stuff because people will cut your line. The mission here is to catch fish and get them in as soon as possible, and if you're struggling with a four-weight bamboo rod with a 1940s reel, you're going to be in a world of hurt. Once you hook up, the people on each side of you will usually move back. If you're lucky, someone will get a net to help you land him. If not, you're going to have to drag him up and get him up on the shore. Best way to do this is to start slowly walking backward and reeling in at the same time.

Once close to the shore, you just give it a huge yank, and up he'll come up—usually! I think the average down there is for every five fish you hook into, you'll end up landing one.

So in case you missed it, if you're going to be fishing the rivers and spots where everyone else will, leave the light gear at home. Instead, go out and get a ten-weight, nine-foot Ugly Stik with a good reel and some fast sinking eight- to ten-weight fly line. From there, all you need is to pick up some Russian River flies at any store in Alaska and a few different size weights, and you're ready to go. Don't forget to get at least a spool of thirty-pound leader to put between your fly line and hook. I usually run about five feet of it, then tie my hook at the end. Then I run a three-fourth-ounce lead shot up about three to four feet from the hook. And if you're wondering what color fly or type to use, check the fishing regulations, for certain areas use certain hooks, and you can get a fine if you're using the wrong one. If you're just fishing the Russian or took the ferry across, look for or ask for a Russian River fly. They are everywhere and in a variety of colors although after eighteen years, I'm kind of partial to the neon green myself. I've seen people pull fish after fish on the banks with just a hook, so don't get too caught up in the whole color thing. Once you get all of this together, all you need to do now is get your feet in the river and start yelling, "Fish on!"

Something else you might want to remember is to bring some good rain gear. If it's not raining when you leave or get there, somewhere along the line it will. If you took the ferry across to the Russian, you'll have to make a trip all the way back, and that could mean losing a good spot. And unlike a lot of places in the Lower 48, there's not going to be an espresso or hot dog stand where you're going so bring a snack or some serious food if you're a big eater or hypoglycemic. Last but not least, don't forget to have a good time. A man once told me that being alive don't mean you're living. If you're in Alaska and standing on the bank of any river, you're living so enjoy it!

Fish on!

6

HEY, BOO BOO

It was July 2006 when I finally pulled the dusty case out of the basement. I hadn't shot my bow since last year this time, and as I pulled it out and blew off the dust, it felt like I was holding a long-lost friend.

One of the best-kept hunting secrets in Alaska is what's referred to as the "Haul Road caribou hunt." The Haul Road is the only road going north to Prudhoe Bay and the oil fields. If you've ever watched *Ice Road Truckers*, it's the same road without all of the ice. What's supposed to be a two-lane road in the show normally turns into a one-lane gravel and mud path in the summer. It is, however, the only way in or out of Prudhoe Bay and Deadhorse with the exception of a small airport. Originally built with the sole purpose of supplying the pipeline, it was restricted to commercial trucking and corporate vehicles for years. Unlike other parts of Alaska, once you get across the Brooks Range, it's like the largest unfenced zoo in the world. There are millions upon millions of caribou that travel in herds and at any given moment can cross the road. Because of this and

Herd of caribou

the fact that there were more than three hundred trucks totaled and eleven fatalities in less than ten years, they opened the road up to hunting in 1998, and it's been open ever since.

Lone caribou bull

Because of the proximity of the pipeline to the road, hunting was first restricted to the use of bows only. Then they later opened it up to firearms as long as you were five miles away from any portion of the pipeline. Although that doesn't sound hard, what people forget until they get up there is that the terrain is nothing but tundra. If you've never walked on tundra, it's like walking on a really soft bed for hours and hours. The first time I tried it, I had spotted a small herd of caribou about a mile from the road.

I thought, *No problem, I'll just walk out there and put a stalk on them.* I made it about a half mile from the road; then because my thighs were burning so bad, I had to turn back. By the time I got to the truck, I was completely spent and could hardly walk.

The first time I hunted it was back in August 2001. I had heard about it for years but never had the time or opportunity to go. Then John, a friend from work, asked me one day if I'd like to go, and that was the start of my obsession. He had done the hunt a few times and swore by it, so it was kind of a no-brainer for me. Because it would take at least one day to get there and one day to get back, we would only have two full days to kill something. We packed his S-10 full of gear and blasted out of Anchorage after work on a Friday night. Eighteen hours and a whole sixty-four-ounce thermos of coffee later, we were there. It was about 10:00 a.m. when I awoke to the force of the seatbelt catching me when John slammed on the brakes.

"What in the—" I started to ask when I realized why he had stopped. There was a herd of caribou crossing right in front of the truck. We were in the thickest fog I had ever seen, and the caribou had come out of nowhere. Now just inches from the hood of the truck, I watched in amazement as the herd slowly meandered around the truck looking at us. John said they were all too small as he eyed one for his wall.

Caribou on a lake

We finally made it to Deadhorse about noon and stopped into the Caribou Inn, one of only two places to lodge if you had a reservation. It fills up quick in the summer due to the many birders who ride around in buses trying to spot a pepper-speckled pickle popper or some other rare bird. Guess there's a lot of them out here because we passed at least two busloads of people on the way in. John had talked about the food in this place since leaving Anchorage, so it only seemed fitting that we try it out. Nothing more than a huge cafeteria, I made my way through the line with oil workers, engineers, and scientists.

"That will be twenty dollars," the lady at the checkout said.

I looked down at my bowl of soup, an egg-salad sandwich, piece of pie, juice, and coffee and asked, "Did you say twenty dollars?"

"Dat twenty dolla, sir," she said again.

Not wanting to look like a tight wad, I pulled a twenty out of my wallet and reluctantly handed it to her. John was back about four people looking at me now, wondering what the holdup was.

He made it to the table a few minutes later when I asked, "Was yours twenty dolla too?" He just laughed as we dug into the grub.

Later, John gave me the fifty-cent tour as we rode around the confines of Deadhorse. It was nothing but a shanty-town-looking conglomeration of old oil rigs mixed in with square weathered tin buildings. It was probably an ugly sight when it was all new, yet after all these years. We turned the corner at the main intersection where under a "Welcome to Deadhorse" sign laid the biggest caribou I had ever seen. John stopped as I clicked off pic after pic. Because there was no hunting within the confines of the "city," the caribou would come in and relax wherever they wanted. Actually, everywhere they wanted, for as we turned another corner, there in the middle of the entire complex was a huge herd of them. They were everywhere. Walking up and down

Caribou in Deadhorse

the roads, in the back of alleyways, lying down in the parking lots—everywhere. It was unbelievable, and as I continued to click away, John pointed to a clump of grass just off the road.

What looked like a grassy bush at first suddenly started to move. As it turned toward the truck and stood up, I could now see it was a bear. It was just a little guy but had a beautiful blond, almost-white coat and was chasing a prairie dog around the base of a hole.

Grizz chasing a mole just outside of Deadhorse

We hunted hard the next two days but never spotted any trophy-class bulls. We were heading back when out of nowhere a small bull jumped right out in front of us.

"That's it, John," I said. "I'm shooting that bastard!" I bailed out off the truck, put the twenty-pin on his brisket, and let it fly.

Faaaawack!

The sound of the arrow whistling through the air followed by the sound of cracking bone was not the sound I was looking for. I had unfortunately hit him in the head, and as he now wandered aimlessly into the tundra, I knocked another arrow and gave chase. He was about thirty yards out now when I let another one fly. Unlike the first, this one went right under his belly.

"Dammit," I muttered under my breath.

I knocked another arrow and let it fly, this time skimming it right off the top of its back. He took off again just staying out of range of my fifty-yard pin. I followed him across the open tundra and up to the edge of the only hill in the arctic, where I lost sight of him. As I looked at my quiver, I realized that I only had one arrow left and no gun; if I were to come across a bear, I was screwed. The ridge was just south of pump station 2, and I could see the entire Sagavanirktok (Sag) River from the top.

"Where in the hell did he go?" I asked, standing there trying to catch my breath. I hiked all over the hill and along the edge of the ridge but didn't see anything.

The brush was about a foot to two-feet high. Green, yellow, and red-spotted tundra bush with patches of small berry bushes. He could be hunkered down in any of it, I thought as I made my way up to another hidden gorge. I was just standing there admiring the view more than I was hunting when just beneath me, I saw something move. Thinking it might be another prairie dog, I looked and waited for it to move again. Then, just like that, the bull stood up, looked straight back at me, and jumped off the edge. I let one go as the bull leapt straight off and into the air below. I watched the arrow pierce its back and exit its chest as he disappeared below me. Seconds later, I heard the sound of its crash and breaking bones as it tumbled farther down the hill.

Not knowing for sure what I was going to find, I ran up to the edge and peered over to see the now-dead bull lying on the shelf of a really steep ledge.

"Yeah, baby," I yelled in triumph. "Yeah, baby, he's down," I continued to yell. Then as I turned and looked back down the hill to the truck, I realized that this was going to be a really long day.

The bull was about halfway down the really steep hill and had gotten caught of a small shelf. Because the hill was almost vertical, we were going to need a rope and maybe even a winch. I started the trek back to the truck, which now seemed to be a lot farther than I remembered. After explaining to John where the bull was, he just rolled his eyes and shook his head. A few minutes later, we were both making the trek back in to retrieve the bull.

Standing on top of the ledge now, John peeked over, looked back at me, and said, "Ya, couldn't have made this any harder, that's for sure."

There was nothing to tie the rope off on, so we would both need to scale the face and drop down on the shelf. No sooner than we had started down the hill when John started a slide.

"Hang on," he yelled.

It was an avalanche of earth, and as I held onto the now-moving hill, all I could do was wait for it to stop. We came to a stop just short of the bull, but still needed to sidehill to it. Problem was, we were on the steepest part of the face now, and it was straight down and about one hundred feet to the bottom. I tried not to look down but did while trying to find my footing.

"Holy crap, John," I uttered. "That's a long way down."

"Don't look down," he called back.

"Yeah, thanks, John," I said back. *Good timing*, I thought as I slowly crawled along the flaking rocks of the hill.

We were almost there, and as I watched John jump down to the shelf that the bull was on, my right foot gave way, and I was heading down the hill again. On my stomach now, I clawed at the dirt above me and found a root.

"Whew, that was close," John yelled back. "Stop goofin' off and get your ass over here."

Moments later I found myself standing on the edge of the tallest hill in the Arctic National Wildlife Refuge (ANWR), staring down at the first caribou I'd ever taken with a bow. I took a moment and looked across the vastness of the arctic, then looked down again, and backed up really quick.

"How in the hell are we going to get this thing out of here?" I asked John.

He took his hat off, wiped the sweat from his brow, and with a serious look on his face said, "Helicopter. We're going to need a freaking helicopter."

We spent the next hour or so slicing and dicing the bull up on that small, tiny unstable shelf. With everything stuffed now in and on my pack, we headed back up the face of the hill. To my surprise, it was a lot easier going up than it was coming down. Like a big spider, I just lay down on my stomach and used all fours to crawl back up. We got to the top about an hour later and back to the truck another hour after that.

My first boo with a bow.
Note the mosquitos all over the meat. Yum!

It was early evening as we packed the meat into the cooler, washed up along a stream, and started the journey back to Anchorage. We got to Coldfoot about 1:00 a.m. and just in time for the buffet. The only stop between Fairbanks and Deadhorse, Coldfoot was nothing short of an oasis out here. A truckers' paradise open 24-7, sporting hot showers, coffee, wide-screen TVs, and a midnight buffet to kill for. We tanked up, got some grub, and hit the road again.

As usual, there were several wildfires burning in and around the road, and the closer we got to Fairbanks, the thicker the smoke got. I grabbed a shirt and wrapped it around my face, rolled the windows up tight, and began passing open patches of forest that were burning. The smoke was thick and getting thicker when we came up on a truck flashing its lights. The truck was rolling up when I noticed a burning ember stuck in the grill of his hood.

"Hey, do you know you're on fire?" I said, pointing to the front of his truck.

He jumped out of the cab and emptied an extinguisher on it. "Thanks. It's getting kinda iffy farther up. You might want to turn around. It's jumping the road in a few spots as you can see," he said while smiling the whole time.

John was awake now and looking for something to cover his face with when he asked, "We're almost there, aren't we?"

"Yeah, John, go back to sleep, I'll wake you when we get to Faibanks."

A few hours later we were in some of the scariest stuff I'd ever seen. Fires were burning on both sides of the road, and you could feel the heat as we flew past the patches of flame-engulfed spruce. Funny thing about the wildfires up here is unless life or property is in imminent danger, you won't find anyone fighting them. There was nobody out here except us, and if the truck broke down, we were toast—literally. We were going about as fast as we could and going across a really narrow bridge when through the smoke I saw this huge black dog standing in the middle of it! I locked up the brakes and skidded to a stop as the dog just stood there broadside looking at us. I was just about to get out of the truck to see if I could maybe catch it when it hit me.

There's no dogs out here. That's a freaking wolf! I thought.

John was just starting to come around when the wolf walked up to his window, stopped, looked right at us, and disappeared into the smoky night. That was really freaky, I thought as I found first gear again and popped the clutch.

"What's going on?" John now asked. "Why are we stopping?"

"Go back to sleep, John. It was just a wolf—just a wolf," I said.

We made it to Fairbanks around noon, had some lunch, tanked up again, and changed our smoke-saturated clothes. We stunk so bad that the first thing the waitress asked was, "Are you guys firefighters?"

"Nah, just idiots," John replied.

The rest of the trip back was all highway, and after a stop in Nenana at a small coffee shop, we headed south again and made it into Anchorage about 10:00 p.m.

John moved out to the valley about a year after that, and like so often happens with people who move out that way, we kind of fell out of touch. His daughter Maggie who is only six now is hunting and took her first black bear a few months back. I know this because her picture is all over the boards at the Sportsman's, and there's even a picture of her with a bear in the current hunting regulations. Not sure what it was for John, but that hunt was pretty darned awesome for me. It was only because of him and him alone that I got to take and retrieve my first caribou—a caribou, hunt, and friend that I will never forget.

Another bull taken the year after

7

THE HOW-TO GUIDE FOR HUNTING KODIAK BROWN BEARS

So you did it; you finally drew a tag to hunt the great Kodiak brown bear. Now what?

Nothing like a nice bath and a salmon dinner!

Unlike planning for most other hunts in Alaska, putting together a Kodiak bear hunt is a little harder than most. For one, the only way to access the hunting area is either by plane or boat, or a combination of both. Both have their advantages as well as disadvantages; however, having done both, I opt for working off of a boat. Here, you spend the majority of your time on a nice, warm boat cruising in, out and along the inlets and bays glassing for the elusive bruins. Once you spot one, a skiff is used to put you on shore and hopefully within range. A few advantages to the boat is that you can stay dry, cover more terrain, and not have to worry about the elements or bears getting you at night. If the weather gets bad, you duck into a bay and get out of it. If you get wet, which you will, you have a nice, heated cabin to dry off in. The best part about working off of a boat, though, is being able to sleep at night without worrying about becoming a statistic—hate when that happens! Although bears are really good swimmers, there has never been an account of a brown bear crawling into a boat—especially a thousand-pound Kodiak brown bear!

On the other hand, if you fly in and get dropped off, you will need an abundance of gear to include a really good and heavy tent, cook gear, rations, and all of your other gear. And don't forget a raft or skiff to get around in, for more than likely, you will not be able to see anything unless it's on the same beach or in your camp. As with the shore hunt I did a few years back, every bear we saw was just across the bay, but we couldn't get to them because we didn't bring a skiff. Talk about a frustrating hunt! Then don't forget the most important piece of equipment when doing a Kodiak hunt on land: a bear fence. They are curious creatures by nature, so it's a given that you will be visited by bears at some point in your hunt. Whatever you do, don't forget where the fence is at when you wake up in the middle of the night for a nature break. Trust me when I say they work!

For those of you who are like me and really aren't crazy about boats, the good news is, it's not that bad. In fact, once you get out of the coastal area, the water is usually calm. Even calmer still once you get into the many passages and bays. Remember that the bigger the boat, the better, so keep this in mind when booking your trip. Personally, I always drug up on either Bonine or Dramamine the day before just in case, then taper off, or go cold turkey after the first day or so. I like Bonine because it doesn't make you as drowsy and wears off pretty quick.

As far as working off of a boat, there are two types of charters in Alaska: the transporter and the guide. Only difference is, the guide will cost you about another $10,000! The average price for a five-day guided Kodiak bear hunt is about $14,000. The average price for the same hunt using a transporter is about $1,500 per person depending on the amenities and services offered.

With the economy as it is, these prices will fluctuate with the price of fuel, so don't be surprised if they are a little higher. As with anything else, there are both advantages and disadvantages to both. A guide will "almost" guarantee either putting you on a bear or getting you one, whereas a transporter merely does just that: They get you to and from the hunting zone. It depends a lot on the guide; however, most cover all the gear, meals, skinning, and shipping; all you need to do is pull the trigger when he or she tells you to.

I have used an old Coast Guard (Coasty) friend of mine who runs a boat out of Kodiak Harbor. I have used him for three different hunts, and he is without a doubt the most knowledgeable and safest captains I have ever seen. Besides knowing the waters around Kodiak like the back of his hand, he and his family are amazingly great people. Sam Catt captains a thirty-two-foot Reinell, the *El Gato*. We initially started out with Sam and a deckhand a few years back, but after learning the ropes, it's just been Sam, myself, and usually one other hunter for the last few trips.

Another bear bites the dust!

So after deciding how you're going to hunt, the next question should be, what to bring? The answer is simple: *everything!* Actually if you're working off of a boat, your list will be surprisingly short depending on the type of charter. I could sit here and suggest some of the things you should consider bringing; however, being a longtime veteran of this hunt, I am going to tell you exactly what to bring, so take some notes.

First and foremost would be to bring some serious painkillers: Motrin, Advil—whatever works for you. If you're lucky, you will spot bears at the get-go; however, if not, you will be spending all day glassing from a moving boat. This in itself should earn you some sort of merit badge, but it doesn't. All it means is that by the end of the day, you will have a headache, neckache, and more. If you want to see what it's really like, practice holding your binoculars up to your face for eight hours, and you will know exactly what I'm talking about. Everything from the top of your head to about mid-torso is going to hurt. Don't forget to bring enough for you and everyone else, for they will be looking for them too.

The next thing would obviously be your gear. What kind of clothes, how much, brand names? The rule of thumb in Alaska is to always go with the priciest gear you can find! *Not!* Sure, you can go out and get the best of everything, but trust me when I say that they don't make any waterproof gear that's completely waterproof! And I'm not going to name any brands like Helly Hansen Impertech II rain gear, but that's about all you'll need to hunt in. The hunting season for these beautiful bears is unfortunately during some of the rainiest months on record; therefore, somewhere in your hunt (if not all of it), you will be wearing rain gear or getting really wet! If your rain gear is solid green, don't worry; funny thing is, bears don't have good eyesight, so when they see a solid dark color, it appears to be black, which in turn leads them to think that you're just another bear. With any luck, they'll come in closer for a better look. If you're in camo, though, and get spotted by moving, it looks strange to them, and they usually end up fleeing. Worth every penny and then some, a pair of Helly pants and jacket in solid dark green is going to set you back at around $140—$170 if they are in camo.

Thus far we have painkillers and rain gear; good start, however, there's more. Next few items on the list would be a couple of pairs of camo pants. I wear one, dry one but usually change out the socks and undies every day. If you don't get the time, you can always turn the underwear around if taco night sneaks up on you. I always pack more camo shirts than pants— one for each day of the hunt to keep down the scent.

So in short, two pairs of pants, a long-sleeve shirt for each day, a pair of socks for each day, and an underwear for each day. In addition, I usually wear a light T-shirt under the camo long sleeve. Then add at least two hats, one warm one and maybe a breathable ball-cap type. I have a Filson hat that has the fold-down earflaps that I have used extensively. Then add in at least one large, warm jacket and another one to layer under it. Layering is the only way to survive up here, so bring a few jackets of different weights. Then add at least two pairs of gloves, for they will get wet, even the rubber-insulated, waterproof ones. It's pretty much a ritual once we get back on the boat to strip off everything from the day and hang it out to dry; everything will get wet, count on it. After a few minutes, the boat will resemble a Chinese laundry junk!

Now for the good part. I have seen many of hunters with really nice, expensive, and waterproof boots do nothing but struggle through the hunt because of wet boots and frozen feet. I bring two pairs of boots and suggest you do the same. One is a LaCrosse 180-gram Thinsulated rubber knee boot with the Burly sole. There are other types of soles that are equally good; however, that Burly sole seems to stick to those slippery, kelp-covered rocks like glue. The other pair of boots is the same, just in the hip-wader version. Trust me when I say these are all you'll need. Oops, that's not completely true. When I get back on the boat, I slide on a pair of dry and toasty bedroom slippers, and that's it.

The next piece of gear is a favorite of mine and is where I draw the line on expense cutting. When I first started hunting in Alaska, I had an old pair of Tasco Binoculars in an 8×42. A friend of mine had an old pair of Swarovski 8×42s that had seen better days but still obviously worked, for he had killed everything in Alaska twice over. Every time we went hunting, he'd constantly be picking out game like we were in a zoo. I just thought it was because he knew what to look for until I borrowed his glasses one day. The next day, I went to the bank, took out a small loan ($1,000), and bought a pair of Swarovski 10×42s and have been killing stuff ever since. The difference between a good pair of glasses and a great pair is not just the price. It was a night and day difference looking through those Swarovskis. My point is, don't try to spare expenses when it comes to optics. If you can't see the game, you can't hunt it. For those of you who plan on roaming the countryside and getting up high to glass, bring a (good) spotting scope, for you will need it. I have seen bears five miles away come into range in less than thirty minutes. If just working off the boat, good luck—for even on a flat, calm day, the ocean is still moving, and it's almost impossible to see anything through a spotting scope, thus the binoculars. Swarovskis, Zeis, and Leupold are the leaders in optics and rightfully so. Make one of them an addition to your gear list, and watch your trophy room grow.

So now we come to my favorite and one of the most controversial issues of all time: what to shoot with. I have seen everything from handguns to spears kill bears, so when I'm asked this question, my answer would be "Whatever you're comfortable killing things with!" If we're talking rifles, I shoot a .338 Winchester Magnum with a 225-grain Nosler Partition. This combination seems to work well with my rifle and me;

however, that doesn't mean it will for you. Personally, I suggest shooting the largest-caliber rifle you can shoot comfortably and proficiently. If you can shoot a .475 but can't hit anything with it, what's the point? If you're bringing a handgun, I suggest nothing smaller than a .500 with the largest barrel, load, and round you can find. These are amazingly tough animals, and I've seen them take off and disappear into the brush after being riddled with round after round of .475!

I am always amazed at people who shoot one round and wait for the running bear to go down only to be surprised when it disappears into the brush. I equip all of my rifles with one of those cheap, ugly round belts that slide right over the butt. Then I stuff it full of whatever it is I'm shooting. When I hit the shore, the first thing I do is chamber a round, place the gun on safe, and stuff another round back in the magazine, so everything I have is completely full of ammo. Then, if I'm fortunate enough to have a shot at a bear, I shoot until I'm completely empty, don't have a good shot any more, or my barrel melts! This is not one of those one-shot-, one-kill-type animals; this is the largest, meanest, most vicious, and deadliest predator in North America, and if you have ammo, I suggest you use it. They say there's nothing worse than going into the brush after a wounded bear, but there is; there's going into the brush after a wounded Kodiak brown bear! If you remember anything from this article, remember this: Shoot until you can't shoot any more, then shoot some more. You can't patch the holes on a wounded bear, but you can on a dead one!

A side note to this topic is ammo. Do yourself a favor and bring at least two boxes or at least forty rounds of the same ammo made by the same manufacturer. I knew a guy who brought six rounds of .338/378 in different grains and manufacturers, only to be baffled at why he missed all six shots. That and the fact that if you run out of ammo out there and nobody else is shooting the same caliber you are, your hunt is over.

For those of you who are looking at doing this hunt with a bow, my suggestion for you is don't! Being a spot-and-stalk hunt only (no baiting allowed), it's an incredibly tough hunt to begin with. Then add in the terrain, the weather conditions, and the fact that most bears don't go down immediately with a bow and you're setting yourself up for failure and maybe even death. If this is your first bear hunt and you've been reading bear tales and other sci-fi stories, just remember this: Contrary to all you've heard and read, *all* bears can run uphill, downhill, and sidehill really, really, really fast! More than likely, you will have to either find a bear that's sleeping or ambush one to get a good shot. If in the open, your chances of stalking one to within bow range is highly unlikely and then extremely dangerous. If you decide to use a bow, bring a lot of arrows and broad heads, for the shots will not be as easy as they were on the range. Don't get me wrong, I am an avid bow hunter, and one of these days when I have a lot of time and not really interested in success rates anymore, I'm going to take my bow. For now, though, I'll stick with my trusty .338.

And whatever you do, either pack a backup pistol or have a friend with a really large rifle as a backup just in case you don't get a good shot. Even with a good kill shot, they've been known to run at speeds of over thirty miles per hour and die five miles away!

A sidebar to hunting with a bow is this: practice your long-range shots! And when I say long range, I mean distances of more than fifty yards. And remember that they are really hairy creatures and your velocity will drop tremendously after the first forty, so bring some really sharp broad heads. I use the Slick Trick four-blade broad heads for everything I hunt up here and have never been disappointed at their performance.

Once you figure out what you're shooting and what ammo to use, now it's time to get on the range and start practicing. If you're like most folks, you'll hit the range, set up a few targets, and a rest and send a few rounds downrange to make sure your scope is on. If you're smart, though, and really want a bear, you'll bring at least two boxes of the exact ammo you'll be shooting on the hunt and plan on spending at least a day on the range. Again I shoot a .338 with a 3-1/2x14 on it. It doesn't matter what kind of scope you have or even if you have a scope; as long as you can shoot and shoot well, that's all that will matter when the time is right.

I start out by putting up two targets: one at one hundred yards and one at two hundred. Then I'll break out my shooting rest and strap my rifle in. All I want to do at this point is to touch the trigger without touching the rifle. If everything goes right, I'll be about an inch to two inches high at one hundred yards. If not, make an adjustment. Then I'll do the same at two hundred until I'm satisfied with the way the rifle is shooting. Don't forget to let your barrel cool between rounds, for this too will make a huge difference at longer ranges. Then I'll start shooting in the free or standing position, prone, kneeling, and sitting. For me, my best position for shooting is sitting; however, it is different for everyone, so find yours and practice using it. The last thing I do that unfortunately gets a lot of attention is run in place until I begin breathing hard, then shoulder my rifle in the standing position as fast as I can, and shoot the one-hundred-yard target. Call it what you will, but I guarantee that somewhere in your hunt, you will be struggling for air and shaking like a leaf while looking at a bear in your sights. Try it at fifty yards, and after you realize you can't hit diddly, then you'll know why I practice this. The veterans on the range will know exactly what you're doing, but it's the younger, inexperienced guys who look at you like you're crazy. Not only is it an essential way to prepare for what awaits you on this type of hunt, but it's also a great way to make a few extra bucks if you get good at it and your friends are not!

So your charter is booked, you're all geared up, have been practicing your shooting—what else is there to know? Here is where you need to ask yourself one simple question: What do brown bears eat? If you can't answer this without thinking about it, then you're not ready, for you don't know the animal you're hunting. Where do they live? When do they move? How do they move? Where is the kill zone? And perhaps the most difficult question of all, how do I judge a big brownie?

Without a doubt, bears in general are the hardest of all animals to judge on size. Throw in the fact that it will be raining sideways, they're two hundred yards out, and the grass they're standing in is three feet tall, and all I can say is good luck with that. If you're lucky, they'll be on the shore or out in the open where you can see them clearly. Even then, they always look bigger when they're inflated! Can't even tell you how many times I have walked up on what was supposed to have been a "monster" dead bear to realize that ground shrinkage got them! Or the ever-so-common "That's not the bear I was shooting at!" line. I think that when we spot a bear, the adrenalin takes over, making things seem bigger than they actually are. Best thing I can tell you is that there are numerous guides on this subject, and I would look at them all—a lot. My experience has only taught me to look for the obvious: If the bear jumps out at you as being a behemoth, he probably is. Just be careful and take the time to glass him good, if you can. If a bear is walking really slow and hunkering back and forth as he walks, he's probably a big bear. If you can't see daylight between his belly and the ground, he's probably a big bear. If you can see his head and it has no ears, it's probably a big bear. If his eyes are real close, has no ears, and no apparent neck, he's probably a big bear. If he's longer than your ten-foot skiff he's chewing on, he's probably a big bear. If you can't distinguish its arms or legs from the rest of its body, it's probably a big bear. And the all-time, without-a-doubt sign that he's a big bear is if he's charging you in a flat-out run; he's definitely a big bear! If you've never hunted Kodiak, you're in for an incredible surprise, for it's not a question of *if* you're going to see bears, but it's *when* and *how many*.

Kodiak is a big open bear zoo without the fences. Unless you're blind or spend all day sleeping, you're going to see bears—a lot of bears. Hard part is picking the one you think is a good one. If you run after every bear you see, you're just going to kill yourself. Therefore you need to learn to judge a bear and judge them quickly. And if you think you can do that with a spotting scope off the back of a boat, good luck. All I've ever seen that do is make a person feed the fish! So take the time while you're on the boat or in the woods to glass them good before putting a stalk on them. Remember that a lot of bears in the spring will be rubbed, which is really hard, if not impossible to see until it's too late. Look around their sides behind the front shoulders and on their hind quarters; if you see it's lighter than the rest of them or a different color, their probably rubbed. In short, take your time if you can and make sure it's the one you want before pulling the trigger. Another note here is to make sure that the bear doesn't have cubs. Many times the sows will leave the cubs in the woods when foraging. All you'll see is a lone bear unless you take the time to ensure it's *not* a sow with cubs. A fact worth mentioning here is that if you're unfortunate enough to stumble upon a sow with cubs, be ready. She will more than likely charge, and it won't be a false charge; she will be going for the kill! They are extremely aggressive when with cubs, which is why I always have a round in the chamber when hunting these beasts! Although it's not illegal to shoot a sow, it is if they have cubs, so be careful. And whatever you do, do *not* run. If you can't get a shot off and it knocks you down or grabs an appendage, try to act dead. Most bears seem to have ADD and will usually give up pretty quick if they believe you're no longer a threat. If it's still gnawing on you after a few seconds, my suggestion is to say a prayer and try fighting back; that's why I always carry a seven-inch bowie knife! You probably won't win, but they'll remember you!

So what's the best way to hunt these, guys? you ask. There's a couple of schools of thought on this, but if you want my opinion, here it is. First and foremost is to know when they move. During the spring when the bears are starting to just come out of their dens, they move slow, but usually move all day looking for food. Then once their bellies are full, they'll start moving in the very early morning and late afternoon and night. Later in the season, you'll be lucky if you get to see them at all unless they're out in an open area or on the beach. For the most part, though, dusk to dark is prime time, so be ready.

Another tip when using a boat is to stay on the boat until you see the one you want, then figure out a way to get to them. I've seen a lot of hunters go off into the brush like they're running a marathon, only to come back exhausted, frustrated, and empty-handed. The bush out there is their territory, and if you trample in it like you're Daniel Boone, the only thing you're going to come out of it with is a lot of cuts and a dirty rifle. If you want to hunt on the ground or just get off the boat for a while, find a spot up high where you can glass all around you and stay there. Brownies have an incredible nose, so pick a place that's downwind of where you're looking and hunker down until you see one. If you decide to go this route, you will need a (good) spotting scope. Personally, all I ever use and carry are an old pair of Swarovskis in a 10×42; however, if you have a spotting scope, bring it and use it whenever you can.

If you're hunting strictly off the boat, once you spot them, it will be the captain's job to get you on shore or close enough for a shot. Hard part is getting close enough for even that. Once you spot one and get to shore, you'll have to figure out the best way to stalk them. Once on the ground, only two words come to mind: wind and wind! Hunting bears is all about scent, and they have one of the best sniffers on the planet. A bear with a good nose can smell you up to ten miles away. The best you can hope for is that you come across an old record-book bear with a bad eye, bad leg, and a bad nose. If you're not downwind or the wind is swirling, they will smell you and probably run. The younger bears may not based on just a new smell or different smell; however, the older, larger, or mature bears will associate a different smell to danger and will run. Likewise, if there is no wind, you may as well just stay on the boat, for that is the worst condition you can have when hunting bears. Even though there seems to be no wind, our scent is swirling about and making its way wherever there is air. So no wind is actually worse than being upwind. With any luck, though, you'll be able to get within range and make a good shot. If you're fortunate enough to bag one of these behemoths, the fun has just begun. With the average brownie weighing around five hundred pounds, the good news is you don't have to pack out the meat. The bad news is that the average hide will square eight feet and weigh at least 150 pounds. Not a big deal if you shoot him on the beach; however, when you decided how beautiful the countryside was and walked for two miles into it, now it's a *huge* deal! I had a buddy who shot one about a mile away from the shore, and it took us two days to get him back on the boat! So how do you pack a five-hundred-pound bear out of the woods? you ask.

    The obvious answer here would be "Any way you can!" Actually, how you get them back to the boat or camp depends on a lot of factors, most importantly the size of the bear. If he's a ten-foot boar that's been eating really well, his hide alone is going to weigh at least two hundred pounds and skull about another fifty! This is where the words *game skidder* come in handy.

Nothing more than a really tough sheet of plastic with some eyelets around the edges, the game skidder is the most important tool you'll ever use when hunting brownies. I have seen people construct these themselves; however, I buy mine online at Cabela's for a mere $25. The rolled-up, one-pound piece of plastic will fit into just about any day pack and even comes with a pull cord. Once your bear is down and hide is off, you simply fold and roll the skidder around your hide and skull, cinch up the edges, and start pulling; the skidder will do just that—skid. The first time I used one, my buddy had bagged a huge bear that took us two days of pulling on a skidder to get him out. If it wasn't for that little piece of plastic, we would have had to cut the hide into at least two pieces. So unless the guy or guys you're hunting with are bodybuilders or in really good shape, the game skidder is the only way to go. I have seen people even use snow sleds; however, they are big, heavy, and bulky and hard to carry around. The game skidder is part of my pack every time I enter the woods.

The only other way is to roll up the hide into a ball and attach it to your frame pack or backpack and throw the skull in your buddy's pack. I was with a guy who shot a seven-footer and thought he could lug the whole thing out on his frame pack. He was only thirty-seven at the time and in pretty good shape. I thought it would be no problem for the ex-army grunt that I'd seen throw iron around in the gym like it was nothing. We were only about a mile from the shore, and I thought it would be pretty easy. I was carrying the skull in my day pack, and he had the hide. We made it less than one hundred feet when we had to make the first stop and adjustment. Then about another two hundred feet for the second, then the third, then he just about passed out when we started back up a small hill. We decided to wrap it up around a small spruce tree and put each end over both of our shoulders.

Three hours and a lot of aches later, we broke out of the thick alders and onto the black, sandy beach. Point being, either bring a lot of people to help lug it out or get yourself a game skidder.

Once the hunt is over and you get back to town, the immediate question of "Now what do I do with the hide and skull?" should be the first thing that pops in your head. The answer is pretty simple although the choices can be complicated. If you did everything right and bagged a bear, before you stuck it in the bag, you should have salted it really well so that the hair doesn't slip. After that, you kept it in the coolest place you could find without actually freezing it. All you need to do now is decide on what you want to do with it. Depending on how much time you have will ultimately drive your choice process, so let me make it easy on you. If you want a nice rug, full body, or anything else done, with the bear, take it to a taxidermist in Alaska. Not only do they know how bears are supposed to look, but they also do them all of the time. If you have a buddy down in the Lower 48 who's done a few, all I can say is good luck. I've seen those bears, and they're embarrassing.

Although there are a number of well-reputed taxidermists in Alaska to choose from, my suggestion is to take it to Knights Taxidermist on Arctic Boulevard in Anchorage. You may have even seen their TV show *Mounted in Alaska*. They have a team of expert taxidermists there who are without a doubt the best in the state. Just a short drive from the airport, all you have to do is get it there, and they'll do the rest. They'll seal it, work it, and then ship it to wherever you want when it's done.

For years now I have brought all my work there and have been awestruck every time I see the finished product. They are true artists in every sense of the word, and it shows in everything they do.

So in case you missed it, start gearing up and go as light as possible. Start practicing your shooting skills, for they will be tested. Learn about the animal you're hunting and know where the kill zones are for any given angle. There is an unlimited amount of information on the state web page (state.ak.us) as well as other sites, and knowing what you hunt will only help you seal the deal. Last, in all of the chaos and excitement that will surely be part of your hunt, don't forget to take the time to appreciate the fact that because of responsible game management, these magnificent creatures are still around for all to enjoy.

Below is a gear list for a five-day brown bear hunt:

1. Painkillers (enough for everyone)
2. Medications (enough for the trip and another week past it)
3. Cash money
4. Credit Cards
5. Hunting licenses/permits
6. 1 rifle with ammo (at least 1 rifle)
7. 2 boxes of ammo (at least)
8. Great binoculars
9. Spotting scope
10. 2 pairs of camo pants
11. 5 camo shirts
12. 5 T-shirts (to layer)
13. 5 socks
14. 5 underwear
15. 2 hats (1 wool or very warm hat/1 lightweight)
16. 1 light jacket
17. 1 medium jacket
18. 1 heavy jacket
19. 1 set of rain gear

20. 2 sets of gloves (rubber if possible)
21. 1 set of long johns (under armor if possible)
22. 2 pairs of rubber boots
23. 1 small day pack
24. 1 small first aid kit
25. 1 small flashlight, laser pen, or headlamp (to signal boat for pickup)
26. Hand warmers (couple of packs)
27. Portable boot warmer (to dry out boots if wet)
28. Gun-cleaning kit (bore snakes are great)
29. Slip-on slippers (for the boat)
30. Batteries (for cameras and headlamps/flashlights)
31. Extra pair of vision/reading glasses
32. Scent spray (not a must-bring item)
33. Skinning knives/saws
34. Cameras/film/discs, etc. (no stores available in sound)
35. Game skidder (Cabela's)

Here is a just-in-case (emergency) day-pack list:

1. First aid kit
2. Fire-starter kit
3. Emergency (Space Blanket)
4. Knives (one for skinning, one for chopping)
5. Bone saw
6. Flares
7. Emergency locator beacon (ELB)
8. Satellite phone
9. Protein bars

8

HUNTING THE HUNTER

I guess it goes without saying that after hunting Alaska for the last fourteen years, I've accumulated a few tales. Some of which, when I look back at them now, still find hard to believe. This is Alaska, though, a land of relentless beauty, adventure, and danger. A land so vast that there are places where man has never walked and maybe never will. A land untouched by the hands of time, where the variety of wildlife is paralleled only by its diverse and majestic landscape. This is the land I love, the land I hunt and fish, and the land I call my home.

It was September in Alaska, which, to the rare few who live here, means moose-hunting season. My bud and longtime hunting partner, Troy, and I had been hunting together for years and usually ended up north past Fairbanks this time of year, usually out in the middle of nowhere or west toward the old Middle Fork camp during moose season; that's a whole other story. Because of time constraints and Troy expecting a new addition to the family, we decided to stay close to home and hunt some of the local areas. The winter before this season had been unusually mild compared to most, so the moose populations weren't effected as usual. According to Fish and Feathers (a.k.a.

Fish and Game), the numbers had actually increased in the unit we would be hunting, so we were pretty psyched.

There's a lot of different ways to hunt Alaska, and depending on the time of year, type of species, and area you're hunting, you may use one, none, or, in some cases, all of them. Some of the choices include, however, are not limited to the roads, air, water, railroad, backpacking, horses, or a combination of all of the above. First, foremost, and most widely used would have to be our extensive and extravagant road system—*not!* We have no road system, and what we do have is anything but extravagant! What you will find is pretty much a road that goes north, and we call that one North. Then a road of similar or lesser quality that goes in the opposite direction and we call that South. From the variety of those two choices, the options of where to turn off and start hunting are just about endless. Problem is, once you get off the actual road, you're going to need a 4×4 truck, four-wheeler, or some other sort of tracked or amphibious vehicle to go anywhere else. So when we talk about road hunting in Alaska, we usually mean staying on the actual road for whatever the duration of the hunt may be.

Kind of funny when I think about it, but I do know a few really lucky folks up here who have taken every animal in this state by just going back and forth to work. Others like myself have never seen anything on the road unless it was already dead or dying. This hunt was going to be a road hunt, which also meant hours of contributing to the gas shortage while looking for a moose in the middle of the road or signs of the like.

Now you might think that because you would be riding around in a nice, warm truck out on a public highway, you wouldn't have to worry about much as far as gear and preparation were concerned. Think again. This is Alaska, and that meant we would still need to be prepared for anything. Spare tires, water, food, gasoline, tent, sleeping bag, cookstove, firewood, signal flares, GPS, batteries, rain gear, clothes, boots, satellite phone, and whatever else we could cram into the backseat of Troy's truck.

For the type of hunting we would be doing and area we were going, none of this would probably be needed except for maybe the guns and ammo; however, you'll just never know out here. Like all hunts in Alaska, you have to be completely prepared for everything, and I mean everything. Even then, the chances of things changing and going horribly wrong are almost certain. Most hunts up here are basically expeditions, and even the ones that didn't start that way usually end up that way. If you go out half-cocked in this country, chances of you running into some really bad luck are really good. As the records show, we lose at least one or two hunters a year due to poor planning or lack of proper equipment. Either something stupid like the guy who caught a .375 slug with his head when he raised it at the wrong moment directly between the brown bear and the guy shooting it. Or like the ones you hear about where folks just end up getting lost or overextending themselves; the bears usually find them first. And if you say or think it can never happen to you, better think again.

A few years back I was getting ready for a bear hunt out of Seward into Prince William Sound for black bear. I had spent the normal month or so before putting it all together and rechecking everything twice—as I always do. It was my turn to buy the king crab for the trip, and halfway down to Seward I realized I had completely forgotten it. Good news was, they had just finished the new grocery store in Seward, so I got lucky and picked some up there. Now we were ready, so off to the dock we went.

After what seemed like hours of loading the boat, we were throttled up and heading out. Once the boat is out of port and under way, we usually start prepping for an evening hunt on these trips and start the endless digging through our gear to sort things out, while the captain heads for the hunting area. Today, however, the weather was really bad, and doing anything besides holding on for dear life was out of the question. After about four hours and one hundred miles later, we arrived at the first bay. The seas were fairly calm, and we still had plenty of daylight, so it was go time; at least that's what I thought!

Seemed that somewhere in all of my infinite wisdom and detailed preparation, I left my rifle in the backseat of the truck, which was now strategically parked in Seward. After a few choice words from the inner sanctum of the void I called my brain and some rightfully earned ridiculing from the captain and crew, I managed to compose myself enough so I would not publically cry or scream like a baby! Lucky for me, the captain let me borrow his .300, which, imagine that, I had brought plenty of ammo for.

Anyhow, good gear, preparation, and a lot of luck can mean the difference between life and death in this country. Nowhere else have I ever hunted compares to the endless challenges Alaska will throw at you. The weather alone is enough to make a grown man cry, which I have actually seen. From freezing temperatures, to rain and windstorms, floods, and even blazing heat—these are all possible within the same day! Then you have the most inhospitable terrain known to man. Raging rivers a seasoned guide couldn't read or navigate through. Mountains made of nothing but bone-crushing slippery shell that even goats can't climb. Thousands of miles of swampland and tundra that has never been seen or touched by man. Now throw in swarms of mosquitoes so big that you can hear them flying a mile away and black out the sun like an eclipse. And don't forget the biggest, meanest, and fastest bears I've ever seen, and yes, contrary to popular belief, they can move quite well.

Then throw in a pack of wolves known to kill a full-grown two-thousand-pound moose, and you have a formula for disaster knocking at your door; and that's just with the land-bearing animals! So unless you are staying at a lodge where you can get in and out of the elements or a nice spike camp, you're going to experience something out of the ordinary when hunting in Alaska; this you can be sure of!

Well, our day started of at Troy's house with a cup of coffee and some of them nasty chocolate doughnuts in a box. You know the little ones you can eat about a dozen of and about a half hour later hope you make it to the restroom or any other place in time! Troy was never known for his promptness, so after an hour or so of watching him try to figure out what boots to wear, we were off and running. He had been shooting a .338 Win Mag with 180-grain Nosler Partitions for years and had killed just about every species in Alaska with it. I had a .300 A-Bolt Stainless Stalker Browning I liked to push the same round through and was kind of fond of, so we were ready. Now if you're like most people coming to Alaska and wondering what kind of gun to bring, you will find that there are many schools of thought on this one particular subject. Personally, you need to have at least a 30-06 or anything larger that you can effectively shoot well. And by *effectively*, I mean that whatever you are shooting, you need to ensure that you can make and consistently hit a target within at least a twelve square inches or circle at one hundred, two hundred, and three hundred yards. If not, then you may as well bag the hunt because I guarantee you that somewhere in your hunt, no matter what you're hunting, you'll have to make at least one of those shots.

If you go out and buy a 375 H&H and can't shoot it because you flinch every time you pull the trigger, then scale down. Sure, it will do the trick on anything in this country, but if you can't shoot it, what's the sense? So when you get to the range, set up targets at one hundred, two hundred, and three hundred yards. Use a *good* rest and the same type of ammo you'll be hunting with and start with shooting groups of three at each target.

rward you can count three shots on each target, you're ready to really start shooting; this is the fun part. You need to dress in exactly what you're going to be hunting in: boots, gear, everything to include range finders, binoculars, and hat. With all this gear on, now you need to shoot the same targets standing, sitting, kneeling, prone, and any other position you can think of you might get into. You will be amazed at the things you'll discover, like how your glasses or hat get in the way. The field is not the place to realize how things work, and I know many of folks who have learned this the hard way. Sitting seventy-five yards away from a world-class moose with your range finder tangled up in your scope is not a good thing! I even recommend running in place while holding your rifle until winded, then line up on a target, and shoot. If you've never tried this, it's a must and quite the eye-opener. Most people whom I have had try this can't even hit a fifty-yard target afterward. This is a great exercise seeing that a lot of our opportunities up here are only present for a short period of time and normally after running, crawling, or even swimming to them. So unless you're hunting bear off of a tree stand, I can just about guarantee that you will have to do some hustling somewhere along the hunt. People always ask me about the stainless thing. If your rifle is stainless, that's great; however, if you don't take care of it, it doesn't matter what it is, but it's going to rust. And for you few who are coming north to hunt in the winter, don't overoil your weapon. In fact, don't oil it at all. I've seen, heard, and experienced actions freezing up due to extreme cold temperatures.

If you have to, use some lip balm to lube the bolt but leave the rest alone. And get whatever oil that's in your barrel out of it. For those hunting around saltwater, Kolpin makes a great rubber gun boot that goes for about $30. If you can't get one, bring a soft case that you can use to transport your rifle from the boat to the shore with. This is where most weapons get trashed; the

ride from the boat to shorelines can be anything b
sometimes even deadly. I rode one in one time, and r
we hit the shore, a wave came in and swamped the whole boat. I
and three others, including all of our rifles, gear, and equipment,
were soaked—not a good thing with saltwater! Since then, I
always keep my gun in a boot until the last minute or at a place
I know it and I are not going swimming.

The weather was pretty typical for that time of year—cloudy, overcast, and cold. Not cold enough for the rut to start but cold enough to maybe see some movement. We took an old logging road out of town a bit and stopped where the power lines crossed. This was a pretty good place to walk in undisturbed, and there was a good trail where we had seen moose before. After getting all of our gear on, we decided to split up and try two areas about a mile from each other. Troy and I had hunted for years together, and for the most part, we usually stayed together. This time, however, we decided that we could cover more ground to look for sign and increase our chance of bagging a moose. After all, this area was fairly close to town, and the chance of seeing any predators this time of year out here were slim to none.

That's a big bear!

Troy went east, and I went west following an old trail through the spruce trees. Within minutes, I lost sight of Troy and couldn't see the power lines anymore. There was a small hill about a half-mile away that looked like it would be nice for glassing, so I made my way for it. As with hunting anyplace this time of year, the dead leaves were making it almost impossible to be quiet, so what I learned a long time ago was to move like a moose moves. Walk a little, stop, eat, walk a little more, stop, and eat. The whole time you're stopped you're doing nothing but listening and looking for movement yourself. Repeating this process works really well in fooling a moose if one is in the area. The only drawback to this method is if you need to get somewhere, it's going to take you awhile.

No sooner did I get to the hill, drop my gear, and started to get my glasses out did I hear a shot go off.

Unbelievable, I thought as I contemplated the scene of Troy dropping a moose. By far, Troy was about the luckiest guy I had ever known when it came to hunting. He had bagged just about everything in this state twice and then some. I waited for a second shot, a sign of anything else, then decided I better go, and check. Once I got back to the power lines, Troy was running toward me and at the same time pointing off into the distance. When he reached me, he bent over and was gasping for air as he tried explaining how he thought he had shot a moose until it turned and came out of the alders. At that point he realized it was not a moose at all; it was a bear—a really, really, really big bear!

As all hunters know, there are state, federal, and local rules and regulations that all hunters know and abide by. And then there's all the others that you will not find in any print, however, hold more weight most of the time than a lot that are! One of which is that if a hunter wounds an animal, they will do everything possible to "dispatch" that animal as soon as possible to avoid any undue suffering on the part of that animal.

As a hunter, you can only hope for that ultimate one shot that delivers the kill to the animal instantly and as humanely as possible. However, anyone who has ever hunted long enough also knows that this is unfortunately not always going to be the case. And on this particular day, we now had one of the biggest, meanest, and dangerous species known to man running around with a bullet in him. I have unfortunately hunted and tracked plenty of wounded animals in my day; however, this was fall in Alaska, and the ground that's not covered up by leaves will soon be, and the rest is either water or moss, which makes tracking literally impossible due to its bright, blood-red, speckled patches. This was going to be fun.

As stated before, Troy was one of the luckiest hunters I had ever known, and like many times before, he got lucky again in being able to see the spruce thicket where the wounded bear had run into; this was the good news. The bad news was that if anyone has ever been in a spruce thicket in Alaska, it's not the greatest place to be when you're looking for anything, especially a huge wounded brown bear! If you're lucky, you may be able to see within a ten-foot radius of your face. If not, then you may be lucky to see anything past five feet unless you crawl along the ground and under the thick spruce branches. Looking back at it now, we probably should have just waited him out. From where we were, we could see almost all sides of the thicket that he was in except for a small area on the backside. That probably would have been the best move; however, being young, dumb, and full of adrenaline, we decided to go in after him!

As we both sat there scanning a good entry point, we loaded up everything we had. At the time I used to carry a .44 Magnum with six shots of custom-made 350-grain Kodiak bear-bonded rounds made specifically for killing bears. Popular with hikers as well as hunters, they are without a doubt the most uncomfortable round to shoot through anything, especially the Smith & Wesson Model 629 with a four-inch barrel. The good news is, you can rest assured that whatever you hit with one is definitely going to be dead. A few minutes had passed, and I now had six in the .44 and four in my .300 Win Mag; we always chamber one and feed three, or as many as we can hold up here, especially when hunting bear. Troy took a sip off his water bottle and passed it to me.

"No, thanks," I said. "I try not to drink anything when I'm about to piss in my pants!"

It was about noon, and around this time of year we would have light until about ten thirty to eleven, so light was not a factor. As we made our way to the line of spruce trees bordering the thicket, I could feel the veins in my forehead popping out on every beat of my now-racing heart. It seemed like the closer we got, the more I could feel it.

We were at the edge now and decided to do one last check of all our weapons before going in. Round in the chamber, three in back of it, safety off, scope at lowest setting, finger on the trigger. My S&W 629 full and holster catch unlatched and stowed to the side to prevent hang-ups when drawing. Turn my hat around so I can see 180 degrees vertical, finger back on the trigger, and I was ready. I raised my rifle and brought the side of my barrel up to my right eye and peered down its twenty-four-inch span; sometimes they're closer than you want, and a barrel shot is all you'll have. Trying to find him in your scope at ten yards can cost you your life! It's good to know how to shoot this way just in case you ever have to. Troy was still fidgeting with his scope, so as usual, I thought, what better time to crack one of my usually stupid jokes to break the seriousness of the situation.

I never saw Troy real serious about anything, but as he looked back at me without cracking so much as a smirk and gave me the look, I couldn't help but to laugh even more!

"This is not a good time for joking," he angrily whispered.

By now I could feel the veins on both sides of my temples pulsating, and it felt like my heart was coming out of my chest. I think the thing that was scaring me the most was the fact that I was really liking this! The sound of my beating heart was radiating through my brain so loud I thought for sure that at least Troy could hear it if not the bear!

As we slipped in with guns raised, pointed, and ready, a warm tingling sensation radiated through my body from my head to my toes. I think it was a huge dose of adrenaline, but whatever it was didn't make matters any better. I felt sick, had to pee, and was starting to sweat profusely. The farther in we went, the thicker the brush got until we couldn't see more than a few feet in front of us. If the bear was stalking us and lying low (as they so often do), we may as well just splash a little salt and pepper over our heads, for there would be nothing we could do if he charged. We got into about the middle of the thicket without hearing or seeing anything—no blood, no bear, nothing.

We took up a knee and were listening for movement when from what sounded like it was off to our right side and really close, we heard the blood-curdling sound of a bear cracking its jaws together—a noise they usually make right before they attack! Not sure what my blood pressure was before this, however, after hearing that sound and realizing how close he was, I doubt if there's a machine known to man that could have read mine. Because we still couldn't see him, all we could do is just sit there and listen while trying to get an exact fix on his location. For those who have never been in close proximity of any bear, no less a wounded one, the best way to describe what we were listening to would be to first take two baseball bats and smack them together real hard. Do this over and over again in short burst. Now add a few low-level guttural grunts followed by some loud snorting, moaning, and a lot of brush rattling. Add the sound of someone digging a huge hole and dirt flying everywhere, and you have what we had about fifteen yards to the right of us.

The bear knows we're here, I thought, *and he's probably looking at us right now.*

Troy and I were back to back now, trying to figure out where he was and what we should do. If it were to charge, we would be lucky to even get a shot off. We had to get a visual on the bear, plain and simple. The old rule about "you cannot shoot what you cannot see" was never more true. We could have just opened up on him in the direction of the sounds; however, in that thick of brush, the chances of a round connecting were slim to none—a chance neither of us were ready to take. And for anyone who knows about or has ever hunted rhino and bears too have been known to head right for the smoke after they've been shot at. We decided to move downwind flanking the bear while trying to get a good visual on him. With Troy on point and me taking up the rear, we slowly made our way through the brush to a small clearing where we could turn if it came at us. Again we took a knee and rested while still listening to the horrid grunts of this wounded monster. The sounds now seemed to be coming from directly in front of us, so Troy stood up and began looking for him while I stayed low and used my scope to scout the brush from underneath the spruce. From out of nowhere and about ten yards in front of us, a huge cloud of dirt flew up. As I stood up and peered through my scope, I spotted what appeared to be hair!

"I think I got him, Troy," I whispered in excitement and fear at the same time.

"Where?" Troy asked. "Where is he?"

I tried explaining to him the position, but from where Troy stood, he couldn't see him. He slowly and frustratingly moved around me trying to see what I was seeing but couldn't get a fix on him. After what seemed like forever and trying to keep my sights steady on him, Troy said "Take the shot, take the shot!"

It was almost as if the bear heard Troy say that, for as soon as he got to the last letter of *shot*, the bear turned, stood up on all fours, and was now looking directly at me! My scope was on three-power; however, because he was only ten yards away, all I could see was his huge eye just staring at me. We peered at each other for what seemed like eternity, the whole time my finger slowly squeezing the trigger of my .300 Win Mag.

Crack, went the first shot followed a half second later by Troy's .338, then another .300, and another .338 and another *crack, crack, crack, crack, crack, crack, crack!* We let out a volley of everything we had and between the both of us and had completely emptied our rifles and my revolver into the bear in probably less than six seconds! As soon as I took the first shot and started cycling the bolt for another, I remember watching this huge light-brown mass screaming toward me and feeling as if these may be my last minutes on earth. He was in a full charge now and mowing down trees like they were twigs while closing the already-narrow gap. All we could do after the first shot was to keep firing in its general direction.

Seconds passed as we gave him everything we had, and I was still squeezing the trigger of my empty .44 when Troy grabbed me and yelled, "He turned, he turned!" There was smoke everywhere, and we couldn't see anything.

"He turned, he turned," Troy kept yelling.

We were both pretty deaf at this point from the barrage of fire we had just laid down. Somewhere in all of the excitement, the bear had turned 90 degrees to the right and was now heading out of the thicket and into the open flats. I quickly holstered the .44 and began stuffing rounds down the .338. We were both frantically trying to reload and at the same time trying to figure out where the bear had gone when my concentration was broken by the sound of bullets whizzing by our heads and slamming into the brush around us! For those of you who have never been in combat or an actual firefight, or for those who have not had the unfortunate experience of being shot at, the sound of a red-hot, whistling bullet radiating past your head leaves a distinct and unforgettable sound. And it is true, you don't hear the gunshot until the bullet has hit or passed you, which for us, was fortunately the case.

Seems that when we initially opened up on the bear, it did a ninety-degree turn to the right and headed out of the spruce and into the open flats. What we nor the bear knew at the time was there were two other moose hunters out in the flats past the spruce who had no idea what was going on. As we later learned, Brian and Tom were just walking along when out of nowhere shots rang out.

Brian later said, "We were just walking along trying to get past the mud in the flats when all hell broke loose! It sounded like fifty guys in there with automatic weapons!"

They had no idea what was going on, and when they turned in the direction of the fire, the next thing they saw was a huge, brown bear coming right at them! Brian was shooting a .308

BAR (Bolt-Action Rifle), capable of laying down semiautomatic fire at about two rounds per second. All Tom had on him was a .44 Magnum like mine, but he let the bear taste every round.

As Brian explained, "It kinda went without saying that when we turned and saw this bear coming right at us and closing the gap of about thirty yards real fast, we just opened up on him."

Troy and I were busy trying to figure out where the bear had gone and reloading when it became Brian and Tom's turn to throw down some lead.

Brian drew down on him pumping out four rounds of .308, hitting him in the back and chest, while Tom let loose his six rounds of .44 Magnum, hitting him once in the head and once in the shoulder; the rest of their rounds (four .44 Mags and two .308s) made their way past Troy and me. What seemed like an eternity of chaos and confusion was now over.

For a second, there was nothing but silence; then rejoicing voices in the distance could be heard yelling and hollering, "We got him, we got him"! As Troy and I made our way out of the brush, the sight of the biggest brown bear we had ever seen began to take shape. As I made my way closer, I couldn't believe the size of this monster bear. As surprised and confused as us, Brian and Tom quickly introduced themselves and began telling us their side of the story. They too were amazed at the size of the bear, and after what seemed like one hundred pictures, we all joined in on pulling the hide.

We learned later from the taxidermist that the bear had a total of thirteen holes in him, although it looked like only eleven were actual hits. Between Troy, Brian, Tom, and myself, we had expended more than twenty-four rounds of high-powered ammunition at a brown bear that measured out at ten feet eleven inches. The skull unfortunately received three substantial hits from what appeared to be .338, .300, and .44 Magnum rounds, rendering it almost impossible to measure. However, after an extensive effort on part of the taxidermist, the skull measured an impressive 28.93 inches. Unfortunately, to qualify for any record, the skull must be fully intact to attain a precise measurement.

Funny thing was, we never did see or get a moose that year. It's been years now since Troy and I have hunted together. I went overseas shortly after that experience, and when I returned, Troy's family had grown, and he was and still is busy being busy. I've heard soldiers talk about the bond between men in battle and how afterward the experience of their experiences never fades. I guess sometimes it's the same with hunting because that day among many that I have hunted seems to be as vivid now as it was that day, and the bond we shared hunting the hunter can never be undone.

9

IT'S NOT YOUR TURN!

I don't consider myself to be a superstitious man by any means, but I have to admit, the more I hunt, the more I believe that there actually might be hunting gods who see all we sow and call the shots on all we reap!

Having hunted bears in the coves and bays of Prince William Sound (PWS) and the Gulf of Alaska for the last six years, I have found it to be one of the best hunts in the state. Not only is bear meat tasty, but the hunt itself is also an absolute blast. For all of our trips, we have used our longtime friend Scott Liska who captains the *Viking*, a forty-three-foot Delta built as tough as they come and capable of handling anything Alaska could throw at her. Docked in Seward, it's about a four- to five-hour boat ride to the hunting area, depending on which way you go.

Although the *Viking* can sleep eight, four hunters and a captain seem to work out the best. This trip would consist of my good friend Tom Henderson, longtime hunting partner and bud Sam Ball, his friend Matt Estell, and of course myself. Unlike Matt and Tom who were newcomers to this hunt and type of hunting, this was mine and Sam's sixth black bear trip together. Between the two of us, we had put five bears on our walls and had a pretty good idea on what to expect and when to expect it. Although both Matt and Tom were experienced hunters, they had never hunted bear and never from a boat, so Sam and I decided to split the teams in two. Seeing that Matt was Sam's friend and Tom was mine, those would be the teams. No matter how it all turned out, though, this was going to be an incredible experience for both of them.

Depending on the weather, we try to motor out in the afternoon and reach the hunting zone a few hours before sunset—the magic hours for hunting bears! Bears also love the low tides where they can feed on the freshly exposed sea kelp and other tasty critters the sea leaves behind. So if you're lucky enough to be in the zone a few hours before dark and have a good low tide, chances of taking a bear are pretty good. Once in the zone, there are only two logical options for doing this hunt. You can beat the bushes and hunt the shorelines, or you can motor around and glass from a boat, then use a skiff to get to the shore when needed. If you've never hunted the coastal areas of Alaska, it is a huge understatement to say that the terrain is less than hospitable. If you're even lucky enough to get through the brush-choked woods, the hunt is pretty much over. Having done both options more than once, I try to always go with the latter. We've spotted many of bears from the boat and thought how easy it was going to be, only to be cut off, blocked, lost, and bewildered once on the ground. If you're lucky and the brush is still dormant, you can see about fifteen to twenty feet in front of you. If not, you better have a line of sight on the bear from the time you spot him to the time you drop him, or it's probably not going to happen.

Long story short, we motor around in the *Viking* until we see one drop the skiff and get on them as quick as possible. I have taken three this way, which only means I have lost twice that many during the very long and humbling learning curve!

It was the morning of May 26, 2011, when we piled the last of our gear onto the deck of the *Viking*. I slid quietly past the guys on the deck and down to the hull to call dibs on the best bunk, for this was going to be home for the next four days. Although they were forecasting a front moving in on Saturday, the weather was looking good for the rest of the trip. As I gazed at the hills surrounding the port, I couldn't help to think that we might be a little late this year. They were greening up fast, and if you can't see the bears, you can't hunt them. Knowing that it might be completely different where we were going, I popped the top on my beer, toasted the hunt, and once more asked the hunting gods for their blessing!

My bud Tom Henderson

As usual, I slept the whole way out until Scott spotted a pod of orcas and humpbacks. We were just past Cochrane Bay when he called out from the bridge, "Whales!"

"What do you see?" I asked. He just pointed to the front of the boat where to my surprise was a pod of orcas. "Guys, guys, orcas twelve o'clock!"

We all scrambled to the bow to get a closer look when Scott pointed to another pod. They were everywhere and seemed to be watching us as much as we were watching them. I had seen them before, but never this close and never this many. They were everywhere and so close that you could see the barnacles on them as they swam past the boat. Everyone except Matt was on the bow clicking picture after picture when I asked, "Where's Matt?"

Tom opened his mouth and stuck his finger in it, then pointed to the stern where I could now see Matt, chumming for fish. We watched them for about thirty minutes then continued on toward Herring Bay. Once we got out of the open water and back into the protection of the islands and coves, the water was pretty flat. Matt was starting to come around and good thing, for Sam said he had been chumming since we left Seward.

Time to gear up, I thought as I looked at the land getting closer to the boat.

It would be low tide around 3:00 p.m., and I wanted a rifle in hand and ready to go when the time was right. Scott throttled back and had Sam take the wheel; we were in the zone now and needed to get ready to hunt.

"George, can you help me with the skiff?" Scott asked.

It was time to drop the skiff and have it ready if we spotted something; nothing worse than seeing a bear and not being able to get to it. When you see one, you have to move and move like there's no tomorrow. Once you get on shore, or on the way there, you can come up with a plan, but I've seen a lot of bears lost by guys who couldn't make a decision if their life depended on it.

We quickly dropped the skiff and tied it to the side of the *Viking*; all we needed now was a bear.

Because we had stopped a few times along the way to look at the wildlife, we got into the bay around 4:00 p.m. and anchored up to the right of a long stretch of beach and a glacier-fed river. No sooner had the anchor hit the water when I spotted our first bear along the beach feeding on some grass.

"He's right there," I said, pointing to the little black spot moving around on the beach. Tom and the rest of the guys were all struggling to see what I was talking about when Scott said, "Looks like a nice one."

"Tom, let's go, let's go get him," I said while grabbing my rifle and pack. I was in the skiff and ready to go when I realized I was by myself. "Where's Tom and Scott?" I asked. Looking over the rail I found Tom frantically searching for his rifle and pack.

"Come on, Tom, come on, we're going to miss him."

Tom was so frazzled he nearly fell in the skiff; nevertheless, we were heading for shore. The bear was in the middle of the beach, so we would need to come in slow and far enough away to not get winded. Scott dropped us off at the mouth of a small stream, and we scurried up the steep sandy beach. Now hiding behind the only log on the beach, we both chambered a round.

If I guessed it right, the bear should be about one hundred yards out and down in the grass. Problem was, when we looked up over the log, the bear was nowhere to be found.

Is he down in a gully or ravine? I thought looking through the thick grass with my binoculars. *Or had he winded us and is now long gone?*

We decided to use the steep beach as a cover and scurried down the shoreline to get a closer look. With rifles ready, we slowly made our way down the beach to where we had first spotted the bear but found nothing but a lot of chewed-up grass. The bear was gone, and as it started to rain, all we could do now was to wait for him to come back out. We set up downwind of where we thought he may have gone in and spent the next two hours getting eaten alive by some of the biggest mosquitoes I'd ever seen. I was so glad when Tom decided to pack it in, it wasn't even funny. I had been bitten in the forehead at least five times now, and between that and the rain, I was more than ready to get back on the warm, dry boat.

We spent the rest of that night glassing from the boat, which works out well if you're anchored in the right place. From where we sat, you could see at least three miles of shoreline in one direction, a valley and mountain sides from another, and a valley in the back of that. If anything was out there moving, we would see it.

It was a beautiful morning, and as Scott grilled up some bacon and eggs, I began gearing up for the day ahead. We had no sooner finished breakfast when Matt yelled out, "Bear! There's a bear right there on the side of that hill!"

As we all scrambled for our glasses, Scott said, "He's a nice bear. Let's get him!"

Sam and Tom were still in their underwear, so Matt and I jumped in the skiff with Scott and headed for the bear. The closer we got to the bear, the steeper the hill became, and all I could think about now was if Matt got him, it was going to be a really long day. We were about one hundred yards out when Scott throttled down. The plan was to idle up as close as we could get, then try to get on the shore; problem was, there wasn't a shore! The cliff went straight into the water, and there was nothing to step onto. We were about fifty yards out when the bear spotted us, and with nowhere to go but up, the bear found the only bush on the hill and disappeared in it. It was a waiting game now, and as we bobbed back and forth in the skiff, I couldn't help question the sanity of getting this bear off the hill. The good news was, if we slipped and fell off the cliff, the water would break our fall. The bad news was, we would probably freeze to death before ever getting back in the skiff.

We were just sitting there bobbing back and forth when the bear stuck his head out. The next thing I know, Matt's throwing lead downrange! The bear shot out of the bush and headed straight up the cliff as Matt slammed him with shot after shot! The bear was almost at the top of the cliff when it folded up like a bowling ball and started rolling straight down the hill. My first thought was, "I hope he doesn't stop." Then it hit me like a bad rash: "He's going to fall right into the boat?" The bear was coming straight at us now, and as I glanced back to tell Scott to move, the look on his face told me he was thinking the same thing. Up to that moment, I had always thought that it would be great to just have one fall into the boat; however, that's when I realized, what if it's still alive? Seconds later I just remember seeing a huge black spot hit the water inches from my head!

Matt leaned over to grab him when I yelled, "Stop, he's still moving, hold on a second!" I leaned over next to Matt, thrust my arm into the water, and felt for anything that didn't resemble teeth or claws.

With the back of its head now twitching in my hand, I held it in the water until the rest of its life drained into the icy waters of the bay. It was Matt's first bear, and as we struggled to pull the wet, bloody mass into the skiff, the smile on Matt's face told me everything I needed to know.

Matt's bear

Because Matt had saturated the bay with a zealous amount of gunfire, we decided to motor out and find another bay. It was a beautiful day, and as I fed some fish scraps to a hungry sea lion, Scott pulled anchor, and we were off again. We were heading for Unakwik Inlet and Barry Arm, which was about an hour ride from where we were, so I found a soft spot in the mass of jackets, gear, and guns to rest my head. The next thing I knew, Scott was dropping anchor.

"Where are we?" I asked.

Sam replied, "In Alaska."

Scott had put us in Drier Bay, which was known for its major low tides and abundance of bears. We were all gearing up when Matt spotted another bear on the back side of the shoreline. Not sure how he saw it but he did and, just having shot one, decided to let Tom and I hunt it. Tom was still inside gearing up and missed the whole conversation about the bear when I peeked through the door and said, "Let's go, we have a bear."

The look on his face was priceless, for everything he was wearing was half on or half off. I motioned through the glass for him to hurry as we all laughed watching him trip over just about everything in the boat. Scott, Tom, and I all piled into the skiff and were off after Tom's first bear. As we motored toward the shore, I realized now that this was going to be a tough stalk. The tide was really low, which unfortunately was exposing a huge amount of shoreline, increasing our distance to the bear. The good news was, the bear had its head down in the tall grass and was clueless to our presence. The bad news was, we had a long way to go with absolutely nothing to hide behind. If we could get in close enough, we could corner him and leave him only one option of escape: straight up.

Scott cut the motor and as we stepped onto the slippery rocks and ankle-high water of the tidal flat, I glassed and ranged the bear at just over three hundred yards; this was going to be a tough one.

We decided to use a technique I learned in Africa where the lead person continuously glasses the animal while walking and the shooter maintains a position directly in back of the lead. Not only does this cut down on the profile footprint, but it also lessens the chances of a miscommunication, cuts down on noise, and eliminates different distances to the target, when ranged. When the bear wasn't looking, we would walk, stop, and glass—then walk, stop, and glass. After thirty minutes of this, we were within one hundred yards and on top of a ravine when the bear looked right at us.

"Don't move, don't move," I whispered to Tom. All I could see was his head over the thick grass, but he was sniffing and looking right at us. I figured we were busted, and as my foot sank into the soft muck of the ravine, the bear slowly dropped his head and disappeared. Where we stood gave us a good visual of the meadow he was in, and I figured that if we could close some distance quickly, we might be able to box him in. We began running along the ridge of the ravine, then dropped down along the edge of a creek when out of nowhere, there he was. We were less than fifty yards now, and to my surprise, it had no idea we were there.

Tom had just caught up and got into position when the bear dropped out of sight again. I snuck up a little farther, spotted the bear again, and motioned for Tom to come up. When I turned back to find the bear again, he was jumping up on a rock and heading up the cliff. Using a variety of secret hunting hand signals, I motioned to Tom to "shoot that bastard!" He was still behind me a bit, and when I turned to see where he was, the first shot rang out! The bear continued straight up the side of the hill and disappeared behind a bush. Where Tom stood, he couldn't see it, but I could and pointed to its position.

"He's right there. Shoot that bastard," I now yelled.

Tom's second shot rang out and connected with the struggling bear. We watched as it fell through some weeds and disappeared behind a blind ledge on the cliff.

"He's down, baby. He's down!" I yelled.

What a day, I thought as we knuckled up and did the "dead-bear-down" dance! It wasn't even noon yet, and we had two bears in the boat; not bad for the first day, I thought as we dragged the bear off the hill. The tide had unfortunately dropped even more, which now meant we would have to either carry or drag the bruin at least four hundred yards to the shore. Lucky for us, there was a river that led straight down to the water, so we floated him down to the skiff, then onto the deck of the *Viking*!

Tom's bear

With Tom and Matt's bears in the boat, we decided to motor out and into another bay to let things settle down in this one. We were slowly motoring through a small strait when I spotted another bear in the very back of Eaglek Bay—a small, narrow cove surrounded by tiny islands and mussel bars. The tide was so low that Scott killed the motor, and we drifted to a stop.

"I've got ten feet," he whispered. "We're going to have to row the rest of the way in."

The only thing that was between us and the bear was a tiny island that we were now rowing up to. We got up to the south side of it and climbed up expecting to see the bear but unfortunately could only see another island. We would need to get up to the next one, which meant more rowing for Scott. Within a few minutes, we were on top of the other island, but the bear was gone. We rowed up to where we had first seen him but, again, found only chewed-up grass and a lot of prints. Judging from the size of the front pad, he was about a six-footer, maybe bigger.

Didn't matter now, though; he was long gone and not coming back as long as we were there.

As I wiped the sweat from my brow and stepped back into the skiff, I spotted another bear on a shore just across from where we parked the *Viking*! This one appeared to be lying down and maybe even sleeping. The beach was small and surrounded by huge rocks on each side that jetted into the water leaving us only one option: the beach assault. According to Alaska state law, it is illegal to shoot from a boat under power; however, you can if not. We would have to come in straight at him and ready to shoot when Scott killed the motor. I glassed the bear again at about 175 yards and could see now that he in fact was asleep.

Perfect, I thought as we slowly made our way towards him. We were about one hundred yards out when Scott cut the motor and began rowing in. Tom struggled to find a comfortable and stable position on the rocking bow of the skiff while I continued glassing the bear.

"He's still sleeping, Tom, just be ready to shoot."

We were less than seventy-five yards out when I tried finding a place to shoot from. For those who have never shot from a moving boat, I suggest that sometime in your life, you try it. Even on perfectly flat, calm water, it's a challenge.

Then throw in some waves, current, and three grown men moving around in something that resembles an eleven-foot bathtub with a motor on it and try it again! We got to fifty yards, then forty, and then at about thirty yards, the bear's head popped up. He was facing away from the shore with his back to us but sensed something was up. Through my scope I watched as his nose twitch from side to side trying to pick up a scent. Still on his belly, he gave us no shot. The skiff was now rocking up and down from being so close to the breakers hitting the shore. And then just like that, the bear leaped to its feet. Tom wasted no time sending his first round downrange followed by one from me, but the bear looked as though it levitated from the shore to the woods and was gone! We scrambled up the beach and up to where the bear was lying but found no blood.

Unbelievable, I thought as I pushed back the huge spruce branches and ran into the woods. Like everywhere out there, once you enter the bush, you'll find a labyrinth of bear trails that look like intercity highways. There were trails going everywhere but not a drop of blood on any of them. As we stumbled through the bush, I couldn't help wonder if my rifle was off. Had I bumped the scope somewhere without knowing it? The chances of actually connecting with something while shooting from a boat is pretty slim to begin with; however, when you're only thirty yards away with two shooters, you have to start wondering. We looked high and low for almost an hour but, again, found nothing. Frustrated, we all piled back into the skiff and made our way back to the boat.

After some lunch and a short nap, we again pulled anchor and motored into Whale Bay looking for something else to shoot. Moments later, Sam spotted two bears in the back of a tiny cove. There was at least a half mile of marsh between us and them and, as usual, nothing at all to hide behind. Without anchoring, we piled into the skiff and maneuvered quietly up and through a series of tiny islands until we were about as close as we could get. To our advantage, the tide was out exposing a long shelf of deep channels we could hide in. We made our way up the last rocky outcrop and piled out of the skiff. The bears were about 350 yards out now, but all we could see of them was a little hair of their back.

Must have been down in one of these ravines, I thought as I glassed the surrounding area for a stalk route.

The only way we were going to close the gap was to get in the ravines; otherwise, we would be completely out in the open and exposed. Without hesitation, Sam jumped into the muddy water and made his way toward the bears. About thirty minutes later, we had covered only half the distance I thought we would and were now smack-dab in the middle of the marsh.

"What's the distance?" Sam asked as I struggled to find a black spot in the grass.

"He's at 208," I whispered.

"Let's see if we can get closer," Sam said.

We crawled into another water-filled muddy ravine and slowly made our way toward the bears. Where moments ago there were two, now there was only one and at one hundred yards. Sam took a kneeling position and brought his rifle up.

"Get ready," Sam whispered.

I tried to find a comfortable spot on the wet grass and mud, but it just wasn't working out.

"Ready?" he asked.

"Take him, Sam," I replied.

I didn't realize how close I was to his muzzle until the crack from his 7mm about blew me over. Nevertheless, I reciprocated by sending a 225-grain Barnes TSX downrange with his. I saw the bear jump and thought Sam had connected, but to our surprise, the bear ran into the woods and disappeared along a ridge!

"Did you hit him?" I asked.

"Yeah, I hit him good," Sam said in a not-so-confident tone.

As we were running up to where the bear was standing, the last few seconds played out in my head like an old silent movie. "I hope you hit him, Sam, because I don't think I did."

We looked all over for blood but found nothing, not a drop. With bears, it's sometimes hard to tell because their coats soak up a lot of it. Even if you're lucky enough to get a good heart-and-lung shot, there's no guarantee you're going to find blood.

It was the typical forest-covered canopy with dense brush as far as the eye couldn't see. We both knew that if you don't see them as soon as you enter or shortly after, you're probably not going to. They can be in a hole or a bush right in front of you, and unless they move, you'll never see them. This one, like so many others, had done just that: disappeared into the deep abyssal forest and was gone!

By the time we got out of the woods and back onto the grasslands, we were both tired and frustrated. We made our way over to an old deadfall and were just starting to break out the water when across the grass and behind a bunch of dead spruce trees I spotted another bear!

"Sam, look, there's another one right there." Without saying anything else, I grabbed my rifle and headed straight for the bear. He was only about two hundred yards away; however, we would need to cross a couple of streams, some more ravines, and a fairly large stream to get to him. The good news was, there was a lot of dead spruce between us and him that we could use as cover. Again, using the African buddy method, we got to about seventy yards where I set my rifle on the limb of an old, dead spruce and got ready for the shot. The bear had its head in the grass and hadn't a clue we were there. We had the wind, time, and element of surprise all in our favor. I ranged him again at just over sixty yards, stuffed the rangefinder back in my shirt, and put him in my scope. All I could think about was that this bear was dead; I had so much time that I was even working out the logistics of getting it back to the boat. I took one last breath, slowly let it out, held, squeezed, and let the hammer go. Through the scope I could see nothing but smoke and a black blur running into a small spruce knob to the right.

We waited a minute talking about the shot and listening for a groan or movement from the brush but got nothing. As we made our way into the spruce, we again found nothing: no bear, no blood—nothing. All I could think of is I must have jerked the trigger, or maybe my scope had actually been bumped. Either way, Sam and I had just missed taking two incredible bears and had no answers why. The only thing worse than second-guessing yourself is second-guessing your equipment, and right now, Sam and I were doing both!

We got back on the *Viking* and motored into another bay that Scott had seen some big bears in before. We anchored up on the mountain side of this beautiful bay whose beach stretched for miles. Hard to describe in words the beauty of this place without seeing it, but it was nothing short of spectacular. In the back of the valley was a huge glacier, which cut its way through an endless valley of spruce and alders and drained into the bay we were now anchored in. On the left side were jagged, green, moss-covered peaks that shot up out of the sea and disappeared into the mist. On the right was the largest span of untouched and pristine shoreline I had ever seen. Miles and miles of secluded wilderness filled with an endless and unequaled abundance of wildlife. The water was so clear, you could almost see the anchor that, according to Scott, was sitting just shy of one hundred feet.

It looked like a scene straight out of *Jurassic Park*, and if one didn't know any better, it could be.

This is why I live here, I thought as I took another sip from my beer. *This is why I put up with eight months of winter and continuous darkness for three. This is why I pay five dollars for a gallon of gas and four dollars for a gallon of milk. For without a doubt, this is the Last Frontier in all its splendor. This is* Alaska!

We had dropped some lines earlier in the day just to see what would bite and were playing around with that when Sam called out, "Bear! Right there on the far side of that hill."

I could see him with my eyes but picked up the glasses to get a better look. He was a nice-size boar skirting the edge of a cliff and stream. This would be a tough one, for we only had two options: come in from the far right using the beach or come in on the left using the cliffs to hide behind. Thankfully, Sam chose the latter, and off we went. We cut the motor and rowed in around the side of a cliff wall using it as cover. We bailed out at about fifty yards offshore into the knee-high water of the bay and hugged the face of the cliff until we got to shore.

Unfortunately, we could see everything except for the bear, so Sam stuck his head out to take a peek. I completely expected him to see the bear; however, he just shook his head and gestured for us to move up and around the corner. My safety was off now, and as we rounded the corner, I was expecting to have a bear in my face, but there was nothing. Sam turned and raised his hands if to say, "Where did he go?"

As I looked farther out and around the rock that Sam was crouched behind, I saw a black spot and pointed. "He's right there, Sam, right friggin' there!" He had been behind a cliff ridge where we couldn't see him and was now a little closer than we'd have liked.

Sam and I both raised our rifles at about the same time and let loose a volley of fire. There was so much smoke I wasn't sure who hit what, but Sam started running toward where the bear had been standing. I quickly followed when I saw him pointing his rifle up and into an avalanche chute. As soon as I looked up, I saw the outline of a bear through the smoke, pointed my barrel in its direction, and fired. Seconds later we were both crawling up the chute trying to find the bear.

"Where did he go Sam? Did you see him?"

"He went up the chute and to the left, I think," he replied. Pointing to a small cut in the timber, Sam said, "I think he went this way!"

With rifle ready, I scanned the area from side to side, ready to fire on anything that moved, but nothing ever did. We looked everywhere for this bear but, as usual, found no sign of anything, anywhere. As we stood in the snow of that icy chute trying to catch our breaths, I couldn't believe what was happening before us. Were we even hitting these bears or missing them altogether?

Maybe it was because we were so close that the rounds were passing through without expanding properly? The questions were racing through both our minds, and as we headed back to the shoreline for a pickup, you could have heard a gnat fart!

I think the worse part of the whole ordeal was when we got back to the *Viking* with nothing in the skiff. There was no end to the barrage of questions that Tom and Matt where throwing at us. "I don't want to talk about it right now," I told Tom. "Just give me a minute," I asked politely.

I cracked the top on two bears and handed one to Sam, who was feeling it too but was a lot better at hiding it than me. Tom and Matt continued to drill us with questions that I just didn't have answers for.

I was madder than hell and ready to head back to Seward when Tom asked again, "What happened, man? We heard the shots."

I was at my breaking point and went stupid crazy on Tom. "Didn't I just tell you that I don't want to talk about it? What part of that didn't you freaking understand?"

Both Tom and Matt amazingly disappeared somewhere into the confines of the forty-foot *Viking*. There was no way to explain what was happening out there, and I was way past being frustrated. We motored into a small rock-protected cove for the evening and broke out the rest of the beers. It was a surf-and-turf night, and I was ready to do some serious unwinding. The beer and food just kept coming as we played with the lines we dropped over the side earlier.

"Tomorrow we will kill," I remember saying before pouring myself into my bag. "Tomorrow we will kill!"

The morning came way too early as I tried opening an eye to peek at the time. It was around 9:00 a.m., and everyone except me was already up and ready to go. The smell of bacon and coffee was overwhelming as I listened to the thunderous sounds of three very awake men going about their day. All I wanted to do was crawl back into my bag and forget about the way I was feeling, but knew that wasn't going to happen. I crawled up to the galley and sat on the bench watching life before me as the boat seemed to spin.

"What in the hell did you guys do to me last night?" I asked.

Sam just laughed as Tom took a picture.

"Come on," Sam said, "we've got bears to kill!"

Scott handed me a nice cup of hot coffee, and I made my way to the still-swaying stern. Seemed like a good place to be with the sun coming up and sea lions playing about; that and if I hurled, it might bring in some fish! According to Scott, we would have a really low tide in about an hour, so the plan was to motor around and try to spot one on the shore. We pulled anchor and motored out across a long open channel and back into a narrow strait with tiny coves and beaches on both sides. About halfway in, I spotted a bear on top of a pile of logs in a small cove about a mile away.

Gotta love those Swarovskis, I thought as I settled back into the seat on the bridge.

We motored up and anchored in a cove opposite of where the bear was. He was still on the beach in a really small cove that would be tough getting into. Imagine that! Good news was, the water was flat as glass, and there was a small hill on the left side of the cove that we may be able to get on. Glassing the cove a little more, we could see that there was no way of getting the skiff straight in. We would have to come around the left side and maybe use the shore rocks to hide behind. That or go across the top of the small hill and drop in on him from the other side. Either way, it wasn't going to be easy. Matt having bagged two bears already was out of the game, and Tom seemed content on just observing, so Sam and I were off again. We got up and along the shore in the skiff and hugged it just shy of the cove; any farther out and we would be in plain sight of the bear. Only option now was to get to the shore and over the hill to drop in on him from the other side—if there was another side.

We hit the woods running and quickly found a bear trail leading straight up. Call me surprised, but the hill was a lot larger than it looked from the boat and seemed to incline further with every step. It was the typical spruce forest crisscrossed with moss-covered deadfall.

Must have been a huge windstorm awhile back, I thought as we climbed up, over, and through the branches and limbs of another blocked path. It looked like God himself had taken his hand and wiped it across the side of this hill.

We were about halfway up and skirting the edge of a really steep hill when we came to a tangled mess of overgrown deadfall. We had been out of sight of the bear now for probably a half an hour.

Not good, I thought as I looked for a way out of this mess. "We have to go back Sam," I gasped. "Gotta pick up that trail that goes up a little farther." I couldn't believe how big this hill was. Seemed that the farther up we went, the farther up it went.

Where is the end? I thought as I struggled for more air.

Sam was jumping through and over it like a mountain goat, but for some reason, I was struggling; funny how at the time it didn't even occur to me why. With one foot in front of the other we finally made it to the top but couldn't see anything but a little bit of the beach when we got there. We would need to go down now, and down was really down. It was at least a seventy-degree decline littered with devil's club and alders. The good news was, we only had about seventy-five yards to traverse to get to the shore, then maybe another fifty to get to where the bear was.

Piece of cake, I thought as I slid down on my butt across the jagged rocks and slippery roots of the cliff. I slammed into a spruce tree about halfway down and was pulling my rifle out from behind me when I spotted the bear in the back of the cove. In the excitement and chaos of it all, I had left my rangefinder back at the boat so didn't have the advantage of getting an exact distance on him. I sat there a moment as Sam slid up to where I was.

"He's right there, Sam. Do you see him?" I asked.

I estimated the bear to be about two hundred yards out, and we were still about forty to fifty yards up. We would need to close the distance some more, so off we went down the last bit of rock. We got to the shore and scampered along the shoreline to a pile of logs we first sighted the bear standing on. The wind was good, and as we slowly made our way up, over, and through the maze of dead logs, I found the bear again. He was about fifty yards in front of us and just grazing along the shoreline of a small pond. Using a branch from the log I was hiding behind, I slid my rifle over the top of it. Now concentrating on slowing my breathing, I watched the bear in my scope meander through the thick tall grass of the meadow. I had him dead in my crosshairs and now could see how beautiful of a bear he actually was. I cranked my scope to fourteen power and settled into the scope. He was a bruiser of a bear and had a beautiful coat on him.

Everything was coming together now, and as I slid my finger across the cool ridges of the trigger, time seemed to completely stand still. I waited until he was broadside and put my crosshairs dead on the back portion of his left shoulder and slowly began squeezing the trigger. The shot rang out like thunder in the small, narrow cove, and through the smoke I could seen him running for the woods. I cycled another round and let it go right before he hit the brush.

"Sam, did I hit him? Did you shoot? Where did he go?" I wasn't wasting any time with this one and ran up over the logs to see where he had gone. The grass where the bear had been standing just seconds before was as green as green got, and there wasn't any blood anywhere!

"What in the hell, Sam? What in the hell is going on?"

Sam was still on top of the logs as I looked back before heading into the woods. I looked high and low but found nothing again, nothing at all. I went up a trail and down a long a stream, then up a river, and back to the pond but found nothing. As I looked across the pond where Sam was standing, he was pointing to a limb and was motioning for me to come over.

When I got to where Sam was, he said in a somber tone, "I think I found your first shot."

As I looked at the log he was pointing to, I couldn't believe what I was seeing.

I had completely missed the first shot and hit the branch of another dead log! I went back to where I had shot from and realized that I would have hit the bear if the stick had just been a one-eighth-inch shorter. Because I was on fourteen power, I couldn't see the stick in my scope! I had made a huge mistake and lost another trophy bear! If there was ever a moment that I could change in time, this was definitely it. The count was now six for me and three for Sam, and as we made our way back to the boat, I couldn't help think about what I had done to piss the hunting gods off.

This time when we came along side of the *Viking* with nothing in the skiff, nobody said anything. We motored up again and headed all the way toward the back of Barry Arm and cut the motor. There was a great south-facing slope, so we decided to drift with the tide and eat lunch while glassing. It was a beautiful, hot day and not a cloud in the sky. Only thing missing,

I thought, was us skinning up another bear. I was just starting to wind down when Tom spotted another bear in a rock slide. We glassed him for a while, but he kept coming out and going into what looked like a deep ravine or stream. I told Tom that if he wanted it, he had better make up his mind, for this time of day they're usually on the move or not moving at all.

We piled into the skiff again and headed for the shore. On the way in, I had momentarily looked over to another ridge when I lost sight of where the bear was only to arrive at the shore not knowing which chute the bear was in. What looked to be only one chute from the boat were now four, and which one he was in was anybody's guess. Tom and I slowly made our way along the shore at the base of the chutes the whole time looking up and around the boulders and rocks.

"I lost him, Tom. Do you remember which chute he was in?"

"No, man, they all look the same to me."

"Yeah, I know what you mean."

We skirted the shore for about a mile, then turned back, and made our way back to where the skiff was. Like they so often do, the bear had disappeared into the hills and was gone. We piled into the skiff and headed back to the *Viking*.

No sooner than we came alongside when Matt and Scott told us that there was another bear on the ridge in front of us.

Great, I thought as I climbed over the rail and onto the deck.

I was so tired of chasing bears at this point I couldn't even tell you. The only bear I wanted to see right now was the one trying to hop in our boat carrying a keg of beer and a pizza! He was up, really up high crawling through a rocky avalanche chute, so we all decided to just watch him for a while. With the sun setting fast, Scott decided to motor into Alpen Cove for our last night of the hunt. We anchored up, dropped some lines, and settled in for our last night in paradise.

Left to Right:
Me, Sam, Tom and Matt

The morning came early with the sun glaring right in my eyes. It was our last day, and after breakfast, we slowly motored out glassing for one last time the bays and coves for one last bear. Before I knew it, we had passed the last bit of land and headed out into the gulf; the hunt was officially over. About an hour later, Scott cut the motor over his favorite black rockfish hole. Tom had been looking forward to fishing from the first day out, so this was a welcomed relief to almost a week of humping the bush; at least that's what he thought! No sooner did his line hit the bottom when he had a fish on.

"Fish on," Tom called out.

"Fish on," Matt yelled as if he had snagged a whale shark.

"Fish on," Sam called out as I felt my bait getting slammed over and over again.

Scott was running around like a one-legged man in a butt-kicking contest when I yelled, "Fish on." It looked like the days of the old tuna boats where guys were just chucking fish into the boat one after the other. The only words you could hear was "Fish on, fish on, fish on!" It was sheer chaos as the deck quickly filled with our limit of rockfish. I glanced over at Tom who was staring at me with a "holy crap" look. He was sweating pretty good and still had a fish on but was loving every minute of it.

"Wait until we get to the halibut hole!" I said when the look on his face turned from shock to terror.

There were fish flopping everywhere, and as I tried chucking my last fish over the side, I slipped on another and lost the one I had. I was getting back up when out of the corner of my eye, I noticed a figure standing up on the back rail of the boat. The next thing I know, Scott's diving into the icy-cold water of the Alaska Sound.

What in the hell, I thought as I looked over the side to see Scott swimming away from the boat. Seemed that in all of the mayhem, Scott had lost his $75 gaff and decided he wasn't going to lose it. There were lines going everywhere, the boat was drifting, and Scott was now being swept out to sea.

Where is the video camera when you need it? I thought as I put my rod back in the holder.

In the two seconds it took me to get across the fifteen-foot beam of the *Viking*, Scott was already out of reaching distance, and you could now see the panic in his eyes. At the last possible second, Scott grabbed the tip of Tom's pole and was pulled to the boat. We all had to help him in, for his muscles were already starting to cramp. With fish still on, we all returned to fishing like nothing ever happened.

Only in Alaska, I thought as I gaffed Tom's last fish and hurled it in the boat, *only in Alaska*.

Tom's yelloweye rockfish

Once Scott thawed out, we motored farther up to one of his favorite halibut holes. Again and no sooner than the first hook hit the bottom when we all had fish on. It was like déjà vu as we all struggled to haul in the run. Tom was again in complete awe as he cranked in fish after fish. We were limited out in less than an hour, and the deck was littered with fish flopping everywhere.

"Get that one," Scott yelled as a lone halibut slid across the deck. We were in the swells now and struggling to stand up while pulling in the last of our catch. "Reel up, reel up," Scott yelled. "We need to turn the boat into the swells, reel up!"

No sooner than the last pole was up when a huge swell broke over the bow. "Holy crap, that was intense," Tom said in a shaken tone. "Is it always like this?" he asked.

"With the exception of almost losing our captain, pretty much," I replied, cracking open the beer and chips, "pretty much."

We now had a six-hour ride to Seward in front of us, and as I settled back into the bench on the back deck, a pod of porpoises started playing with the boat. We all got up to the bow and watched as they gave an incredible show. With speeds reaching fifty miles per hour, they shot back and forth like little black-and-white torpedoes. Don't know why they like boats but they do and were now riding the wake like a group of surfers. Then as quickly as they had appeared, they were gone. What a privilege it was to see these incredible creatures, I thought as my mind again drifted back to the hunt. I always try to do a mental "lessons learned" for myself; however, this time, I couldn't come up with anything except to maybe get a bigger gun!

The more I thought about it though, we had pulled off at least five incredibly stalks that put us within yards of all the bears we missed. We did, however, help both of our friends take bears, which was more gratifying than I ever expected. This alone should have been enough to call the hunt a success, but it wasn't—at least not for me. For no matter how great someone says a hunt was, there's no reward like a "dead reward," and that just didn't happen on this trip.

To this day and every time I see Sam, we still give each other that "what in the hell happened out there?" look. Somewhere in all of our conversations, "it" always comes up like a nasty wart you can't get rid of. How could two experienced bear hunters, shooting two different rifles that they've both killed everything with, miss six different bears at distances of less than seventy yards? After anxiously waiting a week to get on the range and check our rifles, both Sam's and my rifle were dead on! Everyone I've shared this story with has come up with their own version of how it could happen—everything from jerking the trigger to high barometric pressure and then some. None, however, come even close to what I now believe is the truth though. And that is: "When the hunting gods say it's not your turn, it's just not your turn!"

10

THE KINGS OF KODIAK

Whether it's a whitetail or cape buffalo, for those of us who hunt, we all dream about the same thing: that one hunt that will put all of the others to shame. And when it comes to hunting big game, no other place in North America compares to the vastness and diversity of game that Alaska has to offer. For hunters, Alaska offers the unmatched opportunity of hunting some of the wildest and most dangerous game in America. With brown bears that can reach twelve feet, to moose that that measure seventy inches or more, the possibilities of taking an abundance of world-class animals are endless.

Years back and on my first bear hunt in the Brooks Range, I had been bitten by the bear bug and have been infected with it ever since. My favorite of this species is the notorious Kodiak brown bear. Known to some as the Kings of Kodiak, this creature unlike any other ranks number one on the list of dangerous predators and rightfully so. With its unmatched sense of smell, razor-sharp claws, and jaws that have been known to crush a man's head with one bite, this bear is a natural-born killing machine. Contrary to popular belief, all a person needs to hunt this bear is to either have a lot of money, a lot of luck, or both!

This is the story of not one but two *lucky* individuals who drew tags to do just that: to hunt and kill two of the largest, most dangerous bears in North America—the Kings of Kodiak."

Saturday, April 24, 2011
Day 1

It was about two o'clock in the morning, and as we crammed the last of what we thought was about 2400 pounds of gear into Joe's truck, all I could think about was, "Rug or full mount?"

All of our gear

The hellish task of trying to figure out how to put two weeks' worth of gear and crew into a one-week airplane was over. It was go time, and I was more than ready to get this hunt started. Just months before, my longtime hunting buddy and friend Joe Wasielewski and I had drawn tags for the ever-popular and coveted Kodiak brown bear. Having successfully done this hunt together in 2002, we both had somewhat of an idea of what lay ahead.

This time, however, we had drawn a completely different area of Kodiak, which meant the logistics and hunt would be a little different. This time, we would be hunting an area steeped in bear-hunting history and walking the same trails where men like Bill Pinnell and Morris Talifson had made their names as some of the most successful bear hunters in the world. A place lost in time and so remote that like generations before is still only accessible by foot or plane. A place where the largest-known predators in the world roam free among an endless expanse of untouched and pristine wilderness. A small, insignificant, seven-mile body of water in the middle of Kodiak known as Frazer Lake.

After an incredible and unusually smooth eight-hour ferry ride from Homer, we arrived in Kodiak about 7:00 p.m. We were hoping to get in a little earlier so we could get our tags, but that didn't happen, so we would spend the night at the Shelikof Inn and pick up our tags in the morning. I was just happy to finally be in Kodiak and off that damned boat! Nothing worse than a big boat swaying back and forth for eight-hours, no matter how smooth the sways are!

Sunday, April 25, 2011
Day 2

The weather had turned from nasty to complete crap with wind, snow, and ice all blowing sideways the whole day. We stopped in to Fish and Game, picked up our tags, and hit the Safeway for some salt for the hides. The weather was typical for Kodiak—wind, rain, and more rain. So by the end of the day we found ourselves sipping coffee in a local café while watching the rain fall. We later met up with Sam Catt, whom Joe and I first hunted with back in 2002 on our very first brown bear hunt.

A retired Coast Guard, Coasty, as we call them, Sam ran his own charter boat since retiring and knew Kodiak like the back of his hand. He had been to Frazer Lake a few times and had seen firsthand some of the local bears up close—too close from the way he described it.

Unlike Frazer Lake, Katmai National Park is world renowned for bear viewing and is located about 150 miles west of Kodiak. Because most tourists start out in Anchorage, almost everyone who comes to Alaska to view bears ends up there. What a lot of people don't know and what seems to be a well-kept secret is the fact that Frazer Lake has just as many bears, if not more. There is a fish weir at the south side of the lake, which helps the fish from the Dog Salmon River make their way into the lake—a perfect place to watch bears as they try to catch an easy meal. Even though it wasn't salmon season for another couple of months, it didn't take a rocket scientist to figure out that this might be a good place to hang out and look for bears!

Monday, April 26, 2011
Day 3

We headed down to the float plane docks and met up with the crew from Andrew Air who we had chartered to get us into Frazer Lake. They had a fleet of aircraft to include three beavers, a 206, and a Piper Saratoga, so one way or another, we were getting in. Only problem now was the weather, which, as usual, was not cooperating. We were completely socked in, and as we nervously watched our gear being meticulously weighed to calculate the loads, we waited for the weather to break. A beaver can take about 1,200 pounds, and a 206 can take about 800, so that's what we had originally booked: one beaver and one 206. As the scale tipped at 2,100 pounds, we all started to sweat. Twenty-two hundred, then twenty-three, then 2,436 was finally called out. Joe's jaw hung in the wind for a moment as his father paced back and forth shaking his head like a broken bobble doll. Dick, Joe's father, has and probably always will be kind of our good-luck charm and is a natural bear magnet. He had been on our first bear hunt together back in 2002, so it only seemed fitting that he be here for this one. As with our first hunt, he again volunteered to do the filming for this one. I could only hope that this time, the footage would be of something other than the grass growing.

To make a long story short, it was during that hunt when Joe spotted a huge bear meandering along a trail. The bear was coming right toward us and would be passing along the bottom of a hill we had just gotten on top of. Without a lot of time to think things through, we dumped our gear and made our way down the hill to ambush the bear. Joe and Dick set up on the left side of the trail, and for some odd reason, I decided to sit smack-dab in the middle of it—seemed like a good idea in the moment. My butt no sooner hit the dirt, when I realize how bad I had just screwed up. The trail was deep and narrow, and I was now sitting in the bottom of it. All I could see was about thirty feet in front of me and nothing else, nothing! I wouldn't be able to see the bear until he was right on top of me, but it was too late to do anything about it now.

I was just starting to pull myself out of the trail to see if Joe and Dick were ready, when out of the corner of my eye, I noticed a brown spot in the distance. I dropped back into the trail and readied my rifle struggling to find the bear in my scope. That's when I realized I had made another huge mistake. While using my scope earlier to glass what I thought was a bear, I had left the power at fourteen. It was too late now though, and as I peered through the scope, all I could see was a lot of brown hair! Next thing I knew, the bear was looking me dead in the eye!

Bawam!

It was all I heard as Joe's first shot ripped through the bear's right shoulder. I dropped the hammer on my .375, and a volley of fire from both Joe's .338 and mine filled the valley with thunder for what seemed like an eternity! After my first round, the bear was so close that all I had to do is point the muzzle in its direction and pull the trigger. I ran four rounds downrange in about five seconds with Joe matching that in succession. It was like watching a slow-motion film as the bear twisted and turned with each round that ripped through his hide. As if it were his last act of defiance, the bloodied behemoth stood one last time trying to scratch off the barrage of stinging, hot rounds, stumbled backward, and fell into a mangled mess of mud and alders; Joe's first Kodiak brown was down!

I crawled out of the trail and was reaching in my pocket for more rounds when I yelled to Joe, "Reload, reload!"

To my surprise, the bear was still moving, and as I walked toward him, I chambered one more round in the smoking barrel of my rifle. To this day, I will never forget what I saw when I turned to look where Joe and Dick were. At first glance, I thought Dick had been hit by a stray bullet or something, but I realized seconds later that he was just in shock. He was as white as a ghost and just standing there shaking with his hands in the air as if to say, "What in the hell just happened?"

Seemed that when Joe and I let loose the volley of fire from hell, Dick was a bit overcome by it all and dropped the camera in the grass. The only footage we got was that of the grass growing and audio that sounded like something from the Shootout at the OK Corral! To this day, we still laugh and harass him about it every chance we get, and we get a lot of chances!

It only took three hours, but all 2,436 pounds of our gear was finally loaded up into two beavers. Unlike most hunts in Alaska, we were leaving the top ramen at home and were going to be eating and living well on this one. We had booked a twenty-by-thirty state forest service cabin that had an oil-burning stove, living room, dining room, porch, outhouse, and slept four comfortably. So aside from the fact that we would be hundreds of miles from anything, we were going to be living in luxury. The best part was the fact that we wouldn't have to haul our gear too far seeing that the cabin was just one hundred yards away from the shoreline.

Joe and Dick would go in one, and I and the rest of our gear in another; all we needed now was a break in the weather. It was almost noon, and we were getting ready to run into town for some lunch when Sandy, one of the pilots, yelled to us, "Get in and get in now!"

"Go, go, go," the ground crew yelled as they scrambled toward the docks.

Dick was still trying to get one of his hip waders on and was now hopping down the dock.

My pilot Steve blew out of the office and yelled, "Let's go, let's go! Get the lines."

It was mass chaos as we all scrambled down the dock and threw ourselves into the planes. No sooner than my belt was fastened when we throttled up and were taxiing down the shallow, float-plane channel. Joe and Dick were about two hundred feet to our rear, and as soon as we had oil pressure, the throttle was up, and we were out of there like our asses were on fire!

As we banked hard right to avoid a fog cloud, I looked back to see Joe and Dick's plane just getting off the water. We were up and out, and as the beaver struggled to gain altitude, I was overcome with a feeling of relief. Considering that some hunts never get out of Kodiak, we had gotten lucky again, and our adventure had officially begun. Within minutes, we were shooting through snow-covered passages and over the tops of mountains that shot up out of the sea like petrified monsters.

We were on our way, and all I could do now is sit back, shut up, and enjoy the ride. As soon as we got out of the fog, the weather was clear, and you could see forever. Hard to believe it was an island, I thought as we banked left and pointed the nose toward Karluk Lake.

On a hillside just out of Kodiak, I spotted fresh bear tracks going up and into a den. We passed elk, deer, fox, and even a sow with two cubs—what an awesome ride.

About forty minutes later, the pilot stuck his finger out, and said, "That's Frazer Lake. Your cabin is in back of the ice!"

"I'm sorry...did you say behind the ice?" I asked.

"Yep, you're gonna have to pull it in on the sleds," he replied.

We were low and coming in fast, so I would have to wait to find out what he meant by "pulling it in." We flew over the cabin and circled back into the wind when I realized what he was talking about.

Beaver coming in to land on the half-frozen lake.

The cabin that we had reserved was on the south side of the lake and, unfortunately, surrounded by ice. The kind of ice that float planes couldn't land on this time of year. We would have to be dropped off at the water line and then carry our gear—all 2,436 pounds worth—into the cabin, which was now about a mile away—maybe two?

Now the fun begins. Note the ice-line that stretches left from where im standing and across the entire lake

Piece of cake, I thought as the wind under our wings fell out and slammed us onto the lake like a little toy. I pulled my head out from between my legs only to find Steve now looking down at me with a huge smile through his ridiculously large walrus mustache.

"Wind shear," Steve said, still smiling from ear to ear.

We taxied up as far as we could get to the ice and cut the engine. What took over three hours to load took less than twenty minutes to unload. It looked like something out of a bad plane crash movie; gear was scattered all over the rocky shore of an ice-covered lake in the middle of nowhere. No sooner than we finished unloading it started to rain and snow. It was freezing out, and the wind wasn't making matters any better; we needed to find the cabin and find it fast.

The reality of the situation finally hit me as the planes taxied out and the pilots gave a final wave.

This might be it, I thought as the planes throttled up and made their way down and off the lake. This may be the hunt that none of us ever get to reminisce about. Even though I saw it as we were coming in, we had no idea where the cabin actually was. The good news was, even though the ice wasn't thick enough to land a float plane, it was for walking on—sort of. We would use pack sleds to drag our gear in and follow the shoreline to the cabin; at least that's what the plan was. As we loaded the sleds with all of our gear, it started to rain again.

Could it get any better than this? I thought as I pulled the sled along the cracking ice beneath me.

Three trips and seven grueling hours later, we fired up the generator and oil-burning stove and settled into our new home for the next two weeks; we were huntin' now, baby!

Forest service cabin...Home sweet home
for the next two weeks

Tuesday, April 27, 2011
Day 4

It was our first day to legally, hunt and seeing how we still had a lot of gear and a boat strewn all over the shoreline, we would hunt our way there and back through the woods; maybe something had come in from all the different smells. I had woken up around 6:00 a.m., but it was still dark and really cold out, so I crawled back in my warm, cozy bag and caught a few more winks! When I woke again, it was about noon, and Dick had thankfully got the fire stoked and coffee on.

This is heaven, I thought as I slowly sipped the evil bean juice from the warm tin cup.

After a while we all meandered our way down the shoreline again and started hauling in the last of our gear. To our surprise, the ice had receded south and past the cabin, so we just loaded what was left in the boat and made our way back to the cabin in it.

Later that day, we decided to hunt the ridge directly in back of the cabin. It wasn't too high and was just a short trip through the woods; we were all still sore from the day before, so this would work out well. Joe and I spent the rest of that day hiding in tussock holes to stay out of the wind while glassing. Dick had found himself a really nice hole and spent the rest of his day doing "neck exercises," in it.

Wednesday, April 28, 2011
Day 5

Woke up around 4:00 a.m. to about two inches of fresh snow and temperatures around 20 degrees.

Not great bear-hunting weather, I thought as I slipped back into my bag.

We later woke and, after much debate, decided to hunt the valley in back of the cabin again. Joe had pulled a muscle or something in his back, so this would maybe help with loosening it up. It was about 11:00 a.m. or so when we started gearing up when in the distance we saw and heard a plane coming directly at our cabin.

Within minutes, the beaver flew right over us and swung back around toward the lake. We were all standing on the porch now trying to figure out who it was and what they were doing. Couldn't see a tail number when it flew over, so we didn't know who it was. One thing was for sure, though, they were coming in and coming in fast. They banked hard left and almost looked like they were going to do a nose over into the lake when the pilot rolled her out, cut the throttle, and coasted right up to our shore.

I grabbed a rifle and started down the trail to meet them when Dick and Joe joined me.

"Who do you think that is?" Joe asked.

"Don't know, Joe, but the last time I was on a hunting trip and had a plane stop by, it wasn't good. In fact, it was to let one of the guys we were hunting with know that his father had passed."

I was getting anxious now, and as I began to walk a little faster, I began thinking about the worse news I could get. About halfway down the trail I could see three men in waders getting out of the plane.

Was it Fish and Game? I thought as I got closer. Then I spotted what appeared to be either a package or maybe a newspaper? Then I realized from the tail number that it was an Andrew Air service plane and the guy holding what I could now see was in fact a newspaper was Dean Andrew himself—he owner and operator of Andrew Air!

They all had smiles on their faces as we all made the rounds shaking hands.

"Thought you guys might like a newspaper," Dean said as if it was nothing getting it here!

Unbelievable, I thought as I looked back at Joe and Dick who were just as amazed as I was. Come to find out, Steve and Sandy were more than a little worried about our predicament when they dropped us off, so they just flew an hour one-way to check on us! As we stood on the shore shooting the breeze with these guys, the weather started moving in again, so Dean suggested they power up and get back home. As we waved good-bye again, I couldn't help to think how amazingly incredible that was for them to do that. As long as I have hunted and as many stories I have heard from the bush, I have never heard of or experienced a transporter, flying service, or pilot who has ever done what Dean and his crew did that day. Amazing!

We made our way back up to the cabin, had some lunch, and geared back up. After a few more pots of coffee and a lot of procrastinating, we began hiking in on an old trail that later we would learn was an old Pinnel and Talifson trail into the valley between Akalura Lake and Frazer Lake. We spent the rest of the day on a ridge up there just glassing from one spot, but we didn't see anything except snow and rain. It was cold, dark, and miserable, and after about six hours of that, we called it the day and made our way back to the cabin.

Dick and I cutting through the alders

Thursday, April 29, 2011
Day 6

Imagine that, snow again! We accumulated about another two inches overnight, and now the wind was blowing sideways, driving the temperatures to about 10 to 15 degrees. It was our sixth day of the trip, and so far we hadn't seen a single bear. To make matters worse, Joe's back was really bothering him, so we filled up some socks with rice, heated them up on the stove, and used them on his back to loosen things up.

Later that day we hunted the valley in back of the cabin again and didn't see anything except for a lot of eagles. We still had a few hours of light left when we got back to the cabin, so Dick and I took the zodiac up the lake a bit to see what we could see. Up to this point, we hadn't seen or heard of any other people on the lake and thought that we were the only ones out here. It was a beautiful evening, and the water was as smooth as glass.

As we slowly motored down the shoreline, out of nowhere we spotted three hunters on a ridge glassing for bears. Then a little farther up we ran into another group on the lake that had been there for two weeks and only spotted three bears.

Me being stupid in a motorized rubber raft in a really big half-frozen lake in the middle of nowhere!

Then as we looked across the lake on another ridge, there was another party that had set up camp within a mile from our cabin. Come to find out, this was master guide Dennis Harms who alone had six clients in with him.

So much for limiting the pressure, I thought as I swung the boat around and headed for home.

We later learned that at one point during our hunt there were more than nine hunters with tags on the lake.

Friday, April 30, 2011
Day 7

Yeah, more snow! Again, we woke up to fresh powder, blowing wind, and freezing temperatures. If a bear was to make its way out of its den now, it would have to be either really stupid or really desperate or both!

It was about 10:00 a.m. when the smell of fresh-brewed coffee aroused my senses. Dick, who is a really early riser, had been up since the crack of dawn and already been through a pot.

A quick glance out the back window of the cabin confirmed my theory: stay in bed all day because we're not going to see anything in this mess. The wind and snow was again blowing sideways, and every once in a while, the whole cabin would shake and vibrate uncontrollably. Another glance out the window confirmed my suspicion that the loud bang we heard last night was not a bear, but was our outhouse, which was now completely on it's side—toilet covered with fresh snow and ice! Yeah, we were hunting now, baby! Joe and I finally dragged our asses out of bed around noon. Dick had been drinking coffee all morning and by now was wired for sound.

"Are you guys ready yet?" Dick shouted at a volume that could wake the dead.

"Coffee, Dick, where's the coffee?" I asked.

Dick and Joe were of Polish descent and being so, unfortunately, knew a little about making schnapps! Due to the extreme weather and other stressful circumstances encountered over the last few days, we elected to indulge in a bit of the spirits last night to take the edge off. After righting the outhouse, filling up the generator, and cutting up some firewood, I ran down to the lake to check on the boat. To my surprise, I found the entire boat covered with about a two-inch layer of ice on the outside and about six inches on the inside.

Waves must have been pretty big last night, I thought as I wandered back to the cabin to get the ax.

We spent the rest of the day just pretty much recovering, cleaning up, throwing up, and then taking another short nap after breakfast. It was about two thirty or so when the weather finally broke, so we decided to jump in the now-deiced boat and head over to fish weir or fish ladder. Until now, we couldn't get in because the ice was dammed up on that end of the lake, but now it was clear, so off we went. Frazer Lake drains down the Dog Salmon River and then into Olga Bay, and to help the fish get into the lake, the forest service built a ladder to aid in that process. We had heard a lot of bears come down in the spring to see what's there, so it might be a good place to start.

We had been glassing for about an hour when Joe spotted a lone bear sticking his head out of his den. I don't know how he spotted it, for all you could see was just the top of his head sticking out of a snow-covered hole. Unfortunately he was sitting smack-dab in the middle of an avalanche chute that was about eight hundred feet straight up—not the best of options. But we had finally seen our first bear after seven long days in the bush.

GEORGE GARRISON

Bear hunting: 99% glassing, 1% killing!

Bear in the spotting scope

Saturday, May 1 2011
Day 8

It was day 8, and like every other day since the start of this hunt, the weather was less than hospitable. In fact, it was downright nasty out. The good news was, it wasn't snowing anymore; we were just completely fogged in. So after the usual morning routine of coffee, grub, and numerous trips to the outhouse, we poured ourselves back into our bags and took our scheduled midmorning naps.

I woke again around eleven thirty due to the sun shining in my eyes. Joe had been up for a while glassing the hills across the lake from the cabin.

"It's clear as a bell out here. C'mon, let's go," Joe said.

So after a quick lunch and some more coffee, we made our way down to the boat and across the lake to the weir again. We got to the old boat shed by the weir about 3:00 p.m. and set up the spotting scope to start glassing. We all set up in different locations so we could cover more terrain. Dick was looking north; Joe, south; and I was looking everywhere else!

We were about three hours or so into it when Joe jumped up and yelled, "Bear!"

Dick and I jumped up and started looking for what Joe was looking at—which, to my surprise, was clear across the lake.

"Where?" I asked as I tried to get a fix on where Joe was looking. Keep in mind that this unfortunately was not the first time any of us had cried bear. In fact, it was starting to become really annoying, for most of the time they turn out to be just rocks, shadows, or something else completely. So as I stood and reluctantly scanned the area where he was describing, there it was, bigger than life.

"Get in the boat, get in the boat," I whispered as if the bear could hear me over two miles away!

I gathered all of our gear and threw it in the boat the whole time whispering, "Come on, come on, get in the boat!"

Joe was moving pretty good, but Dick, well, for some reason, he was still stuck in slow motion!

"Get in the friggin' boat, Dick" I yelled as I was cranking the motor over. Not sure if it was me pushing the boat away from the shore or if it was Joe yelling at him too, but Dick got in the boat. I twisted the throttle as far as I could, and off we went.

We had a lot of distance to close if we were ever going to get this bear, seeing that the lake is about seven miles long and two miles wide. We were at the very end of the south side and had about a half mile or so of water to cover, then about another mile to get to where we first saw the bear. With any luck, once we hit the shore, we could get up the hill and get the drop on him again. Contrary to popular belief, bears can move incredibly fast and wander aimlessly when they first come out of their dens, so even though our bear seemed to be moving from our left to right, it doesn't mean that's the way he would still be going when we get there.

As soon as we hit the shore, I chambered a round of 225-grain Barnes TSX in .338 Win. Magnum. I quickly tied the boat off and was getting ready to get up the hill when Dick whispered to me, "I gotta poop!"

"Dammit, Dick, we don't have time. We have to go."

"Okay," he said, "I'll stay here, and you guys go!"

It took about a minute to get up on a ridge where we stopped to catch our breath and tried glassing for him again. I heard the snaps on Joe's pack and turned to find him taking a nature break too.

"I got him Joe, he's straight ahead about five hundred yards," I whispered.

Joe scrambled to gear up again, and off we went, running the whole way across the minefield of swamp holes and tussocks.

Finally, we made it up to this nice, grassy knob and to within about 200 yards of the bear. There was an old tree stump about four inches high with nice grass all around it, which made for a great rest. The bear was moving slowly down a hill and straight toward us when I ranged him again at 190 yards. Joe quietly crawled into position and put the bear in his crosshairs.

I ranged him again and whispered to Joe one more time, "One seventy-nine."

The bear was just foraging around in the alders and had no idea we were there. I read the distance out again and was waiting for the shot when Joe said, "I think he's rubbed."

"What?" I said. "Are you serious?" I glassed the bear again and couldn't see any rubs at all. For a moment, I thought Joe might be looking at another bear, so I glassed him again to just make sure it wasn't a sow and cub. Nope, he was all alone, and as I took more time now to glass him better, I realized that he was an absolute brute. His head was huge, eyes were close together, snout straight and wide, and you could hardly make out his ears—all signs of a huge bear!

"Shoot that bastard, Joe. He's a shooter," I whispered anxiously.

And no sooner than the time it took for me too look back up to where the bear was when he disappeared into the brush and was gone.

"C'mon, Joe, I think he's heading south. Maybe we can cut him off farther down this ridgeline." We were running as fast as we could through and over a maze of scrub brush, tussocks, and alder, trying to get in front of him and cut him off.

We had gotten about another five to eight hundred yards out when I stopped to catch my breath. Joe was in back of me about thirty feet, and as I struggled to catch my breath, out of the corner of my eye, I saw something move. Joe had caught up and was attempting to pass me when I grabbed him by his coat.

"Don't friggin' move, Joe. He's right there, right in front of us!" We both stood there motionless for a minute as Joe tried to find the bear. Trying to talk without moving my lips, I whispered, "Don't move, he's looking right at us."

Out of the corner of my eye I could see Joe's head bopping all around trying to find the bear, which now was only about thirty yards in front of us.

"Do you see him?" I asked again, watching his head out of the corner of my eye, struggling to find the bear.

Joe slowly raised his rifle in the direction of the bear as I again nervously waited for the rapport with the rifle. What seemed like an eternity was only seconds when Joe said, "I don't think he's that big." And just like that, the bear was gone again!

"Are you friggin' kidding me, Joe? If you're not going to shoot him, let me take him," I said.

Joe paused for a moment and said, "I'm going up that hill to see if I can spot him again. If you see him, shoot him!"

I was standing there still trying to catch my breath while watching the bushes for any sign of movement when about one hundred yards out, Mr. Brown decided to pop out again! He had gone back into the alders and was a little farther out and in the snow now moving again from left to right. I raised my rifle and put his right front shoulder dead in my crosshairs. There was no time to range him, for there was another clump of alders coming up, and I knew that if he made it there, we would probably never see him again.

He was in about a foot of snow, moving pretty good, so I would need to lead him just a bit. I put my crosshairs just in front of his right shoulder and slowly squeezed the trigger while following him with the rifle. As I slowly started to squeeze the trigger, I wondered if Joe was looking at him too.

Take your time, I thought as I took a long breath in, let it out, held, squeezed, and *bawam!* It sounded like someone smacked a rug with a huge broom as the round slammed into the side of his chest. I saw his back arch and heard him bellow from the hit. I let the second round fly as he was spinning to the right trying to brush off the sting of the first round.

Another *whop* and about a second after that, he did a complete 180 and was trying to get back into the safety of the brush when I heard Joe's shot ring out. It took less than a second for the bear to disappear back into the alders, but nevertheless, he was gone again. I was struggling to chamber another round when Joe came down the hill.

"You hit him good. You smacked the crap out of him," Joe said. We both stood there reloading and filling our magazines with rounds, for we both knew what was next; we would need to go into the alders and find this bear.

Contrary to popular belief, I have found it better to look for a wounded bear in thick stuff than it is to try and find a live bear in it. Once you start closing in on a wounded bear, they will let you know exactly where they are. The best scenario obviously is if you hit them good and they go right down; however, with Kodiaks, this is rare. Or if you're lucky and get a few good hits and end up with a nice blood trail that leads you to a dead bear, unfortunately, this is not always the case either. As if almost instinct, we stood back to back using a 180-degree peripheral as we slowly worked our way across a small stream and into the dark, thick brush.

Joe had the front 180, and I of course had the rest, which works really well seeing that bears are notorious for flanking you or coming in on your back. I hadn't heard the notorious "death moan" that a lot of bears produce just before expiring but knew my first shot was good. Maybe I lunged him, and he couldn't produce a moan? The questions were racing through my mind as we drove farther and farther into the thick, brown alders. It was really starting to get thick now, and as we came around a huge clump of alders, we could see where I had hit him. There was a lot of blood and a good trail of blood that led straight into another patch of alders. The good news was, there wasn't any leaves on the bushes this time of year, so you could see about ten feet forward verses zero in the summer. The bad news was, there wasn't any leaves on the bushes this time of year, so you could see about ten feet forward verses zero in the summer! For those who've ever looked for a brown spot where the only colors are brown and white, it's kind of like looking at a black-and-white picture of a forest; you can't tell what is what. It was reminding me of a time not too long ago when Joe and I had been hunting bear and found ourselves in a similar situation.

It was back on our first bear hunt in 2002 when we had spotted a bear running down a hill and watched it disappear behind a ridge about one hundred yards from our back. We got up on the ridge where we thought he had gone in, but as bears are notoriously known for doing, it had completely vanished. The terrain didn't seem that thick, and I was surprised to see nothing moving as we glassed the entire area back and forth for several minutes. There was a small and narrow elk trail that went through the middle of a row of seriously thick alders. Thinking that maybe we misjudged the ridge that the bear went behind, I suggested to Joe that we cut through the trail and over to the other ridge. We had just about made up our minds to do just that when from down that trail and less than twenty-five yards in front of us, the bear broke out into a full-out run.

To our luck, it was running uphill and away from us, mowing down brush like it wasn't even there. And as expected, Joe and I laid down a barrage or fire cutting down everything in sight, except for the bear. When it finally broke out of the alders and into the open grass at the top of the hill, I let the last round of .375 I had go and dropped it on its tracks; that was my first brownie! That bear was just sitting there the whole time watching us, stalking us as we were stalking it. So when it comes to looking for something in the thick stuff, I'll take a wounded bear over a live bear any old day.

It was late, and we were losing light fast when out of the corner of my eye, I spotted something that was not fitting the rest of the terrain—a really dark spot where a dark spot shouldn't be. With rifles readied, we both slowly made our way side by side to the spot.

"He's down. He's down!" I yelled.

The bear had collapsed belly down just in front of a stream, and the closer we got, the less I could believe what I was seeing. He was a monster and well over nine feet with a head like a Mack Truck.

When all was said and done, we only found two holes in him, so I think he was moving too fast when Joe finally shot. My second round, we later learned, had hit him just above his left knee and traveled all the way back to his tailbone and stopped. Joe found the unexpanded round only because the bullet was so hot when it entered that it had burned the hair around the tailbone where it had lodged. It traveled about a quarter inch under the hide along the fat layer and never hit any vitals. This was the fourth Kodiak brown bear I had seen up close and, without a doubt, the largest. His head was absolutely huge, and there wasn't a rub mark on him.

What a beautiful animal, I thought as I tried to lift his massive head for more pictures. He was an old bear judging from the color and wear of his teeth. The canines were all worn down and brown, which indicated at least a ten- to fifteen-year old bear. The rest of his teeth were either cracked, rotted, or missing altogether. It was late, and after taking the last of our victory pictures, we rolled him on his back and spread him out the best we could to make the cutting easier for tomorrow.

We made our way back to the boat just before dark, and as we dragged ourselves and the last of our gear up the long walk to the cabin, I knew that our work had just started. For now, though, it was party time; and after a nice, juicy porterhouse, baked potato, and slaw, Dick decided to break out some more of the good stuff to celebrate.

Sunday, May 2, 2011
Day 9

Morning came all too early, and after a few trips to the outhouse, I crawled back into my bag and passed out once more. There's an old saying that "a hunt doesn't really start until after the first shot is fired"; for bear, that is a huge understatement! I knew we needed to get back out there and take care of that bear, but my body and especially my head were telling me different! Dick had broken out a lot of the good stuff last night, and in respect for his culture, I had obliged him one too many times. I was just starting to wonder if I was the only one with the same predicament when I spotted Joe on the floor next to my bed.

"Joe! Hey, Joe, why are you on the floor?" I muttered?

"Ughhh," was the only thing that came from the lumpy sack that resembled a human in the middle of the floor.

"Joe, what are you doing on the floor?"

"I'm on the what?" he said in a puzzled tone. The only thought going through my head at this point is that this was not going to be a good day at all.

We finally made it to the bear around one o'clock, and after another short photo session began the slicing and dicing. The more I cut, the more I wondered if we were going to have to cut this hide in two or even make two trips to get it out. There's only a few ways of getting a bear this size out of the woods: you can put it in a pack, cut it into pieces, or drag it in a sled or what's known as a game skidder. From the moment I first saw this bear, I knew he wasn't going in my pack!

We were only about a mile and a half from the boat; however, the terrain was less than hospitable, and even with the game skidder, we were in for a really long day. The terrain was nothing but tussock holes surrounded by patches of muck with moss and water. If you didn't know better, you would have thought that you were in the middle of an old bombing range. The few sections of "good terrain" were just small and short patches of moss-covered tundra that was like standing on a huge sponge or really old water bed. If you were lucky, you could pick up the occasional bear trail, which never seemed to go in the direction you wanted and were always full of water.

Between Joe and I cutting and Dick pulling and holding the hide, we were done with the bear in less than four hours. Unfortunately, it took us just over five hours of back-breaking pulling, pushing, and crawling with about six hundred pounds of bear to get to the boat. We made it back to the cabin around

11:00 p.m., threw everything in the meat shed, staggered into the cabin, and broke out the schnapps.

Monday, May 3 2011
Day 10

I woke up around 6:00 a.m. to the sound of what I thought was rain; however, when I tried to open my eye, all I could see was a blinding bright light like a fireball or something.

Am I finally dead? I thought as I tried to focus. *Either tell me I'm dead and there's coffee in heaven or I'm still alive and Dick's made a fresh pot!*

My brain was still in limbo when I realized that it wasn't raining at all. It was the snow melting off the roof, and that bright light, well, that was the sun! Yep, it was the first time in almost ten days that the sun had come out, and let me tell you, it felt good! The coffee was overwhelming, and as I sat on the front porch in the sun sipping on a fresh cup of beans, a sense of self came over me like a warm, fuzzy blanket; after all we had been through on this trip, we had finally killed a bear and a great bear at that. Now all we had to do is find another one for Joe.

After some home-made pancakes, moose bacon, toast, and taters, we took the boat and ran over to the weir where, to my amazement, we met up with Al Duford who was a coworker of mine. He and a few of his friends had been hunting the hills around the fish weir using the Fish and Game sauna as their base camp. They had spent the whole morning hiking back and forth on the muddy mile-long trail that led to the shore, so they were all pretty spent by the time we got there. Al said that they were on the last day of their hunt when they spotted a lone sow on one of the hills in back of their camp and went up after her. He said it was so steep that when he hit her, she tumbled past him and almost knocked his buddy off the mountain. Turned out to be about an eight-foot sow and the only bear they had seen in over a week.

The sun felt incredible, and as we sat there glassing the hills and waiting for Seahawk air to come in for Al and his friends, the roar of a rotary engine broke the deafening silence as it shot out behind a small ridge on the other side of the lake.

"Man, that guy is low," Al said as we helped him bring the rest of his gear to the shore.

Minutes later, the plane taxied in, and we all helped with loading their gear.

We waited by the shore as they taxied out and headed for the very end of the south side of the lake. You could see the nose lift up and water flying up in back of the plane, but they were so far out that we couldn't hear any sound. Then the sound of the engine made its way to the shore, and they were blasting across the lake. You could tell the plane was struggling, for it was still in the water almost halfway down the lake. The plane was getting smaller by the second when it finally broke the surface. Seconds later they were up and off and looked to be at about one hundred feet when they and the beautiful sound of the rotary engine disappeared behind a ridge at the north end of the lake.

Not sure if it was the sun or just all of the noise we had just made, but the bear we had spotted days earlier in the avalanche chute was now out of his den and taking a look around. Unfortunately, he was still really high and not straying from his den. Making a stalk on him at this point would be really premature given the circumstances. For a minute, we thought we heard the plane coming back when out in the middle of the lake, a small boat appeared. It was Dennis Harms who had taken the day off of guiding to come down and do some steelhead fishing on the Dog Salmon River.

We all stopped looking at the bear in the chute, in fear that Dennis may spot him and come back later. No sooner than he stepped out of his boat when Dennis pulled out his glasses and looked straight up to where the bear was.

"Been watching that one for about a week now," he said as if he'd already tagged him. This guy knew where all the bears were out here. All we needed to do now was figure out how to get him to tell us where they were.

It was the first time I had met Dennis although I had spoken with him on the phone before hunting to let him know when and where we would be—a courtesy that I wish more hunters did. To my surprise, he was a little older than he sounded on the phone but, like most guides in Alaska, as strong and ornery as an ox.

With pole in hand and after a lengthy conversation with Dick, Dennis made his way up the trail that led to the river, without divulging anything about where we could find another bear.

Moments later, that bear came out of his den again and started rustling around as if he might be coming out for good. Joe was frothing at the mouth, and we all had him in our glasses when the bear took a look down, took a look up, and just started walking to the top of that mountain. The distance from his den to the top would have taken us probably a day to cover. This bear, however, was up, over, and gone in a matter of minutes.

"Can't ever tell what bears are going to do, especially when they first come out," I said to Joe.

In all my years of hunting bears, there are only a few traits that I consider are consistent of all bears, and even those are negotiable. So when I hear people talking about bears like they're all the same, I can't help but to laugh, because they're not. They are just like people in the sense that each one is a little different in their own way. There are smart ones, dumb ones, mean ones, gentle ones, big ones, small ones, and even ones that could be considered killers or man-eaters. So when people ask me about bears, the only thing I tell them is what a famous Kodiak bear guide by the name of Joe Want told me along time ago.

THE QUEST

It was the winter of 2001, and Joe's and my first Kodiak bear hunt was right around the corner in May. We had seen an ad in the *Anchorage Daily News* about a bear seminar downtown and decided it might be a good idea to check it out; that and the fact that it was free made it a no-brainer. Put on by Fish and Game, it would host a number of biologists from Kodiak, including the leading bear biologist in the United States Larry VanDale.

Joe and I piled into the crowded theater and sat up front so we could see better. We were just sitting there talking when this old gruffy guy in a pair of raggedy jeans, old plaid shirt, and duct-taped hip waders made his way down the aisle and up to the stage. At first I thought he was just another hunter here for the lecture until he grabbed the microphone like it was some kind of weird and strange toy. After banging it a few times on the podium, he realized that it was working as people scrambled to cover their ears.

"Can you hear me? Can you hear me?" he repeated.

After a vulgar response from the back confirming that even the dead could hear him, he lifted some notes from a table and gazed at them for a moment. "I'm Joe Want, and I'm just going to say this: Whatever you've heard, read, or even think you may know about bears, well, just forget it, cuz it ain't true!" The eruption of laughter was followed by silence once everyone realized that he was serious and not laughing at all. "I'm Joe Want, and as some of you already know, I've hunted Kodiak as a guide for the last thirty years, so believe me when I say this."

Great, that's just great, I thought as I sat there thinking about all I had read and the research I had done. *Who is this clown?* I thought as he rambled on about all that he knew and had experienced while hunting bears in Kodiak.

The guy went on to say that he didn't really have much to tell us; however, two hours and a book full of notes later, Joe and I just looked at each other in amazement. I and everyone else in that room now knew exactly who Joe Want was. This scruffy old shell of a weather-beaten man was the god of bear hunting in Alaska. An icon among icons, a walking, talking, endless open vault of bear-hunting knowledge and outdoor lore and we were sitting just steps away from him. I took the opportunity during the break to go shake hands with him and was trying to pick his brain some more when another voice came over the speakers.

"Hi, I'm Larry VanDale, and I'm one of the biologists in Kodiak." He went on for another hour or so about everything we would need to know and then some.

By the end of the seminar, I had run out of paper and was taking notes on old business cards and my hands.

What an amazing seminar, I thought as we walked back to our cars, which were now covered with a couple inches of fresh snow. I was overwhelmed at the vast amount of knowledge I had just witnessed; now I felt even less prepared than ever!

Years and many bear hunts later, I have come to realize the truth of those words that Joe Want and Larry spoke that snowy day in 2001. I have learned that when you start to think you understand bears, something will happen that will completely change your mind—kind of like people. So now when people ask me about bears, I just tell them, "Whatever you've heard, read, or even think you may know about bears, well, just forget it, cuz it ain't true!"

Tuesday, May 4 2011
Day 11

We spent the next few days hunting pretty hard: up at first light and back in the rack around midnight or so. We were using every bit of light we possibly could and had gone from one of the lake to the other and back—a few times actually! Problem was, we weren't seeing any bears, none at all. We had spotted a sow with three cubs a few days back, and that was all. We did, however, spot and run into a lot of other hunters who were experiencing the same thing. The few bears they had spotted had all been up high and gone across the tops instead of coming down. The bad weather was starting to have its toll on both us as well as the bears. If I was a bear and peeked out of my den to see nothing but more rain and snow, I would go back in too.

Like most animals, bears too have an inherent biological clock that tells them when it's time to do things. However, if it looks, smells, and tastes like winter, its winter, and they're not going anywhere!

Wednesday, May 5, 2011
Day 12

Spent the day just glassing around the cabin and hills in the back. We are all starting to show signs of fatigue, and tempers are on the edge. I thought I'll just hang out and flesh the bear some more, seeing that the sun was out. Dick's on the beach glassing but hadn't moved in quite a while—probably doing more "neck exercises"! I thought it may take the boat along the shore later that evening, and we'll see what's moving.

Thursday, May 6, 2011
Day 13

The sun has been out for two days now, but we still haven't seen any bears—just other hunters. We decided to take the boat all the way up to the north cabin to see what it looked like. It was about seven miles one way, so we packed a lunch and headed out. With the remaining gas we had, we figured that this would be our last long trip out and needed to make it count. Now if you've never tried looking through a pair of binoculars for three hours while moving in a small boat, I'm here to tell you it's not fun!

Even with the occasional stops along the way, by the time we got to the north cabin, I felt like someone kicked me in the head and was going blind at the same time. As we made our way from the shore to the cabin, the closer we got to it, the more I could see the damage. I had heard of and seen destruction from bears; however, I had never seen them try and eat a whole cabin.

They had started on the outside window sills and worked their way to the door, porch, and even coat rack on the porch. Wherever and whatever they could get a bite of, they bit. Wherever and whatever they could claw, they clawed. They even gnawed out the window on the outhouse door; what was once a half moon was now a full moon and then some! The funny part of the whole thing was that the door to the cabin wasn't even locked; we turned the handle and walked right in. The wind had started to pick up, and whitecaps were now forming on the lake, so we decided to eat some lunch and stay out of the wind for a while; that and we could glass from the comfort and warmth of the cabin.

After a few hours and a couple short naps, the wind had subsided, and the waves were down again. If we left now, we might make it back before dark.

Friday, May 7 2011
Day 14

The bad part of hunting this long and not being completely successful is that you start second-guessing everything you do; Joe was way past this point, and it was starting to show. This was it, our last official day of hunting, and we knew without a doubt that if it wasn't today, it would never be. We had spent the last thirteen days doing everything we could to bag two bears but had only been lucky enough to get the one. Joe decided that we would hunt the other side of the lake and work our way just across from the cabin as the day progressed. We would use the sun in the morning to glass the north-facing hills and the sun in the evening to glass the south-facing hills. We had pretty much been doing this all along; however, we never planned it that way. As I rummaged through the shelves in the kitchen, I realized that we still had a lot of food left, so this was going to be a huge breakfast. After having some creative fun with pancake mix; cooking up the last of the moose bacon, taters, steak, beans; and mixing up the last pitcher of Tang, we found ourselves again crossing the lake. It was a beautiful, sunny morning, and as we crossed the perfectly calm water of the lake, I looked down into the crystal-clear water and saw something I couldn't describe.

At first I thought it was a log until I realized that it might be a boat or even a canoe. *Weird*, I thought as we arrived at the other side.

We spent the whole day glassing every nook and cranny until we couldn't see anymore. After two weeks at looking at the same hills, over and over again, you start to see things that really aren't there, I think. Most people think that there are only three species of bears in Alaska; however, and unknown to most people, there are actually seven. There is the black, the brown, the grizzly, and the not so well known—however, found quite commonly when hunting—bush, rock, shadow, and notorious log bears. Unlike a lot of species, you'll never see the latter on the endangered list, for there are millions of them, and they are everywhere.

In fact, I would have to say that between Dick, Joe, and I, we had seen at least one hundred of them in the last two weeks. After a while, you don't even look when someone calls out "bear" in fear that it might just be another one. We were losing daylight quick, and you could see the disappointment on Joe's face. We were all frustrated, tired, cold, and tired of being frustrated, tired, and cold!

It was about 10:00 p.m. when Joe finally called it, and as we made our way back across the lake, I reminisced about all we had done over the last two weeks. All that we had actually accomplished despite the elements, the terrain, everything. If we had never taken a bear, I think I would still have called this hunt a success. To draw a tag like this and hunt in the exact same place where men like Pinnell and Talifson had hunted years ago. To stay in the same cabin, sit on the same stools, and walk the same trails they walked was more than surreal for all of us. It was our last night, and like those before it, we brought it in with the usual flavor—raspberry!

Saturday, May 8, 2011
Day 15

Using our sat phone, we called Andrew Air about 9:00 a.m. and let them know that the weather here was good and we were ready for a pickup. The weather in Kodiak was marginal, so they weren't sure if they could get out or not.

We were all nursing our hangovers, and after breakfast, we started the arduous task of hauling all our gear back down to the beach. It was about eleven thirty or so when we heard the first plane fly over. He flew right over the cabin and was so low that I could see it was Jimmy. He went out around the south side of the lake, banked her in hard left, and was on the shore before we could even say wow!

We had all gotten back into town around 2:00 p.m. and after a short trip to Fish and Game to record the bear, we headed down to the ferry terminal to catch our ride back to Homer.

Unfortunately, while we were gone, our ferry the *Matanuska* had developed some mechanical problems and was down for the count. We would have to fly back now and figure out how to get the truck and everything else back later. As my good friend Sam always does, though, he volunteered to put the truck and gear on the ferry once it was back in commission. We would just need to drive another truck down to Homer to pick it up and get it all back to Anchorage. We took the hide, skull, and whatever else we could take on the plane without paying a fortune and headed for the airport where Sam dropped us off.

We were all just hanging out waiting for the plane, when I glanced up to see Joe reading the paper with his eyes shut. Dick was still reading *Last of the Great Brown Bear Men* and began telling me about a story in the book where two packers working for Talifson and Pinnell had crossed the lake in a canoe to recover a bear that a client had shot the day before. On their way back, the canoe had capsized in the middle of the lake, and the two men, along with the bear, were never seen again. The lake had swallowed them up into the deep, dark void and had become their grave forever. Then it hit me: Was that what I had seen on the bottom of the lake that day we were crossing? Could that have been the canoe those guys had been in? Not sure if it was the fact that someone had just come through the terminal's door or if it was something else, but just about then, the coldest breeze I've ever felt blew through the terminal like a small tornado and, as quick as it had arrived, was gone.

Probably just the wind, I thought as I tried to shake the chill out of my body.

A few months and a lot of stories later, the bear was finally scored and came in at 28 and 11/16 for Boone and Crocket and 29 and 1/16 for SCI. Why, they have different scoring methods I'll never understand. The chief biologist from Kodiak Larry VanDale said it was the largest bear he had seen taken from that area in years and, after looking at the records, the largest perhaps since 1964. Larry put the bear at maybe fifteen to twenty years old, which for a bear is really old. This was one of those bears that people wait all of their lives for—a bear of unequaled quality and proportion and a true representative of the species. But this was just the icing on the cake when I thought about the whole hunt. To have been lucky enough to draw a tag in the first place was incredible enough. Then to have drawn, hunted, and taken a record book bear with Joe and Dick was, for me, as good as it gets.

Unfortunately, because we were successful in filling my tag, I now have to wait four years before I can even apply again. Rest assured, though, as long as I am breathing, Fish and Game will see my name on that list. For nothing, nowhere, could ever compare to hunting these magnificent creatures, the Kings of Kodiak!

So was this the hunt that put all others to shame? I think the answer to that is that there is no answer. The only thing I can say with any certainty is that this was the toughest hunt I had ever done, both physically and mentally. And if there's any moral to this story or any advice I could pass on for a hunt like this, it would be to never give up, never give in, hunt hard, trust your instincts, never second-guess yourself or others, and to just have fun. And of course, never ever, ever bring raspberry schnapps on a hunting trip!

11

SHIT HOOK

It was September '95 when I first got to Alaska after a four-year tour in England. This would probably be my last assignment seeing that I was close to retiring from the air force. I remember the fall smells of dead leaves and cool, crisp air like it was yesterday. I had never been this far north and was seriously out of my element—the city! We drove in from the Canadian border and spent the last three days looking at nothing but miles upon miles of wilderness with absolutely nothing in between but animals. It was both beautiful as well as frightening being out in the middle of nowhere on your own with nothing but a small vehicle for an escape. I remember pulling off at a rest stop and stepping out of the car only to be greeted by a silence I had never experienced. It was almost as if I had gone completely deaf until I could hear again the distant sound of a bird's wing breaking the wind. This was going to be an experience I would never forget as I got back into the car. This was going to be an assignment like no other. As we headed down the endless road toward Anchorage, my mind wandered through enormity and incredible beauty of this land.

Two years later, I was knee-deep in snow and trying to find a reason for being here when I met a man by the name of William

B. Fisher. Billy was a retired technical sergeant in the air force who had been in Nam and was now working as a deicer for the Civil Service. I unfortunately was his and about fifteen other deicers' supervisor. A ragtag group of ornery, old, retired cusses, the deicer crew was comparatively nothing short of the smallest unknown lobbying organization in Washington. With years of union experiences behind them and an overabundance of old-school grit, they were a bunch not to be messed with.

Bill was just a little guy with a big heart and, for one reason or the other, took a liking to me right off. He and his longtime friend Gary Hinerman had been in Alaska for just about forever and had been hunting and fishing buddies for a long, long time. With a lot of downtime between deicing missions, the stories would fly for hours around the break room table. I learned a lot around that table, and as the months passed, I developed a friendship with both Bill and Gary that would endure to this day.

Bill unfortunately succumbed to cancer back in '99; however, Gary and I still remain close friends. We were all sitting around the table one night waiting for an aircraft to deice when Bill started cussing.

"Goddarn it," Bill said as he kicked the leg of the table.

"What's up, Bill," I asked.

"Ahh, just had a guy back out on this hunt."

It was September, and as with every year in the past, this one would be no different. Bill had a hunting camp out in the middle of nowhere that I had heard stories of but was never fortunate enough to experience. From the way the stories sounded, it was quite the feat of getting to, but once there, it was the mecca of hunting. He was short a body now and needed someone to fill the void. Someone they knew pretty well and trusted to keep the location of the camp a secret. Someone good with fixing things, someone just like me!

Moose hunting seasoned opened on the September 20 and ran until October 1, so Billy needed to make a decision and make it fast. I had less than three days to pack when he told me I was going, so I threw just about everything I had that was camo in a dry bag and was ready to go, I thought!

Bill and "Red Thunder"

Little did I realize at the time that this was going to be one of the most incredible adventures I had ever experienced. The hunting party consisted of Bill, his friend Troy, and Troy's cousin Rich who was from Minnesota. A few others, including Gary, would be flying in later at a little airstrip just outside camp. We loaded up Bill's old F-250 "Red Thunder" with just about everything and the kitchen sink! Then we put an old single axle army trailer with more stuff on the back of it. We were loaded to the gills, and all I cared about was killing something, killing anything!

We hit the road early on a Saturday morning and drove north toward the Alaska Range. We hit the Eureka roadhouse for some coffee and pie and pushed north arriving at an old friend of Bill's named Thumper. About halfway there, Bill got on the CB and radioed Thumper.

"Thumper, Thumper, this is Fish Hook. How copy?"

Within seconds, Thumper answered back with, "Hey, is that ole Shit Hook?"

Bill looked over at me as if to say, "Don't mind that stupid bastard." He then replied, "Yeah, I got your shit hook. We're about thirty out. Ya gonna be home?" Billy asked.

"Yeah, we're all here waitin' on ya as usual," Thumper said. Thumper was a jack-of-all-trades kind of guy with a gift for welding monster trucks and big mud rigs. He owned and ran the only Polaris shop between Anchorage and Tok, so he did quite well with that too.

We would overnight at Thumper's, then head north to the town of Slana in the morning, and pick up the old Wagon Trail. We got to Thumper's, had some grub, and built the biggest bomb fire I'd ever seen. It was cold that night, and as I pulled everything out of my bag to find another sweater, it started to snow. We pulled some tops and sat around the fire telling tall tales about days gone by as the snow covered the ground in white.

The sun was shining through the ice-covered window, and as I rolled back the zipper on my 30-plus-degree bag, the cold hit me like someone had thrown a pile of snow in my face. It was 10 degrees above, but between the bag and not having the right gear, I was freezing my ass off—literally. Contrary to popular belief, not everything the military has for cold weather gear is really good. In fact, the stuff I had was not working at all, and as I shook uncontrollably to get more clothes on, I couldn't stop my teeth from chattering.

I ran over to Billy's truck, which still had the keys in it and cranked it up. As I sat there waiting for the heater to kick in, Billy came out of Thumper's house and threw his hands up in the air.

"What in the hell are you doing?" Billy asked.

"I'm freezing my ass off, Bill. What happened to the heat in the cabin?"

"It's not on, ya dork. It's only September," he replied, then walked back into the house. A few minutes later, he came out again and told me to get my ass in there and to shut the truck off. "You're wasting gas, turn it off, and get your ass in here."

I made my way through the foot-deep snow and onto Thumper's front porch where I could already feel the heat coming out of the front door.

"Get in here before ya freeze to death," Bill said in his scrappy, old voice.

After some breakfast and time around the wood-burning stove, we headed out and fired up the trucks. The sun was just starting to peek through the clouds, which were now melting the snow on the ground.

This is going to be a great day, I thought, *for by this time tomorrow morning, we would be knee-deep into the hunt and on our way to the camp.*

I could barely contain myself as we rolled out onto the blacktop again and headed north for Solana. A few hours later, we pulled into the Slana Roadhouse for some welcomed coffee, grub, and gas. This would be our final stop before heading into the bush, so I made sure to appreciate the amenities of the rustic restroom as I washed my hands in the boiling-hot water from the sink. I even made a point to flush the toilet a few extra times to make sure I remembered the sound one makes. With one last look in the antique, chipped, and water-stained mirror, I headed out and into the unknown.

We were a few hours into it now and had only crossed the Slana about four times when we reached a drop-off into the river. Without being able to back up, there was only one way across, and that was straight ahead. Swollen and almost at flood-stage level, the Slana River was at an all-time high. What was normally just a few feet of trickling water was now a torrent of glacial and recent rain furry. The bank we were about to drop off of was about four-foot high and dropped straight into the raging, white water. Because I was on the downriver side, Bill told me to open my door and get ready to bail if things got bad.

"Don't hesitate to get the hell out of dodge," Bill said. "Especially if we start to roll, just get out and keep swimming." There was a glazed look in his eye.

Bandit, Bill's dog, was looking at me like we were all crazy when Bill hit the gas, and we launched into the river! All I remember is seeing Bandit hit the windshield, then looking left toward Bill to see nothing but gray water coming through his window. In seconds, the whole cab was filled with the coldest water known to man, and as my door flung open from the river now flowing through it, I gasped for air from the shock of the cold water enveloping my body!

In slow motion, I watched as Bandit and everything else that wasn't tied down was swept out the door and downstream. We were dead in the water and not moving at all when I looked over at Bill, who was struggling to move the truck.

"Hit it, Bill—hit it," I said repeatedly like it was going to help. Bill, not being of incredible height, was just about engulfed in water as he desperately tried to get the truck out of the river. We were just rocking back and forth when something caught and launched us toward the bank.

"Yeah, baby," Bill yelled like an old cowboy riding a bull. "Get some!" We made our way up the bank of the other side. "Get some!"

We were looking at sky now as the front of the truck hit the bank on the other side. Billy crammed it in low and punched it with everything he had. That's when I learned how Billy got his name Shit Hook. In less than a nanosecond, the sweet sound of the 350 went from sheer joy to complete disaster. With the unmistakable sound of a driveshaft shearing in two, followed by the sound of the remnants bouncing off the undercarriage repeatedly, we were now dead in the water. Seemed that Bill had a knack for gunning it at all the wrong times, thus the name Shit Hook.

The good news was, the cab was out of the river; we just needed to get out of the cab. Because of the angle the truck was sitting at, I couldn't push my door open to get out. I crawled out the window and onto the hood and then off the front bumper and onto the shore. Troy, who was in the other truck, told bill to stay in, and we'd pull him out. It took every chain and cable we had, but after about an hour, Bill and his truck were on the shore.

Bad news now was, Bill had snapped a universal joint and bent the driveshaft. We were in about the halfway point and were now left with a tough decision that could completely change the hunt: Go back to get parts or continue on with one truck and leave Bill's truck until we come back out?

Bill (SHIT HOOK)
Fisher and Red Thunder stuck again!

We were sitting smack-dab in the middle of the river on a gravel bar trying to figure out what to do when Bill said, "Let's just get in, and we can figure out the rest then." Then he realized he had about two thousand pounds of equipment and a four-wheeler still in his truck. "Dammit," he said.

Not sure of what to say or do, I suggested that I stay with the vehicle while they go for parts. Worst-case scenario, if Thumper didn't have the parts, they would have to go to Wasilla or Anchorage, which would only be a day or two.

How bad could it be? I thought as I looked around the area for bear tracks.

Finally, Bill took my advice and decided to go back out with Troy to Thumper's. With any luck, they would be back by tomorrow, and we could be on our way again.

As the back of Troy's truck disappeared into the brush across the river, a sense of complete and utter loneliness overcame me like a wet, cold blanket. A chill shot through every ounce of my being as I sat there listening to the raging water. I was in it deep now. Deeper than I had ever expected.

Had I bit off more than I could chew? I thought as I made my way over to the bank of the river.

As I stood there watching the water flow past me, I looked over to the other bank only to notice a fresh set of bear tracks. Can't really describe how stupid I felt at that moment seeing that my rifle was still in the truck, which was now about one hundred yards away. I had just started to turn to make my way there when out of the corner of my eye, a dark-brown spot appeared on the other side of the river. They say that you shouldn't run from a bear, but I'm here to tell you, I don't even remember how I got to the truck, but I did.

I pulled my rifle out of the scabbard, chambered a round, and slowly made my way back to where I had seen the bear, but he was gone. Standing on the edge of the bank now, I looked for more sign to where he might have went but only saw the one set of prints.

Because I had to stay with the truck, venturing off like what I wanted to do was out of the question. Even though the possibilities of seeing anyone back here was slim to none, it was still a possibility, and we had too much in the truck to lose. Minutes turned into hours when it started to get dark. With light fading fast, I would need to get ready for a cold, cold night. Bill had left me the keys, and the truck still ran so the plan was to rack out in the front seat and use the heater when needed. I pulled a tarp over the cold-soaked seat and threw Wiggy's bag and another blanket on top of that.

Between the heater and everything else, it shouldn't be bad at all, I thought. The sun had all but disappeared, and as I looked out through the fogged-up windshield of the truck, I saw another brown spot moving in the distance. With rifle in hand, I sat and watched as the bear got closer. He was in range now as I slowly started rolling down the window to rest my rifle on. Then I remembered the hunting regulations. Could I legally shoot from a vehicle? Could I shoot from a disabled vehicle in the middle of a gravel bar while being harassed by a brown bear? The questions were shooting through my head as I watched in amazement as the bear got closer.

Not sure what happened, but the bear was about fifty yards out when he stood up, took a whiff, and hightailed it for the woods. I pulled my shirt up to smell my pits, but they seemed okay to me. Oh well, I thought, maybe next time.

I was awakened by the sound of yelling in the distance followed by someone calling out my name. Wiping the dew and ice from the window, I could now see Troy's truck coming across the river.

Trucks crossing river

They were back, and as I slid out of the nice, warm cab, I was greeted like a hero with coffee and doughnuts.

"Ya made it," Bill said with a smile on his face. "We got the parts, shouldn't be a problem now." After a few hours, a lot more coffee, and some scraped-up hands, we were on our way again.

We drove along skirting the Slana for most of the way, only sidetracking when the water was impassable. It was the first time I had seen country like this, and it was nothing short of spectacular—deep gorges, surrounded by rolling green hills that turned into majestic vistas, filled with moose, caribou, bear, sheep, goats, and just about every bird known to man. It was incredible, and as we slowly cut our way through the landscape, I knew that this is where I belonged. This is what hunting was all about. An expedition more than a hunt, this is what I had always envisioned hunting in Alaska would be like, and I couldn't believe I was finally doing it.

Trucks going through the pass

It was late afternoon when we arrived at the camp. We were cutting our way through another mud bog and then came out on top of a sandbar when Bill cut the motor.

"What's up?" I asked still kind of dreamy from the whole ride in.

"We're here, ya moron, time to wake up and get to work!"

I crawled out of the truck looking around for a camp when I noticed a bunch of old air force missile containers lying in the bushes.

Arrival at camp

Bill pointed to them and said, "There's camp, better get to it."

Troy had been here and done this before, so I just followed his lead. A few hours and a lot of putting the pieces together later, I stoked the fire with another log in the seventeen-foot army surplus tent that would be our home for the next two weeks. Because you're not allowed to have any permanent structures on BLM land, the camp was set up and broken down each and every year. To my amazement, though, once it was all set up, it was really quite nice. Bill had an old army surplus tent that could easily sleep twenty men; however, with all of our gear, supplies, and whatnot, it was set up to comfortably house about eight.

A few feet from the entrance was an old wood-burning stove we would use for cooking as well as heating, and heat it did. It could be forty below outside, and with just a few logs burning, you would have thought you were sitting on the beach in Miami. With a huge picnic table in the middle and a Budweiser pool table light above it, meals were enjoyed in warmth and comfort. Just above the table and attached to one of the main tent support poles was a shelve that held the VCR and DVD player. On the list of favorite movies was *Jeremiah Johnson*, *The Cowboys*, and of course *A Bridge Too Far*. Spread out around the walls of the tents were eight cots that had individual shelves above all of them.

The back of the tent was filled with fifty-five-gallon drums that held all the food, water, and supplies. In the front of the tent and to the right of the entrance was a full sink with cutting board and hot-and-cold running water. Over to the front and left of the entrance was Bill's bunk, a regular radio, and the CB radio, which was his baby. Once in camp, Bill loved to just hang out and talk to everyone else who was out there. The lights ran off a portable five-kilowatt generator, which also ran the water pumps for the sink. The whole nine yards was up on pallets keeping everything high and dry.

Why would anyone want to be anywhere else? I thought as I took another sip on my ice-cold beer.

We rounded off the night with some Porterhouse steaks, home-made mashed potatoes, and corn. For desert, we dined on apple pie with whip cream and caramel sauce.

This is heaven, I thought as I changed out the movie and ran outside to make one last beer run. As I lifted the flap to get out of the tent, the cold slapped me like my long-lost ex.

It is freezing out here, I thought as I reached in the cooler for a few more beers. That was when I looked up and saw them: the northern lights. It was unbelievable, and as I stood there mesmerized by them dancing among the stars, I yelled back into the tent, "Lights, we have the northern lights!"

Everybody flew out of the tent, and we all watched the show for what seemed like hours. I had never seen them dance like that before and never in so many colors. They were green, blue, red, and yellow mixed with white and were just going crazy. Every inch of sky seemed to be covered by them, and even though I took a lot of pictures, it just wasn't the same as being there.

The sound of Bill screaming at the top of his lungs killed the best dream I'd had in a long, long time. I jumped up thinking we were being attacked by a bear only to find Bill dancing around in his underwear with broom in hand, yelling, "Damn porkies, get outta here!"

Seemed that somewhere in the night, the porcupines got in through the space in the pallets, and Bill was not happy with that. I didn't know whether to help or laugh as we all watched him dance around the tent in his skivvies. Troy just smiled, rolled back over, and returned to sleep. That was the first time I realized that there was just something different about Troy. In the twilight of the morning, I wasn't sure what I had seen when Troy rolled over, but something was just not right. I spent the next few hours trying to discount and erase what I thought I might have seen; however, when morning broke, the truth was blatantly obvious.

Troy was what I like to call a "manly man" whose nickname was Ponytail due to the fact that he had a long black ponytail. Being somewhat of an exhibitionist at heart, Troy unfortunately had no problem with others seeing his body. The unfortunate part for me now was that I had to hunt with a guy who hunted in thongs! Not the flip-flop kind, but the kind that 'ride up the crack of your ass" kind! When he rolled over last night, all I saw was a leopard print followed by what looked like a piece of rope wedged in the crack of his ass. At first I was hoping that maybe it was just a piece of rope from his bag or something. Then when he rolled out of bed this morning and started doing what men do in the morning, there was no mistaking the leopard bag. Not sure whether to laugh or cry, I said, "Nice G." And pulled my bag up over my head.

The rest of the morning was uneventful as we meandered around the tent trying to stay warm by the fire. It had snowed all night, and the ground was covered in snow.

"Good thing," Billy said as he wrote in his hunting journal.

After a breakfast of eggs, pancakes, bacon, hash browns, and coffee, we decided to finish setting up the rest of the camp and hunting the afternoon. We still had a cutting table, shed, and shower to put up, so our day would be a busy one. The shower and bathroom was like an oasis in the middle of the desert. With hot and cold water anytime you wanted it, life was tough out there in the bush! Using a series of small electric water pumps, we piped in water from a nearby stream and up to a holding tank that was heated with a weed burner.

From there, another pump would send the hot water to the showerhead so you could have a nice, hot shower anytime you wanted. The toilet was an old camper toilet equipped with a flush handle; however, it was just for looks, and "someone" would have to change out the bag every so often. We drew straws for that job. With a shower up and running, shed roof on, and cutting board cut, it was hunting time, and I was more than ready to get some!

It was about four o'clock in the afternoon, and after a short nap, we all decided to head out to see what we could see. The whole time I was getting ready, I couldn't help thinking about that stupid leopard G-string. *Was he really going to wear that thing hunting?* I thought.

We headed out about 5:00 p.m. for a ridge at the back of the camp about a mile or so. It would be an easy hike through the now-blooming fireweed, alders, then spruce. Troy had been up there before, so it would just be a matter of following him. No sooner than we arrived at the first steep hill did Troy's G-string pop out in my face!

"Jeez, dude, doesn't that thing hurt to hike in?" I asked.

"No, it's actually quite comfortable. Wanna try it?" he replied with smile.

The rest of that night I couldn't think about nothing else but that damn G-string.

We had waited too long and now were making our way back to camp in the dark when the wolves started to howl. They were close, really close, and there were a lot of them. All I could see was the whites of Troy's eyes, but the look on his face told me we needed to get back.

"Sounds like a big pack," he said in an acknowledging sort of tone.

"They just sound hungry to me," I replied.

"Yeah, that too," Rich said, "that too!"

We were about a hundred yards out, but I could already smell the chicken on the barbie! It was heaven to my senses and stomach, which was past the point of growling.

"Where in the hell have you guys been?" Bill said. "I've been waiting for ya forever, thought I was gonna have to send the search party out!"

Just joking with us, Bill rustled up some grub out of the pans, and we sat down to brazed chicken with raspberry sauce, wild rice, and black beans. As we watched the last part of *Jeremiah Johnson*, I couldn't help to think that this was just the coolest thing I had ever experienced, with the exception of the G-string!

Through the blinding light of his headlamp, all I could see was the outline of Troy's head and the fog from my breath, but I knew what he wanted.

"Get up, man, it's time to go," he said.

It was 5:00 a.m., and we had forgotten to stoke the stove last night. I knew this because I was freezing my ass off and still in my bag. Troy stumbled over to the stove, threw in some logs, and came back to shake me again.

"C'mon, dude, we're gonna miss it if we don't get going," Troy said.

I grabbed my clothes and ran over to the stove shaking while I donned the rest of my gear. A half hour later, we were making our way up a small game trail that led up to another ridge. From there we could glass a nice valley and hopefully spot something moving. We were surrounded by darkness with no moon in sight when Rich froze in his tracks.

"Did you hear that?" Rich said.

"I didn't hear anything," I replied.

We sat there for what seemed like forever, when I heard the bushes start to crack. Whatever it was, it was big and right in front of us. "Holy crap, Troy, what in the hell is that?" I asked.

"Think it's a moose," Troy whispered back. "Don't move."

Every time we moved, it would move. Every time we stopped, it would stop. It was a bad cat-and-mouse game that I was getting tired of playing. Besides not being able to feel my toes, fingers, or ears, things couldn't be better. The sun was now coming up warming the back of my head and fingers as I tried standing there motionless. If we could just see what it is, we may have a chance if it's a moose.

Troy slowly turned to me and whispered, "I think it's a bear. Be ready to shoot if it charges."

On the edge of being hypothermic now, I slowly moved my shaking finger across the safety of my rifle and pointed it toward the bushes. Moments passed all to slow as the sun seemed to take its time coming up. My glasses were now fogging up, and as I went to wipe them off when whatever it was that was in front of us broke into a run and disappeared into the forest. The incredibly loud sound of trees cracking and brush flying sounded like a herd of stampeding buffalo in a china shop; then as quick as it had begun, the sound dissipated in the brush and was gone. We were all just looking at one another as if to say, "What in the hell was that?"

A few hours later we were basking in the sun on top of that snowcapped ridge, glassing for anything that moved when Troy spotted a bull. Problem was, it was clear across the river and about five miles away.

"Good spot, Troy," I said in a derogatory tone. I mean, what were we supposed to do now? Manufacture a boat out of our rifles, float across the river, then hike another four miles, and shoot it? I actually think Troy would have tried it if I had suggested it, but we spent the rest of the day just glassing and sipping on hot cocoa that Bill had made us. It was a beautiful day, and even though it was really cold, the sun had taken most of the bite out of it. The sky and air was crystal clear, and you could see forever. With three mountain ranges in one little area, the view was incredible and looked like something out of a nature postcard.

It was getting late now, and as we gathered our gear and started packing up, Troy spotted a lone cow moose just across the meadow. We waited awhile in hope that a bull might pick up her scent, but nothing ever came in. Unlike the night before, we started the trek down early so we would not get caught in the dark again. Not that walking in the dark with a headlamp is a scary thing; it's just that you can't see the things out there that are seeing you!

Call me surprised but when we got back to camp, Bill had cooked up some chili and rice and had made some homemade garlic bread in the oven. I stuck in a copy of *My Alaska* and warmed up over a hot bowl of moose-meat chili! Bill was in a festive mood tonight, so after dinner, the beer and cards were out on the table. We drank and played cards into the wee hours of the morning only to be awakened again by them pesky little porkies!

After a couple pots of coffee, bowl, of cereal and another short nap, we decided to take the four-wheelers upriver to see what we could see. Because you never know what's going to happen out here, I packed a bag with just about everything in it and then some. If we got stuck out, we would at least have fire and food. After another short nap, we jumped on the wheelers and headed west along the Middle Fork River. Back and forth we crossed until we hit a plateau that leveled off into a series of small valleys. It was tough going as we hopped logs and broke trail through miles of spruce, alder, and birch.

After a few hours, we were above tree line now and could see both the Slana and Middle Fork Rivers. Reaching into the cooler, I pulled out three beers and handed one to Troy and Rich; we were hunting now, baby!

The hours flew by as the beers did, and after another short nap on top of my wheeler, we decided to head back. We had gotten off the ridge pretty quick and were skirting the river when I spotted a set of really huge bear tracks. I stuck my boot in one and took a picture to show Bill when we got back. It was a huge bear, maybe eight or nine feet judging from the front pad, which was seven inches across. The track was fresh, so I took my rifle out of the gun boot and slung it over my shoulder.

If we see this guy, it probably wouldn't be for long, so we would need to make a quick decision and shot if we were going to bag him, I thought.

We were crossing the river again, and I was busy looking at the water in front of me when Troy stopped and pointed. It was a bear but not the bear whose tracks we had seen. It was just a little boo, moseying along the bank looking for fish, I guessed. We watched him for a minute, then watched him turn and run into the bushes as we got closer. Cute little thing, I thought as I wondered where his mother might be!

Back at camp, I showed the picture of the print to Bill, who was in awe. "I never seen anything that big out here—nothing!

You guys need to watch your backs with this one. He didn't get that big by being stupid."

After another great meal and movie, I lay down in my bunk to just stretch my back out when the next thing I knew, it was morning. Guess I was more tired than I had thought and passed out while still talking to Troy. I crawled over to the stove and threw a few more logs in and slid back into my nice, cozy bag. As I listened to the seasoned timber crack and pop, I listened to the porkies rustle beneath the pallets. It was almost funny as they tossed and turned eating the yummy wood beneath us. I could see through the slit in the door that it was a nice day outside, and as I fumbled around trying to get dressed, the porkies caught wind and hightailed it out of dodge. It sounded like a bunch of trolls in a fire drill as they scrambled from under the pallets.

Bill cooking up another gourmet meal.
Troy hiding in the background

Sticking my head out of the tent now, I could feel the warmth of the welcomed sun as it slapped me in the face.

Ahhh, what a great feeling, I thought as I stood there taking it all in. I had just about pulled my head back in when in the distance I heard a grunt. *What the—*, I thought as I now stepped completely outside. Wasn't sure what I had heard, but I was sure it wasn't a squeaking tree or something else. It was definitely a moose, and as I picked up the fiberglass moose call, I heard it again.

It was a bull, and not knowing exactly where the call was coming from, I stuck the call in the wind and reciprocated with a somber cow call, "Errrrrrrrrrahh! Errrrrrraaaahhhh!"

The next thing I know, the bull calls back from straight out in front of the tent. *Holy crap*, I thought. *I need to get the rifle and wake the guys.*

Troy had heard the calling and was already getting ready, but Bill and Rich were out and none the wiser. Troy and I now sat outside the tent and were playing the bull for all he had. I would call, and it would call back. Troy figured the bull was about a half mile out, but it sounded like it was right in front of us to me. We called for more than an hour but never could get a visual on him.

Pretty exciting, I thought as I looked back at Troy, who was still in his G-string and hunting boots.

"Dude, that's just wrong," I said as I walked back into the tent and put some coffee on.

After breakfast, we decided to hunt the wagon trail back to an old airstrip and mine. Troy had seen some caribou in there and wanted to try it. We saddled up the wheelers and headed out along the east side of the river and picked up the trail again. We were about four miles from camp and just cruising along a really and overgrown trail when out of nowhere, two caribou shot in front of us! I locked up the brakes so hard I killed the motor and skidded to a stop.

The caribou had almost hit us, and still in shock, I popped off the top of my gun boot, ripped out my rifle, chambered a round, and was trying to find them in my scope now. The woods were thick and high, so jumping up on my wheeler, I spotted one caribou just standing there looking at us. I took the safety off, put my crosshairs on him, and started squeezing the trigger. The next thing I know, it's not in my scope anymore and now running full out and away from us. I found him again and was following him in my scope when the shot rang out!

The boo disappeared in the smoke, and though I thought I had hit him, second later he popped up about a hundred yards out, looked back, and was gone. Troy and Rich were still pointing at something, but I knew the boo was gone. I holstered my rifle, cranked up the wheeler, and rode up to where they were.

"Did you see that?" I asked like they could have missed it. Troy thought I may have hit the one, but saw it again a little farther out moving along with the other one.

"That looked like a good shot. Are you sure you missed him?" Troy asked.

"Yeah, pretty sure. He was moving pretty good afterward."

"Oh well, let's find some more," Rich said as he jumped off the seat of the wheeler.

We were slowly moving down the trail when troy stopped, looked way across the river, and called out "bear." We were on the north side of the Slana River looking south when I realized he was talking about a bear that was clear across the river and on a hill about five miles away.

"Troy, are you on crack or what?" I said while looking through my glasses. "I don't see anything."

"Rich, can you see it?"

"No man, I don't see ——," Rich said.

Just then, I finally found what Troy had spotted. Because of the distance, all I could really see was a really big, dark spot moving around on a hill. I couldn't see any definition or anything else, and I was using my brand-new Swarovski 10×42s. Troy wanted this bear though, and as we made our way toward the river, I couldn't help think that this was going to be a really long, long shot.

About an hour later, we were at the base of the hill that the bear was on. Because of the grade, we now couldn't see the bear but had last seen him in the same spot about a half hour ago. We would need to get up the hill and past the tree line if we were to ever see the bear again. As we made our way through a thicket of spruce and shrubs, we broke out in front of the biggest wall of alders I had ever seen. They were at least ten feet high and thick as molasses.

The good thing about alders is the way they grow: out, downhill at first, then they shoot straight up into the sky. The bad thing about alders is being on the downhill side trying to get through them. With my rifle strapped to my back, we all started the grueling trek through the endless expanse of behemoth alders.

A half hour later and still in the middle of the alders, Troy asked, "What do you think, should we keep going?"

I was too busy trying to catch my breath when Rich took off straight up through the alders. "Guess so," I said as we both followed Rich up the hill.

We broke out of the alders and onto the open expanse of the mountaintop, only to not see the bear. We all sat there on the edge of the alder line catching our breaths and sucking down water when I spotted a goat on top of a ridge at the back of the one we were on.

"Look, a goat," I said between breaths.

Troy glassed him for a minute and said, "If we don't get this bear, we'll get that goat."

From where we sat, you could see forever. It was incredible, and though I just wanted to sit and enjoy the view, I knew we needed to find this bear. We had come out downwind of where we thought we had last seen the bear, so that was the good news.

Bad news was, the bear was nowhere to be found. We made a skirmish line across the hill slowly working our way upwind and across the face of this mountain. Rich was up high, I was in the middle, and Troy was down below.

We had gone about a quarter mile when out of the corner of my eye, I saw Rich lie down.

"Troy, Troy," I whispered, pointing at Rich.

We both ducked down and made our way toward Rich, who was now watching something through his scope. I crawled up to the left side and Troy up to the right of Rich. It was obvious now what he was looking at, for just less than two hundred yards out stood the bear. It was just turning up rocks looking for moths and had no idea we were there.

"Take your time," Troy whispered to Rich. "Take your time."

I put the bear in my scope and cranked the power up to nine . "Rich, I got your back. Let me know when you're ready," I whispered.

I watched the bear for what seemed like forever as it turned up huge boulders looking something to eat. I was just getting into watching it dig a huge hole at the side of the mountain when the crack from Rich's rifle blasted me. Having my finger on the trigger the whole time, I pulled the trigger a nanosecond after Rich, who was now cycling his second round.

I saw the bear jump completely off his feet and spin in the air to swat off the stinging sensation in his chest. I could hear the bolt on Rich's rifle cycle again as he let the third round go. I watched as the dust on his back flew up with a spray of red, indicative of a good hit. Then and to my surprise, the bear lunged forward at least fifteen feet and started running downhill. In less than a second, it disappeared into the alders and was gone. We all jumped to our feet and started running to where it was.

"You hit him good at least twice, Rich," Troy said.

"I think I hit him too Rich," I said while feeding another round in the chamber.

We got to where the bear was, and the ground was covered with blood. Rich had hit him good at least twice, maybe more. We would need to find him now, one way or the other. Troy wasn't a fan of looking for anything in the alders; however, being a new hunter, I jumped straight in and started looking for blood. Wasn't long until I picked up a good sign and followed it out into another opening on another ridge. With Rich just behind me, I came up on it first but didn't want to say anything until Rich made his way up. He broke out of the alders and spotted the now-downed bear lying on his back.

This was Rich's first bear ever, and with a smile on his face that went from ear to ear, I realized that this was the first bear I had ever shot too. It was about a six-footer with a beautiful chocolate coat and with a blond patch on the back. As we rolled the hide, we found one hit in the chest and one in the side and one in the left front toenail. The guys wasted no time making fun of the fact that I had wounded him in the toenail, but it was all good. After all, it's tough trying to hit something that's dancing around like its ass is on fire.

We got back to camp around 10:00 p.m. and slapped the bloody bear hide across the table. Bill looked for a second not sure on how to respond; he then yelled out like a little kid in a ballpark, "Who in the hell shot that?"

Troy and I just pointed to Rich as he slowly raised his hand.

"Congratulations, you friggin' chechako," Bill said as he made his way out to get the beers. "It's always the friggin' new, guys." He was walking back into the tent with some cold ones.

Bill and I celebrating

"Jesus Christmas," Bill said looking at the bear. "Who in the hell shot him in the nail?"

We all broke into laughter as we popped the tops on our beers and toasted the kill!

As I stood brushing my teeth along the stream whose edges were now crusted with ice, I spotted a dark spot in the distance coming my way. At first I thought it was a bear until I realized that it was a lot closer than I had thought; if it were a bear, it would have been a little boo. The beaver was heading my way as if it had to be somewhere soon. I stood still along the bank as he started crossing right in front of me.

Halfway across, the beaver looked me dead in the eye, stood up, shook his head a bit, and continued across and right up to the foot of my boot. Not sure whether to stay or run, I stood motionless as he sniffed around my feet, then slowly backed up as if I stunk or something. He took a few more paces back, took another whiff, and then slowly walked away like nothing ever happened. I had never seen one up close, yet alone that close and never realized how big their teeth or claws were. I did realize now, though, why people trapped and hunted them, for his coat was a beautiful, glossy brown and looked as smooth as silk. If I had startled that guy when he was at my feet, no telling how it would have turned out. Pretty cool though, I thought as I made my way back to the tent and put the coffee on.

Rich was up and looking for some pans when I got back in.

"Watcha doing?" I asked as if it was a logical question.

"Gonna make some breakfast burritos," Rich said.

Bill was pretty much the unofficial camp cook because he just liked doing it, but Rich, who by trade was a hazmat inspector, was an excellent chef as well. About an hour and pot of coffee later, we all rolled out into the brisk air of the Talkeetna Mountains. Bill had set up his spotting scope a few days earlier, and as Troy fiddled with the settings on it, he jokingly called out "sheep!"

"No way," I said. "Are you serious?" I asked.

"Serious as a heart attack. Take a look," Troy said. As I struggled to focus on the little white dot in the viewfinder, it finally came to focus, and I could now see the beautiful Dall sheep.

"Holy crud, Troy, it may as well be on the moon," I said pessimistically.

"I'm going to go get him," Troy said as if he'd just be a minute.

Bill was up now, and as Troy started packing for the journey, I couldn't believe what I was witnessing. The sheep was at least five miles out and, without a doubt, on top of the largest mountain in the valley. Was Troy serious about getting this guy, or was he just playing? I walked back into the tent thinking I'd find Troy just sitting there when, to my amazement, he had already packed a bag and was heading out.

"Rich, do you want to go?" Troy asked.

Rich looked over at me with the "why wasn't Troy asking me?" look, when I said, "Don't look at me. He's your cousin!"

Rich got on the back of the wheeler as Bill and I wagered how long it would take them to get to the hill. Looking through the scope again, I bet Bill that they'd never make it at all. Bill shook my hand and confidently said, "You watch—that SOB will be on top of that hill by noon! You obviously don't know Troy that well!"

I looked through the scope again and couldn't fathom how anyone could ever make it to the bottom of the ridge, no less to the top of the mountain. As the crow flew, it was at least three miles across the river, then another two to three miles to the base of the mountain. Then there was at least a mile of tall spruce, followed by a mile of alders that looked as though they dissipated into the steep, shale hills and cliffs of the mountain. Looking at the TOPO map that Bill had, the ridge the sheep was on was just shy of 5,700 feet. At least 3,000 of that was nothing but sheer cliff and rock. Didn't know much about how this day would turn out, but I did know it wasn't going to be a boring one.

Sipping on my coffee and listening to the caribou clatters, I watched for any movement as the hours ticked by. Bill wandered over to take a look, then went back in the tent to take a nap.

"This whole hunting thing is stressful," Bill said, stretching his arms back like he had been working out or something.

The caribou clatters were the only station out here, and even though it came in a little scratchy, you could still make out what they were saying. It was a local radio station that provided the service of broadcasting messages to those in the bush. They were great to listen to, for you'll never know if you would get one or not. Anyone could send one by calling the station. Only stipulation is you had to keep whatever you wanted to say at a minute or less. It was funny listening to a lot of them and trying to figure out what some of them meant. People would use codes and verbiage only those receiving it would know, so deciphering them was half the fun.

I was just about ready to go make some lunch when I thought I'd take one last peek. To my amazement, I saw Troy shimmying across a rock ledge about a thousand yards below the sheep.

"Bill, Bill, you gotta see this," I yelled.

"That will be fifty dollars," Bill said with an "I told you so" tone. "He's a friggin' goat that SOB. Where's Rich?" he asked.

"Don't know, I could only find Troy."

"Ahh, he's probably down by the wheelers."

"No way he could ever keep up with Troy. Nobody can."

It was incredible, and as we both watched him make his way back and forth across the steep edges of this mountain, I could only imagine what it was like.

Troy was on a small grassy plateau and about two to three hundred yards from the sheep when we spotted Rich. He was down on all fours, crawling slowly up to Troy on the plateau. About a half hour later, they both disappeared behind more rock when the sheep popped up, turned in their direction, and bolted straight up the rest of the mountain. It never even slowed down as we watched it shoot over the top and disappear into the clouds.

As I watched through the scope giving Bill the play-by-play, I couldn't help but wonder if those guys could even see the sheep. Did they know it was gone or think it was right around the corner? A few minutes later, I could see Troy standing where the sheep was. I could almost see the disappointment in his posture as he shouldered his rifle and headed back down.

It was dark when in the distance the sound of a wheeler coming up the trail was heard.

"Where's dinner?" Troy yelled walking into the tent.

"I'm starved!" Rich shuffled in a few moments later looking like he had been in a boxing marathon.

"You okay?" I asked.

Without saying a word, Rich just rolled his eyes around and fell in his cot. He didn't even take his rifle off, and as he rolled over and grabbed the sheets, Bill said, "Make sure the safety is on."

The next morning we were scheduled to pick up Bill's son Robert at the airstrip, so after a quick breakfast we saddled up the wheelers and got ready to go.

Bill got a call on his UHF earlier that morning saying they would be in around 10:00 a.m., so we had a little time to kill. We would need all the wheelers, which meant we would need to wake Rich up.

"He's all yours," I said to Troy. "He's got a gun in there too."

Bill was revving his wheeler up right next to Rich's bunk when he stumbled out of the tent. "What in the hell?" he said. "C'mon, ya big pussy, we got work to do."

Rich straddled his wheeler and sat down really slow as if the seat was made of steel. An hour later, we were sitting at the end of the strip when the 206 buzzed overhead and circled back around. The plane hadn't even stopped yet when the doors flew open.

"Get me outta this thing." I heard Gary yell. Bill Jr. and Gary took all of about five minutes to unload their gear—and good thing, for the weather was going south and fast. The 206 blasted us with rocks as it roared down the strip and shot up into the air just shy of hitting the trees at the end. For a second you could see the entire top of the plane until he dropped the nose back down.

Whew, that was close, I thought, watching him bank hard left and head toward Gulkana.

It was raining hard now, and as we loaded up the rest of Gary's gear on the wheeler, a bungee popped back and knocked my glasses clear off my head. I picked them up and wiped the dirt off, but they were all bent to hell. We got back on the trail and headed for camp moving as fast as we could to escape the rain. With drops the size of softballs, it took everything I had to just hang on. At one point, I think it was even hailing, but who cared? I just wanted to be back at camp and around the fire with a nice, cold beer in my hand.

We were just about there when Troy got stuck in a mud bank. It was raining so hard now that I could hardly see in front of me. We pushed him out, jumped back on the wheeler, and damn near rode into the tent.

"Holy ——," were all the words needed to sum up what we had just drove through.

I had never seen rain like that in Alaska. Usually, you just get a constant drizzle that lasts all day or night. This was a storm and a good one at that. No sooner than we arrived at camp when it started in with the lightning. Bill's eyes were as wide as the bottom of a Coke bottle when the first crack hit. It was close, really close, but none of us wanted to stick their head out to look. We all just sat there motionless waiting for the next hit.

Kabam! went the second crack, which now sounded even closer.

"Did we ground the fuel drums?" Bill asked.

Troy looked at me for an answer as I slowly shrugged my shoulders.

"Great," Bill said. "Well, if we take a hit there, we won't have to worry about breaking down camp." He smirked.

The storm passed a few hours later, and we fired up the generator to watch *Jeremiah Johnson* one more time.

"It's pork chops and king crab tonight," Rich said as he wrestled with some pans under the sink.

A few hours later, we were shucking the fresh red meat from the shells of Alaskan red king crab and feasting on pork au gratin. With a side of grilled beans and oven-roasted sweet corn, life was good. Life was real good.

I wasn't even sure what day it was when I awoke the next morning—didn't even care either. As usual, I put the water on for coffee, threw another log in the fire, and rolled back into my bunk. The brewing bubbles and smell of fresh, hot coffee were like magic to my senses, and as I sat on the side of my bunk sipping the hot brew, I couldn't imagine how it could get any better.

Rich had just about fully recovered from the sheep hunt with Troy and started in on making breakfast. The plan today was to head across river and over to Thumper's cabin on the lake. It would be an all-day—if not all-night—trip, so I started getting ready.

It was almost 10:00 a.m. when everyone was finally around the table and ready to go. It was another nice, crisp, cold day; and as we headed out and away from camp, it almost felt as if I was leaving home. It was about 2:00 p.m., and we had made it across the river but still had about another five miles of really tough trail in front of us.

We were just past a gravel bank when I spotted a huge bull caribou. Being third in line with Troy on my tail, I shut the wheeler off and bailed off into the bushes. Troy saw what was going on and did the same. Now kneeling next to me, Troy was glassing the caribou through his scope.

"He's a monster, George!" Troy whispered.

The rest of the guys had no idea that we had stopped, and my concern now was that they would come blasting back and scare him off. I needed to make shoot and shoot soon, and as I took the safety off and put my finger on the trigger, Troy said, "Wait, wait! I think we're in a no-caribou area."

In complete disbelief of what was happening, all I could respond with was, "What?" My eye was still looking at this monster through the scope as I listened to Troy fumble through the pages of the regs.

"Is he good, Troy? C'mon," I hastingly said. I cranked up the power to nine and settled into the trigger getting ready to shoot. He was a beautiful old bull with a huge rack and long, white beard. This was a trophy-class animal, and I was gonna give him a dose of lead poisoning real shortly like.

I could hear the pages stop when Troy whispered, "He's a no-shooter, man. Don't shoot! We're out of the zone right here."

I now took my finger off the trigger, turned to him, and said, "Well, where in the —— is the zone?"

"Dude, it's not my fault!" Troy barked back at me.

As I watched the behemoth bull slowly walk away, I wanted to scream. Moments later, Bill Jr. rode up and asked if we were okay.

"Yeah, we had a bou bull out here, but it was in a no-caribou area." The bull slowly disappeared into the bush, taking his time to stop and look back every now and then as to say, "You can't shoot me. You can't shoot me!"

We made it to the edge of the lake about 6:00 p.m. and just in time for dinner. Thumper and his wife, July, had just finished making some burgers, so as we sat on the front porch of their cabin watching the sun set on the lake, Troy told the story of the bou that got away. As it usually does on trips like this, the stories and booze were flowing like the water in the river as the night turned into day.

"I gotta go to bed," I said. "Good night all."

And as I made my way outside for one last time that night, Troy turned to me and joking said, "Good job on that bou today, George. If it were me holding the rifle, we would have been picking the bou out of our teeth right now!" He just smiled and returned to tossing cards as I tried figuring out if he was joking or not.

It seemed like I had just lay down when Rich's watch alarm went off. There was a small pond about a mile back that we all wanted to hunt, so the plan was to hit it early and hit it hard. We stumbled out about five thirty into the thickest fog I had ever seen. I couldn't even see the outhouse, which I was unfortunately really looking for.

We finally found a small trail that led to the lake and stayed close as we made our way along it. All I could think about was if there was a bear out here, we were all toast, for it would be too late if we spotted him to do anything except maybe to curse. We made it to the west edge of the lake and decided to split up along one edge to increase our odds. Troy went up one side, Rich down the other, and I stayed pretty much where I was.

It was about 7:00 a.m. now, and as the sun was just starting to peek out, I could finally see most of the pond. It was probably a quarter-mile long with an island of dirt in the middle. I had found a nice clump of tall grass to hide in and could see just about every inch of the pond. Once the fog lifted, I tried spotting Troy and Rich but couldn't find them at all.

It was about 9:00 a.m. when I had just about pulled and played with about every piece of grass I could reach when I heard a huge splash. My first thought was a beaver, until I heard it again. Beavers usually slap the water to stun fish and whatnot, but this sounded like someone swimming. As I looked up over the tall grass, I just about had a heart attack. There between the edge of the pond I was sitting on and the island was the biggest bull moose I had ever seen. At the time, this was a spike fork, fifty-by-thirty area, which meant that he could have a spike, be fifty inches or more, or have three brow tines on at least one side to be legal to shoot.

Because of his size, my first thought was to just shoot, but as I struggled to keep him in my scope, I could see that he was not yet legal on the side facing me. I would need to wait and see if he had at least three brow tines on the other side. If not, I would then need to see if his rack span was at least fifty inches. The bull was only eighty yards out and now had his head in the water pulling out shreds of what looked like seaweed. He just sat there munching on it as I tried to find his other tines. What seemed like forever was probably just minutes when he turned right toward me and looked up. Now I could see everything and would need to decide on whether or not to shoot.

I looked at his left, looked at his right, then concentrated on the width between the paddles. He didn't have three brow tines on either side, but from what I could see was definitely fifty across. I settled into my scope, put my finger on the trigger, and *kabam!*

The shot sounded like a fifty-millimeter Canon as I watched the bull buck and run toward the island. Ka-

Bam! went the second, dropping the bull in the water just short of the island.

"He's down, he's friggin' down." I heard being yelled in the distance. Just then, Rich came out of nowhere with the biggest damn smile I had ever seen.

Rich was chambering another round of .375 H&H and said, "Did you see that? I drilled that baby!" He was dancing all around and now making his way to the water's edge when I pulled the round out of my bolt and stuck it back in my holster.

If I would have pulled the trigger just a millisecond sooner, today that moose would be hanging on my wall and not his. The bull measured in at just over fifty-four inches and had the thickest paddles I'd ever seen. That's hunting though, and as we spent the rest of the day up to our shoulders in the blood, mud, and water of that pond, I couldn't stop thinking about how different this could have been.

It was late evening when the last of the meat was hung, and as we cracked the tops on more celebratory beers, I congratulated Rich one more time.

We spent the rest of the next day getting back to Bill's camp. Seemed that it was everyone's turn to get stuck, and we spent a lot of time winching, pushing, and pulling vehicles out of mud, trees, and rivers. We were all spent by the time we got to camp and didn't even turn on the generator. Bill lit a couple of candles, had another cigarette, and rolled into his cot.

The next morning Gary and Bill Jr. left early for their secret spot. I heard them head out but was too damn tired to look or say good-bye. They had both hunted here and taken moose several times, so they weren't divulging any secrets to anyone, especially the FNG. The rest of us slept in till around 11:00 a.m.; then as usual, Rich whipped up some eggs, French toast, moose bacon, and caribou breakfast sausage. After all of that, I just wanted to go back to bed, but Troy wanted to hunt.

"Let's take the wheelers upriver again and see if we can spot some bou," Troy said.

I was still pretty bummed over how my luck was going, so as I slowly put my gear together, I was almost dreading the trip. A few hours later, we were again on another ridge looking for another moose. As much as I was trying, I was having a real hard time with losing that moose the other day. I couldn't stop thinking about how much of a loser I was to not have shot before Rich. Why did I wait so long? The questions were just eating me alive, and as I sat there on top of that hill, I wanted to just start shooting into the woods; at least then, I had a chance of killing something. Between missing the first caribou, not being able to shoot the second, then not shooting the moose, I was wondering now who I had pissed off.

It was mine and Rich's last day in camp, and as I stuffed everything into my duffel bags, I was glad to be leaving. Although it had been a great trip, it had been a long two weeks, and I was ready to get back to my life, girlfriend, and a toilet you don't have to empty. Bill, along with Gary, Bill Jr., and a few others coming in, would spend another ten days, then come back in. We needed to be at the strip about at 1:00 p.m., and because we slept in, we needed to move. I rode on the back of Troy's wheeler, and Rich on Bill Jr.'s. Bill and Gary fired up Red Thunder, and we were off. We got to the strip about twelve thirty and waited for the plane while glassing the hills. About one fifteen, we heard the buzz of a plane in the distance and started unloading gear off the wheelers. A few minutes later, the 206 bounced down the strip coming to a stop in front of us.

We loaded our gear, said our goodbyes, and blasted down the two-hundred-foot strip and into the cloudy skies. We flew low along the river until we buzzed the camp, then turned south toward Gulkana, and climbed to about one thousand feet. We flew right through the mountains and over ponds filled with white geese and beautiful rivers. It was an incredible flight, but before I knew it, Ellis was reaching for the flaps. Because of the high crosswind wind, we crabbed almost all the way onto the runway and at the last second straightened out to catch the pavement square.

The hunt was over for Rich and I. As we drove back to Anchorage, we shared stories like two old-timers who had done this their whole life. Little did I know then that twenty years later, I'd still be hunting. Little did I know then that because of that trip, I was hooked on hunting for life. Little did I know then how much I would miss Bill when he was gone. Little did I know!

12

THE GIMME

If you're like me, you've read, watched, or heard just about every hunting story or show about Alaska. All or most, portraying one of the many seasonal hunts located in the usual desolate, secluded spike camp, deep in the middle of nowhere. This story, however, is about a little known hunt located in the middle of the largest city in Alaska, Anchorage.

Each year there is what's known as the lottery and draw hunts. This is where Alaskan residents and nonresident disabled veterans can apply for a handful of what I refer to as special hunts—hunts reserved in areas not open during the normal hunting seasons or in areas only lottery winners can go. One of these hunts is what they (the military) call DM426: the Fort Richardson Archery winter hunt for a moose of any sex. Yes, that's not a typo—a moose of *any* sex. Located on the army post of Fort Richardson, this hunt is, without a doubt, the epitome of a luxury hunt within the city limits of Anchorage. With a hunting area of almost a thousand square miles, you would think that finding a moose of any sex in the allotted thirty days would be a gimme!

Well, let me tell you a story. The first year I was lucky enough to draw this hunt was 2010. After a short victory dance and some high-fives with a few buds, I realized I didn't even know where my bow was. After a week of looking for it, I finally found my trusty old blue Diamond Victory lying under a pile of old bear hides and a bunch of rusty traps. Purchased in 1998, it was my first bow ever, and I had shot and killed just about everything with it. Unfortunately, time had not been good to it, and after wiping the dust, mud, and cobwebs off it, I knew it was time for a tune-up.

After a few days with the crew at Full Curl Archery in Anchorage, I was driving tacks again and ready to go. I geared up for the long haul knowing that I only had thirty days from December 15 through January 15 to put something down, and being in the middle of the winter, it was probably going to be a tough hunt. The first weekend did not disappoint and was like no other. It was snowing, raining, freezing, and just flat-out miserable.

The second weekend, however, a friend of mine Sam Ball and I got up, had some breakfast in a nice and warm diner, and made the five-minute trip to one of the hunting area access gates on Fort Rich. We geared up and walked in about a mile down a freshly groomed snow-packed road, and about an hour later, I stuck an arrow in a thirty-seven-inch bull. By noon, we were eating lunch at the Burger King on Post and were back home and done with all of the slicing and dicing by 6:00 p.m. That night I took a shower in my own home, cracked the cap on some Maker's Mark, and toasted the kill with Sam as we sat around the barbie eating fresh moose tenderloin.

It was 2014 now, and having drawn the tag again, I quickly came to the realization that this hunt would never be as easy as the first one. What I didn't realize at the time, though, is how hard and incredibly different this hunt was actually going to be.

It was December 15 and about 8:00 a.m. when I rolled out of my nice, warm bed to the sound of Joe's phone call.

"You up?" a rude voice asked.

Lying through my teeth, I said, "I've been up since six, you lazy moron. Get your tail over here and let's go kill something!"

It was warming up and had reached a blistering minus seventeen in town. I threw the pack sled and all my cold weather gear into the back of my truck and tapped once again on my stuck temp gauge to make sure I was reading it right. It was minus seventeen and dropping fast now. Problem was, we were going to an area on the east side of town and alongside the mountains, which meant it would be even colder over there. I grabbed my seal-and-beaver skin hat and headed out the door. We topped off on fuel and some health food at McDonald's and headed for the gate on post, which was only a few minutes away.

Because the gate was less than thirty minutes from my house, we sat there still waiting for the truck to warm up while eating our Egg McMuffins. I tapped again on the temperature gauge to get a good reading.

"Bummer," Joe said after taking a sip of his coffee and looking at the gauge, which was now reading minus twenty-three.

I just hunkered back in my seat and sipped more coffee as we waited for the sun to come up. It was about nine fifteen when we finally rolled ourselves out of the truck and into the bitter harshness of the subzero wilderness.

"Shit," I uttered as I panicked to get my hat on. "It's freaking cold out here, Joe." My teeth chattered in my brain. "What in the hell are we doing out here?" I asked jokingly.

Joe just gave me that "Well, we can stuff our butts back in the truck and head on home!" look. Finally geared up, we looked like two scruffy Michelin men in camo. I could barely move as we made our way under the pole of the locked gate and into the hunting area. I guess the good news was, we were the only ones out here. The bad news was, we were the only ones out here. It was stupid cold and just starting to snow as we made our way down the unplowed access road. The snow was just below our knees, which made the going pretty tough. Thick, wet, and deep, each step was exhausting as we struggled to lift our legs completely out of each hole to start into the next. Unfortunately, snowshoes were out of the question due to the type of dense brush and tree-covered terrain we would be going through. The temperature now was holding steady at about minus twenty-five when Joe picked up the first tracks. Looked like a lone bull that came up and over the road, then went back into the thicket.

The tracks were fresh judging by the feel of the powdery soft edges of the imprint, so I decided to take a look. Like something out of a winter-wonderland postcard, everything was completely covered in snow from a recent snowstorm. It looked like God himself had dusted everything with white, powdered sugar and a lot of it! Beautiful beyond words, it was unfortunately a hunter's worst nightmare, for besides not being able to see anything in it, the snow acts like a natural sound barrier that you can hear a gnat fart in. If not bad enough, before getting hammered with snow, we had a major ice storm that left about a two-inch layer of ice below that, so the going now was just brutal. This meant that besides the fact that it was freezing cold and you couldn't see ten feet in front of you, now with every step we took, it sounded like we were walking on broken glass.

First, you would hear the boot slowly making a soft-sounding-like noise as it passed quietly through the first two feet, only to be followed by the crackle and crunch once it found the ice layer. Then if that wasn't bad enough, next would be the *whoomp* sound, which was the boot, then crushing through the rest of it all until it reached the ground. Because of this, we had to take it really slow, or we'd get busted for sure.

I was only a few yards in and paused to mimic the way a moose travels when I spotted a young bull straight in front of me. From what I could see, he was a nice bull just standing there feeding on the leaves and twigs of some deadfall birch. No more than twenty-five yards from me at that point, I thought for sure that he was going to bust me, but he just continued to feed like I wasn't even there. I drew a twenty-nine-inch 5575 Gold Tip arrow with a Slick Trick 100-grain broad head from my quiver and slowly placed the shaft inside my frost-covered whisker biscuit. I was leveling my bow to make nocking the arrow a little easier when he looked up and straight at me. I stood motionless with my eyes almost closed so he couldn't catch me blinking when he turned and went back to feeding.

Whew, that was close, I thought as I continued trying to nock my arrow.

The bull's back was turned now, and he was quartering left to right when the arrow's nock finally met the string.

Click!

Next thing I know, the bull flew up and over the pile of logs and disappeared into the snow-covered forest. Out of the corner of my eye, I caught another moose who stepped into the picture. No sooner than I had steadied my twenty-yard pin on her when she darted off in the direction of the bull. I followed her at full draw the best I could, but it was like watching an old eight-millimeter movie as her image flashed repeatedly through the open holes in the snow-choked brush. I needed to stop her and stop her now, so I gave her my best bull grunt.

To my surprise, the grunt stopped the moose in her tracks; however, the only thing I had now was a neck shot inside a radius of about six inches at over fifty yards. Standing in waist-high snow and at full draw with her dark-brown neck sitting just below my fifty pin, my frozen, gloveless finger begins to squeeze the trigger when I heard the bull call out. The next thing I saw were two cows in my sights: the one I had the bead on and another that came out of nowhere. They were both running left to right now as I drop my thirty-yard pin again on the first cow. She disappears behind the first, so I switched to the other cow.

Both in a full-out run now and slipping away fast, I dropped my pin again on a brown spot and tried to follow it through, but the brush was too thick. I followed both their flashing silhouettes the best I could just waiting for one to stop, but they never did. Like the bull before them, they disappeared silently into the white of the forest.

Bummer, I thought as I let off and lowered my bow. I made my way back through the twisted maze of fallen trees and to the road about a half hour later but never saw hide nor hair of those three again.

A few hours later and back in the truck, we came across yet another set of tracks that led into a field. I pulled the truck up alongside the road and geared up to do another stalk. It was about 3:00 p.m. when we finally made it in and were following a pretty good set of tracks. Looked like a cow and a calf were staying really close to each other.

Seeing that the hunt was for any-sex moose, we diligently pursued the tracks until they split into two. Having seen this on many occasions, I picked the larger of the two, and Joe took the calf as we split off and followed them deeper into the woods. The area I was in was mostly old growth birch with some willow, which made walking and seeing a whole lot easier than the last spot. Still snow covered though, I could see about fifty yards and had snow about calf high with little to no ice below that.

I was about a mile in when things started to get weird. I was either way in the back of the moose or right on top of it now. The tracks seemed to scatter all over the place and then disappear in the back of a small spruce when I noticed another set of what looked like three smaller moose tracks.

This was getting weird real quick, and as I studied the tracks more, I felt the cold starting to work on me. My body let out an uncontrollable shiver like a dog that just got out of a bath when I realized that I was farther back then I thought. Looking at the hunting area map, I had walked in almost three miles and was almost out of the legal hunting area now. The other bad news was, I was seriously cold and losing daylight fast.

Because you were only allowed to officially hunt from 9:00 a.m. to 4:00 p.m., the question now was, Do I continue on and possibly seal this deal, or do I turn back, stay legal, possibly live but miss the chance to fill my tag? I stood there shivering in my wet, frozen Sorels contemplating the choices when I heard the bushes in front of me move. I quickly nocked an arrow, attached my release, and slowly pulled my rangefinder out. It was so quiet that all I could hear was my heartbeat and the flock of bohemian waxwings swooping over the tops of the trees. They sounded like a small windstorm passing over as they went back and forth just above the treetops.

In front of me though and about fifty yards out was another noise. One I was hoping to hear more of as I moved slowly toward its location. I was about forty yards out now when I heard it again. A crackling, brush-rattling sound followed by what sounded like someone stripping the leaves off of a dead tree. It had to be a moose, I thought as I carefully stepped in for a closer look. Whatever it was, it was right in front of me and behind a huge row of snow-packed alders.

I went to full draw and started moving around to the right when just like that, I was face-to-face with a moose; problem was, he was just a calf. Having a perfect head shot, I was a nanosecond from releasing the fury when I let off. The little guy was just looking at me like, "Hey, what's up?" and had no clue of how close he came to being called dinner. I quickly scanned the area for another thinking this one was too young to be alone but didn't see anything. The moose and I just sat there watching each other when I decided I'd better get back. I was losing light fast now, and in the snow-covered canopy of the birch and spruce forest, it made it even darker. I picked up my incoming tracks and started heading south again when, to my surprise, I stumbled across a bear kill. Not sure how I missed it coming in, but I did and was unfortunately standing smack-dab in the middle of it now.

Contrary to popular belief, not all bears den up in the winter. Some go into their dens and are never seen again until spring, and some don't go in at all. Then you have those that go in on a half-full stomach and find out they needed just a little more in the middle of the winter. Thinking that I wouldn't encounter any bears in the middle of December, all I had on me was my bow and trusty Old Timer bowie knife. I reached down and unsnapped the leather strap on my sheath and headed down the trail. If a bear was to jump me now, I would never have time to nock an arrow, yet put one in it. And walking around with a nocked arrow for a long period of time is about one of the stupidest things a bow hunter can do. I know this because I had met someone a few years back that had done just that. We had come out of the bush after a long and successful moose hunt and were celebrating a bit at the Slana Roadhouse when I noticed this guy at the end of the bar. He was covered in blood and had all kinds of bandages around his head covering his nose. When I asked him what happened, he told me that he was just walking along, ready to kill anything that jumped out when he tripped and fell on his bow. He said the next thing he remembered is something white popping off his face and rolling down the trail in front of him. He thought it might have been his ear, then realized it was the tip of his nose. He held out his hand and started to unfold a bloodied rag when I realized I was looking at the tip of his nose.

"Yep," he said as he slammed back another shot of whiskey, "I'm heading back into town as soon as I kill this pain to see if they can put this thing back on." Since that day, I don't nock an arrow unless I'm ready to shoot.

Back on the trail, it had gotten dark a lot faster than I anticipated, so I stopped for a minute to find my headlamp. I was kneeling in the snow and rustling through my pack when out of the corner of my eye, I saw something move. At first I thought it was a moose, so I quickly nocked an arrow and stood ready to shoot. It was close, but with the light I still couldn't make it out. All I could see was a brown spot moving slow about thirty yards out. The more I watched it, though, the more the pit in my stomach grew, for now I could see that it was a little too short to be a moose. Before I knew it, I couldn't see anything and reached up to turn my light on.

That's when I heard the bushes in back of me crack! I turned around and was trying to find what had made the sound when the flickering beam of light found its source. Crouched down in the brush just yards away from me now was a large, large black bear. Its bright-red eyes lit up like a demons as the light on my head shook and bounced. As I swung my bow up and in its direction, all I could think about was that I hope it didn't charge. I frantically struggled to find the bear through my peep sight and was just starting to sight down the shaft when one of his beady, red eyes again came into view.

I stood there at full draw shaking in my boots as we stared each other down. My first instinct was to let the arrow fly, but I had no shot. His head was down, ears back, and at best, I'd probably just end up wounding him if I shot now. I needed a body shot, and he wasn't giving me one. The next thing I know, he lets out a loud grunt and a jaw pop! When bears are mad or threatened, they sometimes make a woofing sound or crack their jaws to scare their enemies. With no shot and only one thing left to do, I woofed back. To my surprise the bear grunted one last time, and then all hell broke loose! It was as if someone had dropped a bomb as the snow-covered brush exploded in my face! I don't even remember releasing an arrow, but I did, then jumped back, dropped the bow, and pulled my knife from its sheath. I stood crouched and ready for the battle, but the battle never came. Not sure if my grunt was better than his, but I happily listened as he crashed through the brush and away from me like his tail was on fire.

Shaking uncontrollably, I sheathed my knife, retrieved my bloodless arrow, and returned to what now would be a very dark, very cold, and very scary trip back to the truck. I got back to the road about an hour later and to the truck around a half hour after that, so needless to say, I was on the edge of being hypothermic. I struggled to get my tired, frozen body and iced-up clothes into the truck. With the engine now running and heat blasting, I sat there contemplating the last few hours of my life. I had heard that there were a lot of bears out there but until that moment had never seen any sign. It was just my luck, I thought as I sank back into the warm sanctuary and comfort of my truck.

As I waited for my fingers to regain feeling enough to drive, I realized now why the moose tracks had looked scattered. I was beginning to lose my mind back there following all them tracks, but it all made sense now. *Damn bears*, I thought as I threw her into gear and headed down the dark and dreary, snow-covered road to find Joe.

Before I knew it, another week had passed, and I was now looking at just over a week left to hunt. It was Friday afternoon, and I had gotten off work a little early, so I decided to do a little scouting. I swung by the school and picked up my daughter Liv and arrived at the Post about a half hour later. We made our way down the long, snow-packed power-pole road and into the hunting area passing an endless amount of tracks. I had just gotten back into the truck from looking at another set of tracks when Liv spotted something in the distance. "Look, Dad, what is that down there?"

"Wouldn't you know it, Liv, those are moose!"

About a mile out and down the hill were three moose standing right in the middle of the road. I couldn't believe it as I cautiously made my way down the steep and slippery hill. We pulled up to within seventy yards before they even budged, then just took their time as they slowly crossed the road in front of us.

Liv yelled in excitement, "Shoot that one there, Dad. That's a big one!" All I could do is sit there in disgust and admire their poise.

"What are you waiting for, Dad? Shoot that one," Liv said. "Oh, Dad, you don't have your bow with you, do you?" she hesitantly asked.

"Nope, Liv, I sure don't," I said as we watched the moose who seemed to know I was bowless just stand there looking at us. The young bull in the group even came back toward the road as if to taunt me.

"Well, Liv, at least we know there's some moose out here," I said jokingly. We laughed about it later; however, that was without a doubt the longest and quietest ride home I had ever had with her.

Moose in the woods. This (if you're lucky) is all you'll see. Go ahead, take the shot!

The next day, Joe and I had heard that a lot of moose were recently spotted on the south side of the post, so we decided to take a look. Unlike the north side, the south side is roughly 580,000 acres of pristine wilderness and encompasses almost a third of the Chugach National Forest. The only drawback to hunting this side is that you're not allowed to use any type of motorized vehicles. This means no snow machines, four-wheelers, airplanes, boats, or airboats—nothing. The good news is, there are a couple of roads you can either walk or use bicycles on. One of the roads is Oil Well Road, and the other is the Bulldog Trail. Between the two, if you can't drop a moose in thirty days off of one of them, you're doing something wrong. I had done some recon on both roads a few weeks back but didn't see anything, so I got busy hunting the north side, which can be done in a vehicle using the road system.

Seeing that the Bulldog was about eight miles long and Oil Well was about three, we decided to use our bicycles to cover more territory. Believe it or not, as long as the snow doesn't have ice under it, riding a bike on a plowed, snow-covered road actually works pretty well. Joe and I headed out early, for we would have to access a locked gate by either throwing our bikes completely over the barbed-wire fence or sliding them through the gap that the large chain allowed for. Either way, both would generate a huge amount of noise, so it would be best to do it before 9:00 a.m. We stopped again at the Mickey D's on the way out and got to the west gate about five minutes later.

One of the beauties of this hunt, unlike any other hunt in Alaska, was the fact that you could get up, take a shower, grab a meal, and be hunting thirty minutes later. Then after a long day in the woods, you can jump back in the truck and head home for a hot meal and relax in a nice, warm house. Nothing like it!

As quiet as we could, we unloaded the bikes and all of our gear and threaded them through the two-foot gap in the gate. My apprehension about whether this whole bicycle thing was going to work quickly faded as I began paddling down the soft, snow-covered road.

Still too dark to hunt, we huddled up against a snow berm at the corner of Oil Well and Bulldog where a lot of moose had been taken and seen. All we needed to do now was to stay warm enough to actually shoot if something popped out. We were into it for about an hour when my fingers started to go numb in the minus-nineteen-degree weather. I tried shaking and moving them to get the circulation back, but they were past that. Then my legs and arms started cramping up. When I looked over toward Joe, I could tell too that he was starting to feel the splendor of the arctic.

"Joe," I whispered. "Let's ride down the road a bit and see if we can pick up some tracks."

Joe stared back for a minute with a glossed-over look and said, "I'm good. Take off and I'll come get you if I see anything step out."

I had only ridden about a mile south on the Bulldog Trail when I spotted a cow picking at some bushes. Problem was, she was on the east side of the road, which was a no-hunting zone.

Dammit, I thought, *why couldn't she be on this side? How hard could that be?* The good news was, she hadn't seen me yet, so maybe if I waited her out, she'd cross over to this side, and I could put the hurt on her.

I dismounted the bike and belly crawled over to a small snow berm on the side of the road. I sat there lying in snow for about thirty minutes just watching her as she made her way slowly down a tree line packed full of fresh, yummy willow. Ripping and chewing, ripping and chewing. All I could think about now was that I shouldn't have had that Egg McMuffin. Beginning to think I might have to back out of this one for a nature break, I noticed her ears go back and nose go up. Something was up, but I wasn't sure what. She picked it up way before me and walked just far enough into the woods to not be seen.

A contractor work truck from the firing range pulled up to where I was sitting, and as I motioned for him to keep going, he decided to stop anyhow. With my eyes wide open and my teeth clenched, I pointed furiously in the direction of the moose. I even did the antler sign with my hands on my head, but the scruffy old government employee felt compelled I guess to let me and everyone else know he was there. His window wasn't even halfway down when in the loudest tone known to man he asked if I had seen anything. Being the kind-hearted, ethical ambassador of hunting that all hunters should strive to be, I politely told him that if he was still sitting there when I stood up, we would be having a different type of conversation. I watched as he sped away, then looked back at where the moose had been, but it was gone. Imagine that! I waited a few minutes longer to see if she'd come out but never did.

Back on the bike now, the sun was just starting to peek out behind the snowy overcast skies. And as I rode just past the Middle Eastern village they use to train soldiers going to the great sandbox, I picked up a single set of really large tracks. I followed them across the road and saw where they disappeared into the thickest snow-blanketed alders I'd ever seen.

Jeez, I thought. *There's no way in hell I'm going to get through that stuff without waking everything in Alaska up.*

As I stood there contemplating my next move, I decided to go for broke and began making my way into the entangled weave of snow- and ice-covered alders. I was only about ten feet in when my bow got hung up on a branch, dumping snow straight down the back of my jacket. Chills shot through every millimeter of my being as my body struggled to rebound from the shock.

On the tracks now, I made my way through, around, up, and over and even under every obstacle in the forest. I realized that this could go on forever. Faced again with whether to keep going or turn back, I decided to continue.

I tracked the prints about another half mile when they dumped out into an open field used for live firing exercises. I had passed two signs awhile back that read, "Warning, no unauthorized entry. This is a live fire training area with unexploded ordinance." Not really the kind of thing you want to see when you're out hunting but this was Fort Rich, and this is what the army does—blow stuff up!

Not the sign you want to see after stomping in the woods! UXO = Unexploded Ordinance!

I followed the tracks up a little farther and was coming around a bend when—lo and behold—there in all its glory stood a fine young bull! Not sure if he was just smart, or if it was the sound I was making that resembled a freight train coming through the woods, but he had busted me bad and was looking straight at me now. With my trusty Nikon 400, I ranged him at just over seventy-eight yards. Having shot at distances like that, I knew that I could probably hit him, just wasn't sure where I'd hit him. At that kind of distance there's a lot of variables that are out of the shooter's control once the arrow leaves the bow. Things like temperature, wind, the weight of your broad head, and the strength of your arrow's spine—it all comes into play when you're shooting long distances.

I was comfortable and confident at sixty—but eighty? I needed to close the gap and close it soon, for he was watching me like a hawk. Steam poured from his nostrils like a locomotive, and as I watched his ears go back, I knew it was just a matter of time before he bolted. Each step was a major undertaking as I tried to be quiet on top of the crunchy, wet snow. I was at sixty when he turned around and looked like he was going to run but didn't.

At just over fifty yards, he took a few more steps away from me and stopped. I was just transitioning the pin from his rump to his neck when his head swung around and straightened out. Now all I had was nothing but a rump shot. I stood there waiting for him to turn.

Just turn, I thought as I began to feel my arms start to shake. Stepping away from me again I centered the fifty-pin on his rump. I stood there thinking about the outcomes of a shot like that when for whatever reason, he turned broadside, swung his neck back to look at me, and just stood there. In less than a nanosecond, the pin went from rump to brisket, and I let the fury fly. I watched in slow motion as the arrow launched from the mechanical confines of the bow and cut its way through the air like a rocket. Like a tracer bullet, the orange Lumenok left a laser-lit trail of imminent destruction. And then just like that, I watched as the arrow dropped like it had ran out of fuel and passed right under the breastplate of my hard-earned reward. By the time I had nocked another arrow, the bull was gone. I had forgotten the number one rule of bow hunting in extreme-cold weather: arrows drop like rocks.

Moose standing up...you don't see that everyday!

In this case, I hadn't factored in the few steps he had taken right before I shot or the fact that I might need to shoot a little higher because of the temperature. All those and many other factors, however, were quickly realized as I watched the bull disappear into the forest. I quivered my bloodless arrow that was unfortunately buried in the ground, tucked my tail between my legs, and began the long walk of shame back to the road.

A week went by before I was able to hunt again due to an unscheduled slip and fall on the ice. I had jammed my leg under a car I was getting into and had boogered it up pretty good. At first I thought the hunting was completely over until around day 3 when it started feeling a little better. I would be taking it slow, but after all, isn't that how you're supposed to be hunting moose? I geared up once again for another cold, cold trek down Oil Well and the Bulldog Trail. I figured if I hunted there long enough, I'd have to finally land something. It was early Saturday morning and about fifteen above as I struggled to get my frozen gloves on. I slipped once again through the gap in the west gate and started my ride down the Bulldog Trail. I set up once more at the intersection and was just sitting there next to a kill that someone else had taken the day before when I spotted another bull starting to walk across the road.

Dressed in whites today and about one hundred yards out, the bull had no idea I was there as I sat motionless. As if he was checking for traffic, he stopped dead in the middle of the road and looked right, then left, then started up a berm that led into another old growth alder field. I needed to intercept him but with more than one hundred yards of thick, noisy snow between him and me, my best chance was to come in on his trail and hope that he'd lie down along the way.

As soon as the bull disappeared over the berm, I grabbed my bike and high-tailed it to where he'd gone in. I grabbed my bow, and before I knew it, I was on his trail. The tracks were good and were leading straight toward the field where I'd heard they liked to bed down after feeding. I was close now and at one point thought I could actually smell its wild, pungent, musk-like odor. I decided at that point that I may be too close, so I hunkered down for a minute while trying to peek for legs beneath the bottom of the spruce trees that littered the area.

The bull was close now, and as I nocked another arrow, I heard the snap of a branch about thirty yards to my right. I swung quickly in its direction to just see the back half of its body disappear behind a huge pile of fallen trees. As far as I could tell, he had gone behind them but had never come out. I continued my assault and got to within twenty-five yards when I caught the tip of his ear twitching between two limbs. Judging from the way his ears were moving all around, he knew something wasn't right, but he just didn't know exactly what.

Faced now with the reality of having to wait on the bull out, I decided this time that I would try spooking him so I would have the jump on him if and when he shot out. At full draw now, I let out my best dried-mouth cow call, which unfortunately ended up sounding like somebody stepped on a dying cat. What I was hoping to be a slow exit on his part followed by a fast entry on my arrow's part turned into something entirely different. Because he couldn't see me, when I let out the call, he instinctively shot out of there and back the way he had come, which unfortunately was exactly where I was standing!

Within seconds my peep was filled with nothing but moose and a lot of it. I watched as my arrow traveled down the length of its body just inches off of its hide, then bury itself in the trees behind him. He was coming straight at me now in full canter and knocked the bow right out of my hand as he blew by me like a brown, hairy rocket. He was so close that I could smell the snow-soaked dander of his sweaty, hairy hide. All I could see once I lifted myself out of the snow was his back end disappearing into the woods again.

Whew! That was close, I thought as I brushed the snow off my bow and self. Funny part was, by the look in his wide-opened, bloodshot eye, I think he was just as freaked out with what just happened as I was. I dusted myself off, picked up the rest of my gear, and headed out back toward the road.

Before I knew it, it was closing day, and as Joe and I once again stopped for breakfast at a local diner, we both sat there thinking that this had been one of the longest, most grueling hunts either one of us had done in a long, long time. Hell, hunting brown bears on Kodiak was almost easier we both laughed and chuckled at. Between Joe, Joe's Uncle Karl, Sam, and I, we had spent almost twenty of the allotted thirty days in the woods on this hunt. Today would be day 21 and time for something to die. Time for something to be dead and gone and in our freezers. This was the day, I thought as we shuffled out the warm and cozy, greasy spoon and into the face-slapping, "your mama just kicked you in the butt" cold of the Last Frontier.

We slid our bikes through the west gate again and made our way down to one of the firing ranges when we picked up our first fresh track. What looked like a cow and calf had made their way along the road weaving in and out to grab at the accessible alders. They led straight along the road then went in next to a creek surrounded by, you guessed it, more snow-packed alders.

I whispered to Joe, "Why don't you go around on the access road in back, and I'll see if I can get in here? Maybe we can stir them up."

As I stood there contemplating how to get through the labyrinth of what appeared to be some really pissed-off, snow-covered alien plant life, I watched as a cow and calf shook the snow off the trees as they busted out of their hiding place just yards from where I stood.

Joe must have roused them up as he came around the backside, I thought as my heart now began to resume its regular beat. That was cool, I thought as I made my way farther south, while Joe searched the perimeter of the firing range. It had warmed up to negative five and was pretty comfortable as I slowly rode over a fresh layer of fallen snow. I stopped at a swamp to take a break and was just straddling my bike when a fox jumping in the field caught my eye. He was chasing something I couldn't see and was jumping around like a cat with a big ball of yarn when I caught his eye. He just sat there looking at me as if I might be his next meal when he pounced again and pulled from the snow a nice, plump field mouse. He scurried into the bush quicker than you could say boo, and that was that. I rode to the end of Bulldog

Trail now and was beginning to turn around when off to the left I saw a dark-brown blur going through the woods.

At first I thought it was people seeing that we were really close to a housing area; then I realized it was a nice, big bull as it stepped out into a clearing. Problem was, it was again on the wrong side of the road. He spotted me pretty quick when I locked up my squeaky brakes but went right back to eating. I watched as the big bull pulled and tugged at the brush. It was almost like he knew I couldn't touch him until he crossed the road. I threw my bike off to the side of the road and slowly made my way toward the bull. I searched and scanned for a place where he might cross and hunkered down just seventy yards from him. All I needed now was for him to cross.

"Just step over here, Mr. Moosy, and let me put you in my freezer," I uttered under my breath. He just stood there like he had all day, and as the minutes turned into an hour, I began to question my motives and methods.

Come on, you stupid ungulate, cross the damn road, I thought.

And then just like that, he lay down. *You've got to be kidding me*, I thought as he now was looking right at me while chewing his cud. *Come on*, I thought as I stood up to get his attention. I crossed to the other side of the road and was standing on the edge at sixty-five yards from him. I figured he would get up and at least move, but no, he just lay there watching me as if to say, "Not today, buckwheat. Not today!"

Being highly illegal to harass, corral, or coax the game in any way, all I could do was just watch and wait for him to move. Well, you guessed it. That damn bull never got back up—at least not for me. I waited almost three hours for him to move, but he never did.

I was heading north again on Bulldog Trail when I rounded a corner and almost ran into a big cow in the middle of the road. I locked my brakes up hard this time and ended up doing a face-plant onto the road as my front wheel slid out from under me. I thought for sure that when I looked up that she'd be gone, but to my surprise, she was still there. I scurried over to the side of the road and jumped into a ditch to hide, not realizing that the ditch was really deep. I sunk up to my waist but still found the time to nock an arrow and pull out my rangefinder. I could just see her back from the hole I was in, so I started moving up and toward her through the thick firm snow.

The good and bad news were, she had come from the legal side but was now heading across the road and into the illegal side. Shooting across or from the road was illegal; however, if she stepped back over to my side and was off the road, she was going home in a game bag! Being on a bend in the road, I couldn't see what was around the corner; however, I could see her ears were rolled back, and the hair on her back was standing straight up—sure signs of a spooked moose.

With the cow still standing in the middle of the road, I made my way up to her with a freshly nocked arrow and went to full draw. She was no more than twenty yards away from me now when she stepped off and into the no-hunt side of the road. I was now standing in the waist-high snow off the side of the road at full draw and had the bead on her brisket when I let off and lowered my bow. All I could do now was admire her as she trotted quickly into the woods and, like those before her, disappeared.

I finally got back to the house about seven thirty that night and was thinking about what I had done to anger the hunting gods. All the mistakes and missed opportunities were flooding my mind. This hunt, after all, was supposed to be a gimme!

After a really long hot shower, I made my way downstairs and down the hallway filled with years and years of hunting memories. As I sat there looking at those pictures, I realized that all of them had one thing in common: the smile on my face. Even the unsuccessful hunts I still seemed to be smiling in. Somewhere though in the last thirty days, I had forgotten to smile. I had forgotten all that I had learned and became obsessed somehow with just the killing.

This is not what the hunt was about, I thought to myself as I stared endlessly at the wall. The reason I fell in love with hunting was the hunt itself. Day after day my crazy friends and I had trudged through the worst elements on this planet in search of just one dumb moose. Day in and day out we fought off freezing temperatures, ice storms, waist-deep snow, illness, injuries, and more. We had given everything we had into this hunt and at the end of the day, we were unsuccessful in at least filling our freezers.

Without a doubt, though, we were successful in the fact that we all had learned and seen a lot. Successful that we had enjoyed one another's company and camaraderie on more than one occasion. And successful in the fact that we had hunted it hard and given it our all, which is the only thing you can do. With only one thing left to do, I cracked the cap on the Maker's Mark and toasted the next hunt and to the first poor bastard moose or anything else that steps out anywhere in front of me!

13

THE OTHER GUIDE TO HUNTING BLACK BEARS IN PRINCE WILLIAM SOUND

Having probably already read the The How-To Guide For Hunting Kodiak Brown bears, you will probably find that this story will reiterate a lot of the same principles. In fact, alot of it is verbatim from a previous chapter, however, is still a good review of alot of things a person needs to know when bear hunting in Alaska. Hope you enjoy.

You finally decided to hunt the great black bears of Prince William Sound (PWS). Now what? Well, if you're like me the first time I hunted it, you'll throw everything you own in three of the biggest duffel bags you can find only to realize all too late that you forgot your rifle! Or you can read this article and put together one of the best and most memorable hunts of your life.

Unlike planning for most other hunts in Alaska, putting together a PWS bear hunt is relatively easy. For the most part, the only way to access the sound is either by air or by sea. Both have their advantages as well as disadvantages; however, having done both, I opt for hunting off of a boat. Here, you spend the majority of your time on a nice, warm boat cruising in, out, and along the inlets and bays glassing for the elusive bruins. Once you spot one, a skiff is used to hopefully put you on shore and in shooting range. A few advantages to the boat is that you can stay

Viking with skiff ready to go

dry, cover more terrain, and not have to worry about the elements or bears getting you at night. If the weather gets bad, you duck into a bay and get out of it. If you get wet, which you will, you have a nice, heated cabin to dry off in. And perhaps best of all, you can sleep at night without worrying about becoming something's dinner! Although bears are really good swimmers, to the best of my knowledge, there has never been an account of a bear crawling into a boat.

Me and a big blackie

On the other hand, if you fly in and get dropped off, you will need an abundance of gear to include a really good and heavy tent, cook gear, rations, and all of your other gear. And don't forget a raft or skiff to get around in, for more than likely, you will not be able to see anything unless it's on the same beach as you are or in your tent. As with the shore hunt I did a few years back, every bear we saw was just across the bay, but we couldn't get to them because we didn't bring a skiff. Talk about a frustrating hunt!

Then don't forget the most important piece of equipment when doing a shore hunt: the bear fence. Whatever you do, don't forget it's there when you wake up in the middle of the night to relieve yourself; trust me when I say they work!

For those of you who are like me and really aren't crazy about boats, the good news is, it's not that bad. In fact, once you get into the sound itself, the water is usually calm. Even calmer still once you get into the many coves and bays. Remember that the bigger the boat, the better, so keep this in mind when booking your trip.

Personally, I always drug up on either Bonine or Dramamine the day before just in case, then taper off, or go cold turkey after the first day or so. I like Bonine because it doesn't make you as drowsy and wears off pretty quick.

As far as hunting off of a boat, there are two types of charters in Alaska: the transporter and the guide. Only difference is, the guide will cost you about another $8,500! The average price for a five-day PWS bear hunt on a boat using a certified guide is about $10,000. The average price for the same hunt using a transporter is about $1,500 per person depending on the amenities and services offered. With the economy as it is, these prices will fluctuate with the price of fuel, so don't be surprised if they are a little higher. As with anything else, there are advantages and disadvantages to both. A guide will just about guarantee putting you on, or bagging a bear, whereas a transporter merely does just that; they are only responsible for getting you to and from the hunting zone.

It depends a lot on the guide; however, most guides cover all the gear, meals, skinning, and shipping. All you need to do is pull the trigger when he or she tells you to. I have used a transporter out of Seward for the last eight years, and he is, without a doubt, the best captain I've ever known. Scott Liska captains a forty-three-foot Delta the *Viking* and knows every inch of the sound like the back of his hand. We initially started out with Scott and a deckhand who did all the cooking, cleaning, and launching the skiff when we spotted bears, but after we learned the ropes, it's just been us (four other hunters and Scott) now for the last few years, and it's been working really well.

THE QUEST

the Viking

So after deciding how you're going to hunt, the next question should be, what to bring? The answer is simple: *everything*! Actually if you're working off of a boat, your list will be surprisingly short depending on the type of charter. I could sit here and suggest some of the things you should consider bringing; however, being a longtime veteran of this hunt, I am going to tell you exactly what to bring, so take some notes.

Joe and his bear

First and foremost would be to bring some serious painkillers; Motrin, Advil, whatever works for you. If you're lucky, you will spot bears at the get-go; however, if not, you will be spending all day glassing from a moving boat. This in itself should earn you some sort of merit badge, but it doesn't. All it means is that by the end of the day, you will have a headache, neck-ache, and more. If you want to see what it's really like, practice holding your binoculars up to your face for eight hours, and you will know exactly what I'm talking about. Everything from the top of your head to about midtorso is going to hurt. Don't forget to bring enough for you and everyone else, for they will be looking for them too.

The next thing would obviously be your gear. What kind of clothes, how much, brand names? The rule of thumb in Alaska is to always go with the most expensive gear you can find! *Not!* Sure, you can go out and get the best of everything, but trust me when I say that they don't make any waterproof gear that's completely waterproof! And I'm not going to name any brands like Helly Hansen Impertech II rain gear, but that's about all you'll need to hunt in.

The hunting season for these beautiful bears is unfortunately during some of the rainiest months on record; therefore, somewhere in your hunt (if not all of it), you will be wearing rain gear or getting really wet! If your rain gear is solid green, don't worry; funny thing is, bears don't have good eyesight, so when they see a solid dark color, it appears to be black, which in turn leads them to think that you're just another bear. With any luck, they'll come in closer for a better look. If your in camo though and get spotted by moving, it looks strange to them, and they usually end up fleeing.

Worth every penny and then some, a pair of Helly pants and jacket in solid dark green is going to set you back at around $140; $170 if they are in camo.

Thus far, we have painkillers and rain gear. Next few items on the list would be a couple of pairs of camo pants. I wear one, dry one, but usually change out the socks and draws every day. If you don't get the time, you can always turn the underwear around if taco night sneaks up on you. I always pack more camo shirts than pants, one for each day of the hunt to keep down the scent.

So in short, two pairs of pants, a long-sleeve shirt for each day, a pair of socks for each day, and underwear for each day. In addition, I usually wear a light T-shirt under the camo long sleeve. Then add at least two hats, one warm one and maybe a breathable ball-cap type. I have a Filson hat that has the fold-down earflaps, which I have used extensively. Then add in at least one large, warm jacket and one to layer under it. Layering is the only way to survive up here, so bring a few jackets of different weights. Then add at least two pairs of gloves, for they will get wet, even the rubber-insulated ones. Nice thing about working off of a heated boat is that every day, you can come back and dry out your gear.

Now for the good part. I have seen many of hunters with really nice, expensive, and "waterproof" boots do nothing but struggle through the hunt because of wet boots and frozen feet. I bring two pairs of boots and suggest you do the same. One is a LaCrosse 180-gram Thinsulated rubber knee boot with the Burly sole. There are other types of soles that are equally good; however, that Burly sole seems to stick to those slippery, kelp-covered rocks like glue. The other pair of boots is the same, just in the hip-wader version. Trust me when I say these are all you'll need. Oops, that's not completely true. When I get back on the boat, I slide on a pair of dry and toasty bedroom slippers, and that's it.

As stated before, the next piece of gear is a favorite of mine and is where I draw the line on expense cutting. When I first started hunting in Alaska, I had an old pair of Tascos in an 8×42. A friend of mine had an old pair of Swarovski 10×42s that had seen better days but still obviously worked, for he had killed everything in Alaska twice over. Every time we went hunting, he'd constantly be picking out game like we were in a zoo. I just thought it was because he knew what to look for until I borrowed his glasses one day. The next day, I went to the bank, took out a small loan ($1,000), and have been spotting and killing stuff ever since. The difference between a good pair of glasses and a great pair is not just the price. It was a night and day difference looking through those Swarovskis. My point is, don't try to spare expenses when it comes to optics. If you can't see the game, you can't hunt it. Swarovskis, Zeis, and Leupold are the leaders in optics and rightfully so. Make one of them an addition to your gear list and watch your trophy room grow.

Me and another big black bear

So now we come to my favorite and one of the most controversial issues of all time: what to shoot with. I have seen everything from handguns to spears kill bears, so when I'm asked this question, my answer would be "Whatever you're comfortable killing things with!" If we're talking rifles, I shoot a .338 Winchester Magnum with a 225-grain Nosler Partition. This combination seems to work well with my rifle and me; however, that doesn't mean it will for you. If you're comfortable and proficient with shooting a .243, then that's what you should bring. As far as caliber goes, I wouldn't shoot anything less than a .243, but I do know a guy who killed a bear with a .22. Personally, I suggest shooting the largest rifle you can shoot comfortably and proficiently.

A side note to this topic is ammo. Do yourself a favor and bring at least two boxes or at least forty rounds of the same ammo made by the same manufacturer. Again, I hunted with a guy that brought six rounds of .338/378 in different grains and manufacturers, only to be baffled at why he missed all six shots. That and the fact that if you run out of ammo out there and nobody else is shooting the same caliber you are, your hunt is over.

For those of you who are looking at doing this hunt with a bow, my suggestion to you is don't! Being a spot-and-stalk hunt only (no baiting allowed), it's an incredibly tough hunt to begin with. Then add in the terrain, the weather conditions, and the fact that most bears don't go down immediately with a bow and you're setting yourself up for failure. If you decide to use a bow, bring a lot of arrows and broad heads, for the shots will not be as easy as they were on the range.

Once you figure out what you're shooting and what ammo to use, now it's time to get on the range and start practicing. If you're like most folks, you'll hit the range, set up a few targets and a rest, and send a few rounds downrange to make sure your scope is on. If you're smart though and really want a bear, you'll bring at least two boxes of the exact ammo you'll be shooting on the hunt and plan on spending at least a day on the range. Again I shoot a .338 with a 3-1/2x14 on it. It doesn't matter what kind of scope you have or even if you have a scope; as long as you can shoot and shoot well, that's all that will matter when the time is right.

I start out by putting up two targets: one at one hundred yards and one at two hundred. Then I'll break out my shooting rest and strap my rifle in. All I want to do at this point is to touch the trigger without touching the rifle. If everything goes right, I'll be about an inch to two inches high at one hundred yards. If not, make an adjustment. Then I'll do the same at two hundred until I'm satisfied with the way the rifle is shooting. Don't forget to let your barrel cool between rounds, for this too will make a huge difference at longer ranges. Then I'll start shooting in the free or standing position, prone, kneeling, and sitting. For me, my best position for shooting is sitting; however, it is different for everyone, so find yours and practice using it. The last thing I do that unfortunately gets a lot of attention is run in place until I begin breathing hard, then shoulder my rifle in the standing position as fast as I can, and shoot the one-hundred-yard target.

Call it what you will, but I guarantee that somewhere in your hunt, you will be struggling for air and shaking like a leaf while looking at a bear in your sights. Try it at fifty yards, and after you realize you can't hit diddly, then you'll know why I practice this.

So your charter is booked, you're all geared up, have been practicing your shooting—what else is there to know? Here is where you need to ask yourself one simple question. What do black bears eat? If you can't answer this without thinking about it, then you're not ready, for you don't know the animal you're hunting. Where do they live? When do they move? How do they move? Where is the kill zone? And perhaps the most difficult question of all, "What does a big black bear look like?"

Without a doubt, bears in general are the hardest of all animals to judge on size. Throw in the fact that it will be raining sideways, they're two hundred yards out, and the grass they're standing in is three feet tall, and all I can say is good luck with that. If you're lucky, they'll be on the shore and out in the open where you can see them clearly. Best thing I can tell you is that there are numerous guides on this subject, and I would look at them all—a lot. My experience has only taught me to look for the obvious: if the bear jumps out at you as being a behemoth, he probably is. Just be careful and take the time to glass him good, if you can. If a bear is on the beach, walking really slow and hunkering back and forth as he walks, he's probably a big bear. If you can't see daylight between his belly and the ground, he's probably a big bear. If you can see his head and it has no ears, it's probably a big bear. If his eyes are real close, has no ears, and no apparent neck, he's probably a big bear. If he's longer than your ten-foot skiff he's chewing on, he's probably a big bear. If you can't distinguish its arms or legs from the rest of its body, it's probably a big bear. And the all-time, without-a-doubt sign that he's a big bear is if he's charging you in a flat-out run, he's definitely a big bear!

In short, take your time if you can and make sure it's the one you want before pulling the trigger. Another note here is to make sure that the bear doesn't have cubs. Many of times the sows will leave the cubs in the woods when foraging. All you'll see is a lone bear unless you take the time to ensure it's *not* a sow with cubs. Although it's not illegal to shoot a sow, it is if they have cubs, so again be careful.

So what's the best way to hunt these guys? you ask. There's a couple of schools of thought on this, but if you want my opinion, here it is. First and foremost is to know when they move. During the spring when the bears are starting to just come out of their dens, they move slow, but usually move all day because they're hungry. Then once they get their fill of food, they'll start moving in the very early morning and late afternoon and night. Later in the season, you'll be lucky if you get to see them at all unless they're out in an open area or on the beach.

For the most part though, dusk to dark is prime time, so be ready. Another tip when using a boat is to stay on the boat until you see the one you want, then figure out a way to get to them. I've seen a lot of hunters go off into the brush like they're running a marathon and come back with nothing. The bush out there is their territory, and if you trample in it like you're Daniel Boone, the only thing you're going to come out of it with is a lot of cuts and a dirty rifle. If you want to hunt from the shore or just need to get off the boat for a while, pick a spot on the beach where you can see as far as you can see and are downwind of the area you think you might see them in.

I like to sit just above the sand break on the beach where I can see both the shoreline and the trees in front of me. Obviously, the more you can see, the better, so pick a spot and stay there. My only suggestion when doing this is to stay alert. I have taken two bears this way, and both had been sitting just yards ways when I noticed them; I had no idea they were there or how long they had been sitting there until the last minute. They have a habit of coming out of the spruce and resting just on the edges to see what's going on. Once they feel there's no threat, they'll make their way toward the beach to search for clams, crabs, kelp, and anything else they can eat, so stay alert.

If you're hunting strictly off the boat, once you spot them, it will be the captain's job to get you on shore or close enough for a shot. Unlike other areas in Alaska, in the sound, you can shoot off of a vessel if it's *not* underpower. Hard part is getting close enough for even that. Once you spot one and get to shore, you'll have to figure out the best way to stalk them. Once on the ground, only two words come to mind: wind and wind! Hunting bears is all about scent, and they have one of the best sniffers on the planet. A bear with a good nose can smell you up to ten miles away. The best you can hope for is that you come across an old record book bear with a bad eye, bad nose, and gimp leg. If you're not downwind or the wind is swirling, they will smell you and probably run.

The younger bears may not base on just a new smell or different smell; however, the older, larger or, mature bears will associate a different smell to danger and will run. Likewise, if there is no wind, you may as well just stay on the boat, for that is the worst condition you can have when hunting bears. Even though there seems to be no wind, our scent is swirling about and making its way wherever there is air. So no wind is actually worse than being upwind.

With any luck, though, you'll be able to get within range and make a good shot. Once the bear is down, it will be your responsibility of getting it back to the boat. Unless you're hunting fall black bear, you'll be required to salvage all meat.

And contrary to popular belief, spring black bear is really good if they haven't eaten a ton of fish before going into their dens. A good way to tell this is if after skinning the bear you notice that the hide is really yellow, you can almost bet that the meat is going to be a little fishy. If, on the other hand, it's a nice white color, the meat will probably be quite tasty.

Either way, *all* the meat must be salvaged from the field for spring bear and don't forget to leave the evidence of sex attached. If you're unsure of what to do with the meat, skull, and hide, that may be a good indication that you don't have a current copy of the hunting regulations. Unless you go with a licensed guide, you will ultimately be responsible for knowing them, and if you don't, the violations can stack up pretty quick. Besides being the bible for hunting in Alaska, they also provide detailed maps of the hunting areas and Game Management Units (GMUs). Fish and Game publish new regulations every year, so make sure you get and are using the most current. A good example of this is if you look at GMU 7. It extends from Hope to Seward and east to Cape Fairfield, then heads west to Gore Point, Outer Island, and Granite Island.

When we first started hunting this area, the limit was one bear per season. The 2012 regulations have now changed that limit to three bears and no closed season. That means you can take three black bears in the middle of the winter if you wanted. All you need is a hunting license and a harvest ticket that you can get at Fish and Game or any store, gas station, or variety of other places that carry them.

Prince William Sound, or Unit 6D, encompasses everything from Whittier to Valdez, Cordova, and back over to Cape Fairfield. There the limit has been and still is one bear per season, which only runs from September 10 through June 10. Again all you need is a hunting license and a harvest ticket.

Knowing when and where to hunt is just half the battle. You also need to know what you're supposed to do if and when you harvest an animal. On page 25 of the current regulations, it tells you exactly what you need to do with the bear depending on the season and area. For example, if you were hunting on May 31 and you harvested a bear in Unit 7, you would need to harvest the hide, skull, and meat from the field. If, however, you were hunting the same exact area on June 1, you would just need to harvest the hide and skull; the meat could stay in the field. Again, the bottom line is to know and heed to the regulations. Aside from being in every store, gas station, bar, restaurant, and even bathrooms, the regulations are also available online.

The only other thing I would possibly add to the gear list would be the items you need to have in your day pack or just-in-case pack. And when I say day pack, I mean "day pack." Can't tell you how many times I have seen guys try and hunt with packs that look like they're doing K2 for a week! A good day pack for this hunt should run from the bottom of your neck to the small of your back; the smaller and lighter, the better. Aside from the obvious reasons for having a pack, one must remember that not all boats float!

Unfortunately, Alaska has had more than it's share of misfortunes in this area. Therefore, beside the things I know I will need, I also carry the things I hope I never need. If for some reason you have to permanently depart the vessel or find yourself having to spend the night off the boat, you are going to need a few essential items. One of the most important things you should always have in your pack is something to start a fire with. You can make your own kit or buy one on the market; however, if you don't know how to use it, you may as well leave it at home. Before you ever get on the boat, make sure you know exactly how it works. I have seen a lot of different kits work when the weather is good, but don't work at all when it's raining or damp out; and it will be raining and damp!

The next thing should be at least one sixteen-ounce bottle of water or more. Although there are many natural streams and ponds available, beaver fever is very common up here. If you have a light and portable water filter or the purification tablets, those are good too. The next thing is kind of spendy; however, it has saved my butt on many occasions: a satellite phone or (sat phone). If you're the kind of person who can't go five minutes without calling someone or really get into a pinch, these are worth every penny and work really well. There are several places to rent them here in Alaska, so if you can't find one where you're at, don't worry. The costs will vary depending on who you rent from; however, the average weeklong (seven-day) rental is about $150.00. The bad news is, a minute will cost you about $1.90, so if you have a teenager on the trip, you may want to keep it close.

If you don't want to go the sat-phone route, another good option is the emergency locator beacon or (ELB). There's a lot of different names for them, but they all do the same thing: send out an emergency signal for someone to come and get you. If you fire one of these off in Alaska, you can be sure that either the Alaska Air National Guard, Coast Guard, or Civil Air Patrol will find you. I have yet to see anyone rent these; however, you can buy them just about anywhere, and they are relatively inexpensive. One reminder here is like everything else, the more they do, the more they costs.

The next thing I would recommend and should already be in your pack are a few knives. I say a few because that beautiful inlaid ivory-handled four-inch skinning blade is not going to cut you a lean-to if needed (and it will be needed). You should already have at least one skinning knife and a sharpener in your bag. Your other knife should be at least something that you can chop and saw branches with and use as a backup for boning and cutting game. I see a lot of guys carrying the twenty-pound Rambo knife with compass, matches, and rope in them, which is fine; however, I never see them use it. There's nothing worse than deadweight in a pack, so make sure everything can be used. If after all of this you still have room, I'd suggest a ball of 550 (parachute) cord and one of those (space blankets). They're silver and about six inches by six inches but are invaluable for making a shelter or just hiding under to get out of the weather.

Another item worth mentioning is a cell phone. More than likely, you will not get reception; however, you'll never know. Whatever you do, just remember to turn it (completely) off when in the field.

Last but not least, you're going to need a few small flares, some protein bars, and an extra pair of socks. "Socks?" you ask. If you get stuck, lost, or stranded because your boat sank, you're going to be wet. If you have a pair of dry socks, you can use them as such or as gloves or even a hat if cut right. Worst-case scenario is that you'll need them to start a fire; however, you will have them, and they're light. Now that all of this "junk" is in your pack, you'll need to keep it dry. If you don't already have them, I suggest you run out and buy a bunch of those really expensive waterproof cases—*not!* All you need is a bunch of different-size plastic bags. They are cheap, light, and more than do the trick; that and you can use them for a lot of other things like catching rainwater to drink.

The last little tidbit I will give you is this: keep that bag readily accessible at all times. Depending on the circumstance, you could go from wining and dining on steak and lobster to treading water in the Gulf of Alaska in less than five minutes; that bag and its contents may be the only thing that saves your life!

Once the hunt is over and you get back into town, the first question should be, "What do I now do with the meat and the hide?" The answer is pretty simple although the choices can be complicated. If you did everything right and bagged a bear, before you stuck it in the bag, you should have salted it really well so that the hair doesn't slip. After that, you kept it in the coolest place you could find without actually freezing it. All you need to do now is decide on what you want to do with it. Depending on how much time you have will ultimately decide your choices, so let me make it easy on you. If you want a nice rug, full body, or anything else done with the bear, take it to a taxidermist (in Alaska). Not only do they know how bears are supposed to look, but they also do them all of the time. If you have a buddy down in the Lower 48 who had done a few ten years ago, all I can say is good luck. I've seen those bears, and they're embarrassing.

Although there is a number of well-reputed taxidermists in Alaska to choose from, my suggestion is to take it to Knights Taxidermist in Anchorage. They have a team of expert taxidermists there who are without a doubt the best in the state. Just a short drive from the airport, all you have to do is get it there, and they'll do the rest. They'll seal it, work it, and then ship it to wherever you want when it's done. For years now I have brought all my work there and have been awestruck every time I see the finished product.

They are true artists in every sense of the word, and it shows in all of their work. The last question now is, what to do with the meat? Years ago, there were several butchers and meat processors in Alaska who processed bear meat. Today, however, there are only few. The one I have used and am more than satisfied with is Pioneer Meats in Wasilla. They make the best black bear breakfast sausage I've ever had. Yum! And because most of the people in Wasilla commute to Anchorage and back every day, the logistics of getting it there are minimal. A quick call and you can set up a drop or pickup pretty easy.

So in case you missed it, start gearing up and go as light as possible. Start practicing your shooting skills, for they will be tested. Learn about the animal you're hunting and know where the kill zones are for any given angle. There is an unlimited amount of information on the state web page (state.ak.us) as well as other sites, and knowing what you hunt will only help you seal the deal.

Sam's bear

Last and probably the most important thing I can tell you is that in all of the chaos and excitement that will surely be part of your hunt, don't forget to take a moment to just look around and take in the incredible beauty that will undoubtedly surround you.

Somewhere during the hunt, I always make it a point to wake up before everyone else so I can sit on the deck and just listen to nothing! It's the most incredible thing you'll ever experience as the deafening silence washes over you like a soft, warm blanket. I'll watch the curious seals come in for a closer look as the puffins skimmer across the flat, calm surface of the water. I'll look over the side of the boat and watch the luminescent jelly fish gently make their way aimlessly through the crystal-clear waters. Just yards offshore, I'll watch as a cautious sow and her three cubs slowly make their way down to the shore to get their fill of razor clams. I'll watch the cubs play and fight as mom tries to keep them in line, aware of the all-too-present danger.

I'll watch as the sun peeks through the haze-covered bay and lights up the brilliant green, moss-covered hills. I'll watch as an eagle swoops down out of the sky and plucks out a silver salmon for its breakfast. And I'll watch and listen as time slips by in a pristine land touched only by a fortunate few. To say that it is one of the most beautiful places I have ever been or hunted would be an incredible understatement. My hope is that you will find it the same and realize how lucky we are to still have places as beautiful as this on Earth.

Another fine bear taken in PWS

Below is a gear list for a five-day boat trip:

1. Painkillers (enough for everyone)
2. Medications (enough for the trip and another week past it)

3. Cash money
4. Credit cards
5. Hunting licenses/permits
6. 1 rifle with ammo (at least 1 rifle)
7. at least 2 boxes of ammo
8. Great binoculars
9. Spotting scope (not a must-bring item)
10. 2 pairs of camo pants
11. 5 camo shirts
12. 5 T-shirts (to layer)
13. 5 socks
14. 5 underwear
15. 2 hats (1 wool or very warm hat/1 lightweight)
16. 1 light jacket
17. 1 medium jacket
18. 1 heavy jacket
19. 1 set of rain gear (yellow is good—especially if your friends are blind)
20. 2 sets of gloves (rubber if possible)
21. 1 set of long johns (Under Armor if possible)
22. 2 pair rubber boots (Lacrosse with "burly" soles)
23. 1 small daypack
24. 1 small first aid kit
25. 1 small flashlight, laser pen, or headlamp (to signal boat for pickup)
26. Hand warmers (couple of packs)
27. Portable boot warmer (to dry out boots if wet)
28. Gun-cleaning kit (bore snakes are great)
29. Slip-on slippers (when inside the boat)
30. Batteries (for cameras and headlamps/flashlights)
31. Extra pair of vision/reading glasses
32. Scent spray (not a must-bring item)
33. Skinning knives/saws

34. Cameras/film/discs, chargers, etc. (no stores available in sound)
35. Hunting regulations (current)

The following is the day-pack, emergency, just-in-case list:

1. Smallest and quietest day pack you can get all of the stuff listed below into
2. Water (at least one sixteen-ounce bottle)
3. Portable water purifier or tablets
4. Protein bars (enough for you and your bud)
5. Emergency blanket (shiny, light, tin-foil-looking thing)
6. Flares (small emergency type—not road flares)
7. Fire-starting kit (Make sure it works.)
8. Satellite phone (with recently charged battery)
9. Extra socks (1 thick pair)
10. Emergency locator beacon (ELB)
11. Knives (plural)
12. 550 cord (parachute/nylon cord)
13. Cell phone (you never know.)

14

THE REAL DEAL

I was dead tired and ready to just call it the night, but my stomach had other ideas. As I slowly stoked the fire to cook up some pork chops, Joe came over and pulled up a stool.

"How's it looking there?" he said in a somber but authoritative tone.

"Good," I replied. "Looks like the fire's 'bout ready for them chops." I then watched in horror as Joe field-stripped his nose above the now-sizzling pork chops and week-old leftover rice. This was going to be an interesting hunt, I thought as my stomach began to turn.

I had met Joe Want about a year ago at a Fish and Game bear-hunting clinic. He was the keynote speaker and a good one at that. When I first saw him, I just thought he was another hunter until he grabbed the microphone on the stage and began talking. A marine at heart, Joe had on an old, torn green-and-black plaid shirt; some old, worn-out jeans; and a pair of duct-taped Extra-Tuff boots. Hours later, I felt as though I had been baptized by the bear-hunting god himself. He was a walking, talking hunting encyclopedia filled with years of experience and an unparalleled knowledge of Alaska. I couldn't help think that if I could just know half of what this guy knows, I might have a chance at this whole hunting thing!

Weeks later, I found myself and now longtime hunting bud Joe Wasielewski humping the bush and shores of Kodiak looking for bear. Thanks to Joe Want's bear seminar, we put together a really good hunt and came out with two really nice bears for our first time out.

Months later, I was looking for another hunt when I remembered Joe Want stating that he does guided hunts and bear clinics up along the Gerstle River. *How awesome would that be?* I thought as I dug through my "hunting box" looking for his phone number.

About an hour later I was talking with Joe who, unfortunately, was all booked up that year. *Bummer*, I thought as we spoke about the Kodiak hunt.

"Tell ya what, though," he said, "if I get a cancellation, you'll be the first one I call."

"Cool, Joe, that would be great," I said.

A few months passed, and as it started cooling off and getting closer to moose season, my trigger finger started getting itchy. For whatever reason, seemed that everyone that year was either already in a hunt or not hunting at all. Hope was fading quickly when out of the blue, I was awakened by the phone. It was about 6:00 a.m. on a Saturday morning when a deep voice said, "Hey, is this George?"

"Yeah, who in the hell is this?" I said, not being as awake as I should have been.

"This is Joe Want from Fairbanks. Do you still want to go hunting?" I went from a dead sleep to wide awake in about two seconds.

"Hell yes, I want to go," I said.

"Well, ya better start getting ready, cuz we're leaving in two days."

I think my heart actually skipped a beat as the amount of preparation raced through my mind. "No problem, Joe," I said in the best, confident tone I could find, "no problem."

Two days later, I piled everything I had into my minivan—yes, a minivan—and headed north. It was September 19, and the farther north I went, the worse the weather got. By the time I got to Glennallen, it was snowing pretty hard, and the temp was hovering somewhere around zero. I tanked up, cleaned the lights off, and headed out again into the dark and cold wilderness. At several points, I had to completely stop for I couldn't see the road anymore.

I waited about thirty minutes, but it just kept coming blowing sideways now. Joe was expecting me come morning, so I needed to push it a bit, or I might not make it. I crept along at about twenty-five miles per hour for almost two more hours when the weather finally broke. I could finally see now, and as I put the petal to the metal, I now realized that I had another problem: no traction! The road was now snow packed, and although I loved my minivan, the front-wheel drive was just not cutting it.

Once again I found myself creeping along at the breakneck speed of twenty-five miles per hour. As I sat there watching the darkness change to light, I couldn't help to think that I wasn't going to make it. I finally got to the turnoff I needed and started inching my way down a small hill when all hell broke loose!

I should have realized that the clearing of the snow meant that I was probably in a high-pressure area, but with everything else going on, I totally missed it. With a high pressure comes cooler weather, and with cooler weather comes ice! Long story short, I was in the wrong lane on a hillside curve with no steering at all! If there was ever a time where I felt completely out of control, this was one of them. All I could do was hang on and hope for the best.

The road north.
Note, the Alaskan oil pipeline on the left.

I was sliding down at about twenty miles per hour and straight toward a cliff when I began thinking about jumping. If I bailed, I could escape the crash but not the elements. The scenarios were racing through my mind as I slid closer and closer toward the cliff. Then, from around the corner I saw headlights.

Oh crap, this is it. This is where it ends, I thought as the glare of the lights got closer.

The next thing I know, I'm bumper to bumper with a truck, and we're both now heading down the hill! What seemed like forever was in actuality, only seconds as our ice and snow-covered conglomerates of metal slid to a stop. We were in the middle of the road with nowhere to go, but we were stopped. I jumped out of the van only to be greeted by the pavement, which I had somehow forgotten was frozen! I picked myself up like nothing happened and called out to the other driver, "You okay?"

"Yeah, I'm good, we need to get out of the road and quick," the other voice called back.

I got back in the van and threw her in reverse only to hear the sweet sound of the two-liter burning rubber on that ice-packed road. Lucky for us, the truck had chains, so after a long and cold battle with the cold steel links from hell, the truck pushed me back up the hill and off of the ice.

It was late now, and as I sat there watching the wind and snow start to blow again, I realized I wasn't going to make it. I was out in the middle of nowhere, had no cell coverage, and was about three hours away from the nearest gas station. Guess it could have been worse, but at the time, I couldn't see how. Only thing I could do now was try to make it back to Glennallen and maybe wait for the weather to turn.

Three days later, I was back in Anchorage waiting for the weather to turn. Good news was, the snow had stopped, so with my truck, I may be able to make it this time. Joe's other clients had all cancelled due to the weather, so it would just be him and me on this one. I loaded up one more and headed for the highway.

By the time I got to Joe's place off of the Gerstle River, it was late, and as we made small talk about the hunt, I bid good night, rolled up the windows, and passed out in the seat of my cozy, warm truck.

I awoke to the sound of voices only to find that it was Joe talking to his horses and mules. Joe was the epitome of old-school and, as such, didn't believe in all those mechanized gadgets like four-wheelers and whatnot! As with all of his hunts, Joe used pack horses and burro to haul in the gear. Not only are they efficient packers, but they're quiet too.

Joe's rifle (Pre-64 30.06)

So after the crash course Mule-Packing 101, we were almost on our way. Funny thing was, when we were loading up the animals, I couldn't help notice that there was only one horse and three mules, or burro—still don't know what the difference was, but Joe could tell you. We had loaded the three with pack canisters and a saddle on the other.

This is weird, I thought as I got my backpack out from the back of my truck.

"Looks like we're about ready," Joe said. "How ya doin'?"

"Good, Joe, good," I answered. "How's this work here, Joe?" I asked hesitantly, seeing now what the answer might be.

"How does what work?" he replied.

"I mean, do you take them into the spike camp then come back for me or...?"

The smile on his face confirmed what I had feared, and as I stood there in the mud, rain pouring down and looking at my seventy-pound pack, I was really contemplating running. Three hours and about a seven-mile walk later, we reached the spike camp in the middle of the Gerstle River. It was a pretty, nice camp and had three separate wall tents, a cooking area, and all of the outhouses you could find. Being in the middle of the drainage and with a freshwater stream running up along the side, it was the perfect location to glass animals from.

Joe pointed to one of the tents and grumbled, "That's your tent." The rain had finally stopped, and the sun was now glistening off the peaks of the fresh snow on the hills.

Beautiful, I thought as I broke out the spotting scope and tripod. We spent the rest of the afternoon and evening glassing from the camp but only spotted one moose about five miles away.

"We may need to call that one in," Joe said as if he knew its name or something.

The light was fading fast across the hills, and as I broke out the fire-starter kit, I heard Joe say, "No, ya don't. Ya need to start it like a man. None of that girly stuff round here." He grunted.

Then I remembered, this was a bear/moose clinic/hunt; I was supposed to be learnin' stuff! "No problem," I replied as I stumbled through my thoughts on how I was going to do this.

"Er, let me show ya," Joe said.

Grabbing a bunch of old spruce tinder and palm fronds, Joe assembled them in a pit and then pulled out a flint striker. Two sparks later, we had fire. A minute and a lot of spruce fronds later, we had a lot of fire. This guy was good, I thought as the chill in me melted away with the now-blustering flames. I stoked the fire a few more times with some birch and then threw in some mesquite wood for the pork chops. I was dead tired and ready to just call it the night, but my stomach had other ideas.

As I slowly stoked the fire to cook up some pork chops, Joe came over and pulled up a stool. "How's it looking there?" he said in a somber but authoritative tone.

"Good," I replied. "Looks like the fire's 'bout ready for them chops."

While Joe was gone, the bears had gotten into the cooking area, and as I was cleaning up, I noticed a pan with some old rice and grease from the last hunting party. Looked as though both the bears and birds had gotten to it from the teeth marks and bird tracks in the grease. I put it to the side figuring I'd wash it with everything else later when, to my surprise, Joe was now using it to cook those luscious chops in! To top it all off, I then watched in horror as he fieldstripped his nose directly above the now-sizzling chops! Mmmmmm, good!

Morning came way too early, and as I tried rolling the flap of my undersized sleeping bag over my head, I noticed that it was really bright out. It had snowed all night, and we were now covered in the white stuff. Great, I though as I fought the undersized, underrated bag. The crackling sound of the fire aroused my sense, and I could smell the bacon through the thick fabric of the tent. As I lay there thinking about why I was still alive after eating those chops, I couldn't help wonder what he was cooking the bacon in. I made my way over to the stream, cupped a hand of freezing cold water, and threw it on my face.

"Coffee's on," Joe said. "Are you hungry?"

I wasn't sure whether to laugh or cry, but I made my way over to the cook tent and snuggled up around the fire. "See anything moving?" I asked.

"Nah, too early right now."

"What time is it?" I asked.

"I've got 6:00 a.m.," he said as if it was too late and I had overslept. Joe wasn't a big talker, but when you got him going, he was hard to stop. After a pot of coffee and a really good breakfast, the conversation flowed into the day and through the night.

We spent most of that day in camp just glassing the hills and riverbeds while waiting for the snow to melt. The next day we spotted another moose on a ridge, but again, it was too high and too far off. The next day the sun came out, so we packed some lunch and went for a walk. Eight hours and a gallon of water later, we were back in camp, discussing the trials of the day. Joe had led me out, then got me lost on purpose to see if I could find my way back. To my surprise, I couldn't, and if it wasn't for him being there, I would probably still be out there. I had always considered myself a fairly good woodsman; however, after hunting a week with Joe, I was amazed at what little I really knew. I'm sure he spent a lot of time in his tent just laughing at me, for compared to him, I was nothing short of a greenhorn! Joe was an amazing man, a man among men, and I was sitting across the fire from him sharing stories from near and afar.

Pretty much self-educated, Joe had grown up in an era where people took care of themselves or died. I think between that and the fact that he was a tried and true marine, Joe was the real deal! A person of impeccable moral, ethics, and unmatched toughness that only comes with years of being a woodsman, hunter, outdoorsman, and true Alaskan by every sense of the word.

Joe and his flock

We spent the next few days hunting and hiking the backcountry on foot. I learned about navigation, glassing, weather, and just about everything else a person could use in the wilderness and then some. It was an incredible hunt filled with endless stories and adventures he had experienced. Not sure how old Joe was at the time, but I was only forty-two and having a hard time keeping up with him. He seemed to just pass through the brush like a ghost, never touching or disturbing anything, never letting obstacles slow him down or hold him back. He seem to know exactly where and where not to walk. Unlike me, Joe was in his element out here; this is where he belonged. Like the bear or moose, he was home out here, and you could see as much as feel it. Despite his unique campsite etiquette, Joe was simply an amazing man, and I was lucky to be in his presence.

We spent the last day walking the river and scouting the hills but never saw a moose nor a bear. Didn't really matter to me though, for I had learned more in the last four days than in all the years I had hunted. The last night around the fire was spent talking about the numerous events of the week and lessons learned.

Unlike a lot of outdoorsman, Joe was a true educator and had no qualms with sharing his abundance of knowledge with those willing to listen long enough. We were both just sitting there watching the fire die out and listening to a distant wolf's howl when Joe asked me, "If there was one thing you took away from all of this, what would it be?"

As my mind raced through all I had experienced and learned, I was having a hard time pinpointing one single thing. Then it hit me. I said Joe, "If there was just one thing, it would have to be to pass on to others whatever knowledge I have, as you have passed on to me."

He slowly tilted his head back looking up at the stars, smiled, and said, "I think you're ready."

15

LUCK OF THE DRAW

I arrived in Alaska on September 7, 1995, and after becoming a resident a year later, I was now eligible for a hunting license. Being a city boy who grew up on the streets of Miami, I knew pretty much nothing about big-game hunting; however, fishing had always been my passion. The only thing I really knew about hunting was that you had to drink a lot of beer, then go out, and try to kill something!

In fact, I was pretty much opposed to it until 1996 when a friend from work asked me to come on a moose hunt. He needed another hunter and another person to wrench on the three vehicles we'd be taking, so I thought what the heck. Besides, he had mentioned that there would be plenty of excellent fishing along the way, so it was kind of hard to say no. That hunt and everything about it was nothing like I had ever experienced before. As with most hunting up here, they are more expeditions than hunts, or at least turn out to be whether you want them to or not. This, however, turned out to be hunting at its finest in a land and environment I had never seen or experienced in my life. I was hooked.

From 1996 to about 2002, I had hunted everything from moose, bear, wolf, caribou, and just about every fur-bearing creature in Alaska and never killed a thing—nothing. I did, however, help everyone else kill all of them; I guess it just wasn't my turn.

That all came to an end in 2002 when I shot my first black bear in Prince William Sound, and up to May 12, 2009, I had been on a pretty good lucky streak. With trophies that included an Alaskan musk ox, four black bears, one Kodiak brown bear, a Russian boar, seven African plains game trophies, and three caribou taken with a bow, I was riding high on the lucky train, or so I thought.

For those unfamiliar with hunting in Alaska, there are seasonal hunts here referred as "drawing hunts." They're open to both residents and nonresidents, and if you're lucky enough to draw a tag, you get the exclusive right to hunt in areas for game that's only accessible to those with permits. I drew such a tag in 2004 for a Kodiak brown bear and ended up harvesting a really eight-footer. The best part about the whole thing was I had teamed up with a hunting partner who has since become both a really good friend and a great hunting partner. The way the permit system works is if you're lucky enough to draw, Fish and Game (F&G), will publish a list with the names and addresses of those who drew the same area, unit, and species.

So when I drew the same tag for the same area in 2009, I was a little bit more than ecstatic. The hunt area was known as DB-293 and consisted of the southwest corner of Kodiak, which encompassed both Raspberry and Afognak Islands, an area consisting of steep, snowcapped mountains and endless valleys that flow into miles of pristine shoreline and bays. There's no restriction for residents on how you hunt it, so if you decided you wanted to hunt alone, you could. This, however, would mean picking up all of the costs and, if successful, dragging the largest bear known to man out of the woods by yourself.

As with the hunt in 2004, I sent out a short form letter to the other sixteen people who drew. A few days later I received a call from a guy named Carl who explained that he and his friend Brian had drawn the same tag and were definitely interested on hunting it with me.

All we needed now is decide how and when to go. Now, if you're like most people, you're probably thinking, Wow, wouldn't you want to at least know the people you were hunting with, especially for a hunt like this? That would be great; however, with this particular hunt, there are only seventeen permits, which left me only seventeen possibilities of finding a partner. According to (F&G), only half of the people who draw will actually hunt it, which cut that to eight. So unless you like to hunt alone, you can't afford to be real picky when dealing with numbers like that.

When it comes to hunting on Kodiak, there's basically three options: boat, plane, or a combination of both. Like everything else, they both have their obvious advantages and disadvantages; however, I am partial to working off of a boat because you can sleep at night without worrying about being someone's dinner. You can also get out of the weather when you want or, as in a lot of cases in Kodiak, really need to. A boat and skiff, or dinghy as some call them, also gives you mobility into areas that would otherwise be completely inaccessible.

Don't get me wrong, I have done fly-ins, which are great too; however, I just remember always being cold, wet, and tired from not sleeping well. Another drawback to a fly-in is the fact that once you get dropped off, that's it; you won't be seeing that plane again until the scheduled pickup date, and that's only if they can get back in! If we were to do a fly-in into the same area, we would be looking at around the same price; however, meals would not be included, and we would have no mobility besides our feet once we were there. This is why a lot of people who do fly-ins bring a small inflatable skiff and motor to scout the bays. The drawback to this, of course, is that it also adds more weight, and weight equals money when flying.

So, the day I drew my tag, I was on the phone with Sam in Kodiak, who was the transporter we used for the hunt in 2004. If you're wondering what is the difference between a guide and a transporter, it's around $10,000! Actually, if you choose to use a guide, the going price is anywhere from $10,000 to $15,000.

The main difference between a transporter and guide is that a transporter is just that; they can get you in and out of an area and offer you a variety of amenities; however, they are not allowed to hunt with you or even help you in any way with getting a bear. They can't even legally spot a bear for you and tell you about it. There are a lot of strange regulations up here, and if you go to the state website, you can learn a lot more about the dos and don'ts.

A guide, on the other hand, will normally be hunting with you and be there when you pull the trigger. Depending on your arrangement, most guides will also do the skinning, packing, and everything else required to transport the bear; however, all are different, so make sure you know what you're getting.

In our case, Sam Catt had retired from the Coast Guard and operated as a transporter out of Kodiak. He had a nice forty-foot boat and knew the islands like the back of his hand. After a brief conversation, he again gave us a great deal on the boat, which included three meals a day, a deckhand, shower, and a real toilet. What I originally thought would be a hard sell to Carl and Brian turned out to be quite easy once I mentioned that the boat had a shower and toilet on board—ah, life's simple pleasures.

A few weeks and several phone calls later, Carl and I decided to meet at a local diner to go over some of the logistics of the hunt, such as the terrain, weather, equipment, and of course cost. I had no idea what he looked like, but judging from our previous conversations, he sounded like your average-size guy. As I made my way through the diner looking for what I thought a "Carl" would look like, a familiar voice from my right asked, "George?"

As I turned to greet the person attached to the voice, I began trying to comprehend why the voice I had been listening to over the last few weeks wasn't matching the person I was now shaking hands with. Standing about six foot one and pushing close to three hundred pounds, I couldn't help but wonder if this was actually the same person I had been speaking with for the last few weeks. Because of his asthma and bronchitis, he wheezed a bit after every laugh and coughed uncontrollably between those periods. My first and only thought was, *Wow, this is going to be an interesting hunt!*

On a good day, Kodiak is a tough hunt for even those in really good shape; for someone in Carl's condition, this was going to be a real challenge. With the shape he was in, lack of experience, and challenges that lied ahead, I figured we'd be doing well if we all made it from the boat to the shore in one piece! Carl was a rambler who had no inside voice, and after about an hour of listening to him go on and on about nothing, the only thought in my head at that point was what his friend Brian was like.

Since Carl was going to be my backup and I his, we decided to meet at the shooting range about two weeks before departing to get a feel for the way each other shot. Brian, who had just moved to Colorado, was still a state resident and qualified for the hunt; however, we unfortunately wouldn't meet up with him until we all got to Kodiak. Carl told me that they had killed a black bear together a few years ago and Brian was a pretty good shot, but that's all I really knew about him.

So on a clear, crisp, Saturday morning two weeks before we departed, I met Carl out at the range for what I thought would be a simple practice session. He rolled up about an hour late, carrying a slick (no scope) .375 H&H that he had borrowed from his brother and had never even shot. At first glance, I thought, okay, he had probably got some kind of quick disconnects and a scope in the small plastic bag he was carrying. Turned out that the only thing he had in the bag were fifteen rounds of mismatched ammo that his brother had also given him; this was going to be interesting!

If there was ever a time in my life that I knew I was in trouble, this would have definitely been one of them. Carl explained to me that the only way he ever shoots is with iron sights (no scope), and that was the way he would be doing this hunt. Well, after the first four rounds, he quickly changed his mind, for there wasn't a scratch on the one-hundred-yard target. After shooting the (whole) fifteen rounds he had brought and not hitting anything but dirt, I convinced him that he needed to get a scope, a full box of factory ammo, and try this again.

Six days later, we were back at the range with a newly fitted scope and a fresh box of ammo. After an hour or so of adjustments, we had him shooting three-inch groups at one hundred yards. Good enough!

It was showtime—May 4, 2009! And as we departed Anchorage on a frosty Monday morning, I couldn't hold back the rush of adrenaline surging through my veins. The weather in Kodiak was overcast but would be lifting around noon, which could give us an opportunity to get our permits and a safety briefing at F&G and motor out of port to do a hunt that afternoon. By regulation, you normally can't hunt the same day you fly; however, if you flew in on a commercial carrier, you can hunt.

If you then took a private flight/carrier into another area, you would then be restricted from hunting that day. The weather on the flight out of Anchorage was pretty good until we neared the coastline of Kodiak, where things started to get a little bumpy. All I could see was clouds when the captain came over the loudspeaker informing us that it may be a good idea to keep our seatbelts fastened for the impending landing—like that was going to help in this tin can!

Era Aviation operates a carrier service all over the state and uses a lot of small aircraft like the one we were on. There was no cabin/cockpit door, so I could see the small runway through the cockpit window when we broke out of the clouds at about a one thousand feet and a forty-five-degree nose-down attitude. After a few pitches, yaws, rolls, and some awesome zero-g moments, we were on the ground and weaving toward the baggage line. We grabbed our gear, jumped in Sam's truck, stopped by Fish and Game for our permits, and were on the boat and motoring out of port by one thirty. Not a bad start, I thought as we motored along, seeing that the last time I did this we spent two days watching the rain drip off the windows waiting for the weather to break. On the third day, we finally got out of port but got caught in a squall in Marmot Bay that was bringing green water over the bow; I think Sam could have actually applied for and received a submersible license after that trip!

the El Gato

We were off at last on the hunt of a lifetime, an adventure we knew that would be like no other. Once we stepped off of the boat and on to the shores of Raspberry and Afognak Island, anything could happen. We would be in the land of the notorious Kodiak brown bear, the largest and most powerful bear in the world—an elusive creature known for its speed, prowess, and cunning ability to sneak up on its prey despite its enormous size. It was overwhelming to think that in just a few short hours, we would again be standing in the middle of nowhere, surrounded by nothing but elk, deer, and hopefully a lot of bears!

As we throttled up in Marmot Bay, I couldn't help remembering the first time I landed on the north shore of Raspberry Island in 2004. The weather was cold, and the seas were rough, so a tactical assault with the skiff would be required to get us onto the beach. As we neared the shore, the swells grew larger and larger to a point where I couldn't even see the shore over the tops of them. The next thing I remember was Sam yelling, "Get ready, get ready" as we caught the crest of a huge wave and rode it onto the shore. The sound of gravel scraping the bottom of the dinghy was interrupted by the shock of freezing seawater filling my boots from the wave that had broken inside the boat.

"Go, go, go," Sam yelled as he furiously back-paddled off of the shore. The skiff had turned parallel with the shore, and as we were all trying to get out of the surf, I noticed the next huge swell building in the distance. Sam was frantically trying to turn the bow into the wave to keep from capsizing but kept getting sucked back in along the shore. I threw my gear down, jumped into the water, and gave the bow a good push when the wave broke all around us. The bow went straight up, and Sam nearly fell out but somehow managed to fire the motor off and get past the breakers. I was soaked from head to toe and shivering before I had even made it to shore!

Once on dry land and away from the surf, I changed into an extra shirt and pair of socks I always carried, and as we walked from the beach and into the brush, the feeling in my toes started to come back. The pain was unbearable as I struggled to hold back from screaming. Minutes passed, and I had lost all concern for where we were when we stumbled on to our first bear prints in the middle of an elk trail. If there was ever a cure for hypothermia, this could be it, for the surge of adrenaline I got from seeing those prints sent my blood pressure through the roof. I had seen a lot of bear prints over the years; however, these were not from your average bear. These were from a creature of unimaginable proportion—a *monster* by any name. The left front pad was almost eleven inches across, which when you add the inch for measurement purposes meant the bear was at least an eleven-footer.

As we looked around more, we realized that we weren't standing in an elk trail; this was a bear trail. It was more like a bear highway seeing that it was almost three feet wide and about twelve inches deep! As I slowly opened the bolt on my rifle to chamber a round, I remember thinking, *What have I got myself into now!*

It was about four thirty in the afternoon when we arrived at the first bay we could hunt. Like many bays in Kodiak, this one had no name, but we called it Happy Valley, for it was the same place Joe and I had pulled our bears out of in 2004. There's a knob about a mile back that offered a 360-degree view of three huge valleys, so the plan was to get to the knob where we could sit and glass. The weather was considerably different than the last time I was here, beautiful and warm with calm seas. And since it wouldn't get dark until 11:00 p.m., we had plenty of time to hunt. Sean (the deckhand) and Sam readied the skiff and we were off on our first hunt. We took our time and made our way through the dense brush using the convenience of the many Elk and Bear trails that crisscrossed the valley like a massive road system. Although I didn't notice it until we reached the shore, Carl had not stopped talking since getting off of the airplane and was now continuing to ramble in his normal tone of voice.

"Carl, can you keep it down a bit? We're hunting now," I told him.

For the next hour, all I could hear was the sound of the whistling reed grass mixed with the tones of Carl's obnoxious voice. I had given up on trying to explain to him that bears have ears too and that sound travels forever in the bush.

By the time we were halfway up to the knob, I turned to see where Carl and Brian were when I spotted our first bear on the other side of the valley. I gave the get-down hand sign, but I guess they both thought I was just swatting flies or mosquitoes.

Carl climbing another hill.
Note the El Gato in the background

"Get down, get down," I whispered, pointing to the bear just playing in what was left of the winter's snow.

"I don't see it. Where is he?" asked Carl in his normally loud tone of voice.

For anyone who has ever hunted with a partner or group, one of the hardest things to do when spotting game is try and explain to another person the location of what you're looking at. After what seemed like forever, they had finally seen their first Kodiak brown bear. Unfortunately, the bear had picked up on Carl's voice and was now watching us too. We all came to the conclusion that the bear wasn't as big as we first thought. If it was there on the way back down from the knob, we could plan a stalk on him then—a decision we would later regret. Moments later, the bear got up, walked up a ridge, and as they so often and mysteriously do, disappeared into the brush.

This was May, and the weather this time of year was statistically wet and cold, which bears seemed to like. The weather on this trip, however, had been beautiful, sunny, and warm, which was great for tanning; problem was, bears don't tan, and when you're a hungry 1,200-pound brown bear with six-inch fur, the last thing you want to see is warm and beautiful. You want the rain, wind, and even snow, so it's comfortable when you're out turning up logs to find moths, sharpening your nails, and chasing deer and elk, or anything else that comes along.

Because bears are primarily nocturnal, they prefer the early mornings and evenings to wander, feed, and mate, but have been known to move all day this time of year. Because of the heat, the bears were just not moving until late at night or early in the morning. Early morning is ideal because you can try and slip into a location and wait for them to start moving. Nighttime is even better; however, if it's too late when you see them or start a stalk, you could find yourself in a really bad situation with them having the advantage.

It was day 3, and while sitting around the breakfast table taking in a nice, hot meal of eggs, toast, and of course, coffee, we realized that the only way we're ever going to get any bears was to hunt from sunrise to sunset. This would mean some serious long days seeing that morning broke around 4:00 a.m., and sunset was around 11:00 p.m. We stuck with the plan, and over the next ten grueling and frustrating days of hunting every bay, valley, river, drainage, and estuary in our area, we had seen only four bears and very little sign in the areas we had covered. Between the three of us, we only had one stalk on a sow and boar, which was unfortunately unsuccessful.

On day 7, I had woken up early as usual and made my way out to the cold and clammy back deck to make my daily contribution to the Bering Sea water level. I had left my glasses next to the bunk and am pretty blind without them, so when I saw what appeared to be a large black spot moving on the hill next to us, I didn't think much about it but decided to take a second look anyhow. I had just woken up and was standing there in the undies that I had not changed since day 1 scratching when I heard Carl foraging about.

"Whata ya lookin' at?" came from a high-pitched crackling voice deep within the hull of the ship.

"Not sure," I said as I continued to scratch and glass at the same time. "Looks like it might be a sow and a boar."

The big, black spot had actually been two bears "playing" if you know what I mean. This is the season, and those two were making the most of it right there in front of us.

"It's a sow and a boar getting busy up there." I said. "Want to get them?"

The bears were oblivious to our presence even though we were probably less than five hundred yards away. They were just hanging out and having fun about halfway up the side of a really large and really steep mountain. After watching them for a while, I told Carl that if he was ready, he and Brian should try and get them; I never was a good morning person, and besides, I hadn't finished all my scratching yet.

Sean launched the skiff, and within a few minutes, Carl and Brian were heading up the mountain from the steep shoreline. We were all just sitting the watching the show and nursing a good cup of coffee when the bears got their wind and started moving sideways along the hill. It took all of about two seconds for me to see that they were moving straight across and in our direction; if I could get up high enough, fast enough, I could cut them off and maybe land one. We launched the skiff again, and Sean put me right below where we had last seen them; as I made my way up the slippery, steep shale rock cliff, I thought to myself that this may actually work.

My stalk put me halfway up a three-thousand-foot mountain and left me staring at a twelve-foot wall of impenetrable alders. From where I was sitting, I thought for sure that the bears had already gone, for it was impossible to traverse this brush and be quiet at the same time. Like all of Kodiak, there are two kinds of brush: mean and nasty and mean and nastier! It was tough going, and I was spent when I got to a point where we had last seen them. I was sitting on a small ledge between a solid wall of alders and a lone spruce tree where I could see nothing except the water below me; one wrong move and I would be hurting pretty bad.

Taking a break about halfway up.

I sat there as long as I could, listening for anything that would suggest the bears were still in front of me or even in the area. All I could hear were the wind and the waves hitting the shore, so after what seemed like forever, I decided to go to plan B.

I had never successfully used a bear call before but decided that this may be a good time to try given the situation. I figured that if I hadn't scared them away with all the noise I had just made, maybe I could get a rise out of them with a call. According to Sean and Sam who had been watching the whole thing from the boat, as soon as I hit that call, the biggest boar they'd ever seen stood up in the alders no more than thirty yards in front of me. It looked around for a second, then he broke out of the alders in a dead run with the sow, and both of them shot up the other 1,500-feet of mountain like their butts were on fire! Funny thing was, I never heard nor saw anything and had no idea until Sean picked me up on the beach and told me what happened. I didn't believe him at first and thought he was joking when I realized he wasn't. That's when the reality of it all set in, and I realized that I had just blown the only stalk in seven days on a possible record bear! Only those who hunt can relate to what I was feeling then and even now—complete and total numbness, disbelief, and guilt. The what ifs were endless, and I spent every waking hour for the rest of that hunt thinking about all of the things I could have done different that day!

It was day 11, and we were all tired and frustrated. We had put in the time, done the work, stuck to the plan, and hunted hard for the last ten days. We had only seen four bears in eleven days, which was incredibly poor for anywhere on Kodiak. Where were all of the bears? Were we too late, too early, doing something wrong—what? The questions were endless, and after a while, we all started second-guessing everything that we were doing—everything!

It was about 6:00 a.m., and after a quick breakfast, we decided to hit the shore of a bay we had hunted a few days before and seen a few signs that indicated a bear might still be in the area. We followed a river up through a valley where it split and decided that I would stay at the split and use a bear call, while Carl and Brian would go upriver a bit to glass another valley.

Carl jumping stream

The plan was to hunt all day and be back at the boat around 8:00 p.m. so we could motor around the bays and look for bears on the beaches; they've been known to take advantage of a good low tide to eat the kelp and turtle grass.

Around 6:30 p.m. and after a long day of glassing, calling, glassing, calling, I packed it up and slowly hunted my way back along the 2.9 miles of river that wound through the valley like a huge, slithering snake. I reached the shore about 7:30 p.m. exhausted, frustrated, and bewildered why the hunting gods were mad at me. Sean had seen me making my way down a steep cliff that ran into the cove they were anchored in, so after a few minutes, launched the skiff and picked me up. It was around 9:00 p.m., and I had just started on my second beer when the shot was heard. It was a big gun, and the sound echoed through the valley like thunder. We sat and listened for more, but nothing came.

Ten o'clock rolled by, eleven, then twelve. The questions were endless, and theories were starting to formulate. At around one o'clock, we decided to go ashore and look for them. We had no moon, and it was pitch-black. When we reached the shore, Sam yelled to us from the boat that he had seen one headlamp in the distance and about halfway up the mountain. This was good and bad at the same time, for why was there only one headlamp? Had one of them simply left their headlamp on the boat? Sean and I couldn't resist making light of the situation by joking about the possibilities of a bear running around on the mountain with the headlamp in his stomach. If there was only one lamp, where was the other person? We all had lamps for the possibility of a late return; why was there only one lamp?

After about an hour of calling out into the darkness, we heard a joyous shout from what sounded like Carl. A few minutes later a headlamp broke through the thick brush that lined the cliff above the beach, and we could now faintly see two figures traversing the last steep cliff that stretched into the shoreline. Carl let out a scream that could have been heard in Saigon!

"We got him, we got him, he's down, baby," he hollered as he strutted his way toward the skiff. "It's brown, and it's down," he repeated over and over like a kid who just got a new toy.

We all piled into the skiff and made our way back to the boat where the story came to life. Seems that the place where we had split up earlier was where they shot the bear—the same place I had sat for more than nine hours pouring all I had into a stupid little distress call. Yep, it appeared that I had left a little too early. Call me a skeptic, but when you don't see anything anywhere for two days in the same area, then all of a sudden a seventeen-year-old, nine-foot-five-inch brownie with a 27 and 3/16 skull magically appears in the exact spot your were calling, you just have to wonder! Carl and Brian were completely exhausted, but the story played out through the evening like an old broken record.

There was still one day left to hunt, and I was now forced to make a decision to either hunt for another bear or help the guys drag that one out of the bush; needless to say, I didn't get much sleep that night. Six o'clock rolled around before I knew it, and after breakfast we all started getting ready for the day ahead. The weather was again beautiful although it was colder than previous mornings. As I sat there packing my gear, I couldn't help but to overhear Carl and Brian's plan to extract the bear. As much as I wanted to try and take advantage of the last day to hunt, I knew that they would never get that bear out with the plan and experience they had. The best that I could hope for now is that maybe another bear was on the kill or just in the area.

We hit the beach around 10:00 a.m. and started up the long, steep climb to where we would hopefully find the bear. Two hours later we had reached the area but couldn't locate the bear. Had we gone too far back, not far enough, or was it higher than they had originally thought? Things always look different at night, which makes locating things the next day a little tricky sometimes. The best thing to do is either have a good GPS or use survey tape to mark a trail and or exact location. In our case, we had a good GPS, but it was giving us some bad information. A recap of the events that evening put us close enough where after a short wander around the area, we spotted the bear lying belly up in a deep ravine. The guys had talked all night about the scenario of the kill; however, they failed to mention how big this guy really was. As I made my way through the alders and water that lined the ravine, I got my first look at this monster. The details of their story made it sound like they had killed a pretty good bear, but I didn't expect a bear like this.

He was an old boar with an enormous head, beautiful coat, and long ivory claws. I was impressed to see that the guys had gutted him and stretched his limbs out using sticks so when he rigged out, we could still get in and skin him pretty easy. Four hours and several finger cuts later, the bear was all wrapped up in the game skidder like a big, giant taco. A lot of people have different ways of getting bears out of the woods here; however, when you're talking about a hide that weighs anywhere from one hundred to three hundred pounds without the skull in it, you need to come up with something other than a backpack!

Six hours, 2.9 miles, and a lot of sweat later, we made it to the beach where we fleshed the skull and took a long-deserved break while waiting for a pickup; our hunt was finally over.

Now this is a big bear!

The guys with their trophy

Carl and the bear paw

As I told Sam before I left Kodiak, this was the most successful unsuccessful hunt I've ever had. I thought for sure that if anyone would get a bear out of this hunt, it would be a guy like me, an experienced hunter, a man among men. However, and as fate would have it, it wasn't. In fact, it was a person who by nature was the direct and polar opposite of me. A person who in any hunter's book should have never even been on a hunt like this. A person who by right had no business being in the woods, yet being in the woods with a loaded rifle. A person who by any means would be out of their mind to even attempt a hunt like this. But there he was, all three hundred pounds of him talking his way through the brush like he was in Safari World or something. A person whose idea of having the right wind meant lifting a leg when breaking wind. A person who no more than two weeks ago couldn't hit the side of a barn door if it were fifty feet in front of him. A person who when even walking on wet, moist, moss sounded like Godzilla coming through New York City!

So I guess if there's an actual moral to this story, it would have to be that sometimes it just doesn't matter who or what you are. It doesn't matter where you're from or how much experience you have in the field. It doesn't matter if you're a professional hunter or a person who just opened up their first gun box. It doesn't matter if you did everything right or everything wrong. And it damn sure doesn't matter if you're a little bigger than the average person or can't seem talk in a normal tone of voice. At the end of the day, sometimes it's just a simple luck of the draw!

16

THE HUNTER

When I first started writing this book, I realized there was only one way to do it and that was honestly. I also knew that somewhere along the line, someone would be offended by it's content. Please know that none of these stories were in no way meant to offend. This is only to describe my life events as and when I saw them.

I get asked all the time about how I became the hunter I am today, about the number of bears and other critters I've killed and what drives me to keep hunting more. I've pondered this question for years, and the only thing I can come up with is, "I was born to be a *hunter*!"

I believe that the core of what a person is and will be is decided at conception. No matter what that person experiences in life, that core cannot be changed or influenced. Thus, the endless stories of those who were so promising yet failed. Or those who came from nothing yet became everything.

So for me, I believe I was just born to be a hunter. Heck, from the day I opened my eyes, I was on the prowl for something. I can't even remember a time when I wasn't hunting something, and growing up in Miami, Florida, gave me an endless diversity of critters to choose from. Before I could walk, I remember crawling along the floor and chasing lizards, roaches, and these little armadillo-looking bugs. They were fun because when you flicked them, they'd curl up in a ball just like an armadillo. From there it progressed to frogs (and I mean some serious, five-pound kinda frogs), snakes, hogs, and anything else that lived or moved. We lived next to a canal called Snake Creek, which was a major watershed that cut its way through the middle of Miami and was full of everything—gators, frogs, crawdads, snakes, fish, manatees, dolphins, and more. Even found a guy who was sleeping in it one day. Cops came and took him away though, said he had had enough sleep and now needed to take a "dirt nap"!

What began as just a simple fascination for all things living quickly grew into a childhood obsession. First, happy with just finding and playing with things grew into a study into the biological world of every living creature in Florida. I wasn't real smart on a lot of different levels; however, if it moved, slithered, crawled, or swam, I could tell you everything about it and then some.

So if I wasn't fishing (which was pretty rare), I was hunting down something. Even while walking to school I'd look for green snakes and lizards, which there was never a shortage of. Green snakes were fun because they just latch on to a finger with their tiny, little teeth; then you could literally rip them out of the tree. I'd play with them and study them on the way to school, then let them go in this old man's yard across the street from the school. Not sure how many of those things I released over there, but I do remember the animal control van and a bunch of cops out in front of his house one day.

From there, my love for all things (nonhuman) grew, and before I knew it, I was sneaking up on deer and wrestling small alligators. I remember getting so close to a deer one day that I could have reached out and touched it. I was getting good at this whole hunting thing and didn't even realize it. It was just fun to me, and the poor victims were endless. My friend called me one day and said he had an alligator in his pool.

I jumped on my bike and took the shortcut through the alleyway and came in from the back gate to a sight that only could be seen in the south. In the pool and looking quite comfortable was about a six-foot gator. It was just floating there looking at all of us like lunch, sizing us up to see who'd be the tastiest. My buddy was yelling "Get the net, get the net" when I came up with a better idea. All I remember saying was, "Watch this!"

I had just seen *Mutual of Omaha's Wild Kingdom* where Lorne Greene, I think, was wrestling a huge crocodile in Africa, so I was fully trained on what to do. I leapt from the side of the pool directly in back of the little guy and landed right on the middle of his back! To my surprise, not only was the water freezing but that damn gator also did not like me on his back! No sooner than I hit the hard scales of its back and wrapped my arms around its belly when that thing took off like a rocket. The power and speed of that little guy was more than overwhelming, and as that thing shot through the water like a rocket-propelled torpedo, my head was pulled so far back it nearly touched my butt! The next thing I know, the gator and I were out of the water and on the lawn, where I was whipped off him like a bad tick.

Still unable to see and choking from the half pool of water that was just shoved down my throat, I got up and ran as fast as I could in the opposite direction, which unfortunately was back in the pool. I hit the surface and was struggling to find the gator when I noticed the other boys pointing toward the fence. I jumped out of the pool and was making my way toward the commotion but was quickly rumbled to the ground by my friends, who thought that was the coolest thing they ever saw.

"That was cool, man," one of them said as he shook me furiously.

"You were like Tarzan, man!" another one said.

I just remember lying there and thinking that was the stupidest thing I had ever done! Shortly after that I guess was when I got the nickname Gator.

So in 1974 when it came to my first actual hunt with the guys, I more than jumped at the chance. It had been a dream of mine as far back as I could remember, and now it was finally going to happen. I was fourteen then and had never actually hunted with a rifle before, but I was a good shot with one. All I needed was for something to step out in front of me, and it would be down. A friend of my father's in Florida had invited us all up, so all we needed to do now is "get our hunt on!" The men all gathered their gear (mostly beer) and a few rifles, threw it all in the back of the truck, and off we went.

About fifteen minutes later, we pulled along the roadside with seven other trucks. There were about twenty men total and just a few kids, but soon the men had gathered without us to discuss their hunting strategy. I and a couple of other kids meandered around the edge of a swamp looking for turtles and whatnot, while the men readied themselves by finishing all the beer in the back of that one truck; after all, it was pretty hot. The next thing I know, we were all walking into the woods in different directions with no direction at all. We just kept walking and walking and walking until Bill yelled out, "It's over here! It's over here!"

There were people everywhere it seemed as we made our way over to where Bill was standing.

"This is the one," he said as he looked up at a huge oak tree. "This is a beer tree," he said as he gazed up at the behemoth mass of stump. "This be the baby rat heeya!"

Like an idiot, I had to ask. "What is a beer tree, Bill?"

I knew I was in trouble when his son looked over at me and just shook his head. Bill said, "Well, this heeya is a beer tree cuz when it blooms, it puts out beer cans! Now, you watch. Ain't no cans heeya now, but by the time we leave, theya gonna be beer cans uh everywheres!" He threw his 30-06 over his shoulder and started his way up the tree as the rest of us looked on. Next thing you know, Bill's on the ground and cussing like a drunken sailor.

"Gosh darned, stupid tree!" He dusted himself off, took another look at the tree, and headed back up now using the ladder spikes someone had stuck in the tree before. What seemed like forever was only a few minutes, but finally, all of us were in the tree and now hunting. Dad and Bill were on one side of the tree rambling on about business and work, and his son and I were on the other side just watching for deer. We were into it about two hours when we heard a single shot followed by a lot of automatic gun fire from a ways out. Everybody just sat there wide-eyed wondering what was happening. The forest had erupted into a war zone, and there were people shooting from everywhere it seemed.

I looked over at my father, who was giving me a get-down sign when I heard the first round whizz by. It sounded like a high-pitched whirling sound followed by another. The branch next to us exploded, sending pieces flying everywhere.

My father was now yelling, "Get down, get down!"

As I lay there clinging to the tree like a lizard in heat, I remember thinking to myself, *If this is hunting, I don't want anything to do with this mess!*

Finally the gunfire stopped, and the deafening silence once again filled the forest. We spent the next four hours in that stupid tree listening to sporadic burst of gunfire, people yelling, and beer cans falling out of the tree just like Bill said there would be.

As I watched the sun starting to fade, Bill and Dad were starting to make their way down the tree.

"C'mon, ya'll, time to call it the day." Bill had only taken a few steps when he slipped and fell out of the tree again. This time, though, he just lay there moaning and rolling around a bit. "Damn, I think I busted a beer," he moaned as he continued to roll around in the leaves and mud.

Dad helped him to his feet and was brushing him off when he calmly said, "Nope, it's rat heeya! I done saved the las' beer." He popped the top and tossed the tab high into the air like he'd just graduated from something. Then in one last blaze of glory, he held the can high in the air and toasted the hunting gods, then proceeded to guzzle the whole can.

Back at the road, my father and Bill precariously poured themselves into the truck as we listened and laughed at their banter. First, Bill couldn't find the keys. Then my father couldn't find his keys. Then the truck wouldn't start because they had the wrong keys. Finally, Bill got the truck started and even managed to turn it around, and we were off again. To this day, I still don't know how we survived the five-mile trip back to town. I don't think we were even on the actual road for more than five minutes out of the thirty or so. We made it back to the town's intersection, which consisted of a general store, a church, and two gas stations.

Lo and behold, did I not realize until that point that this is where the hunting starts. This was where the trophies and stories were made. This, my friend, was what hunting was all about! We pulled up smack-dab in the middle of what looked like the largest truck show in America! There must have been one hundred trucks and about a million people there as we made our way through the maze of vehicles. We hadn't even stopped yet before a man came over to Bill and handed him a beer.

"Well, well," Bill said. "Looks like someone's done sum killin' t'day, ain't they!"

There were dead deer laid over the hood of trucks for as far as the eye could see! There were blood and guts strewn up and over everything. It looked like a herd of about a thousand had crossed the highway at the wrong time, and this was the results. Hell, even the town sheriff had got him one and was walking around with what was left of it draped over his blood-soaked shoulders.

"Lookie heeya, Bob," Bill said in a somber tone. "Who in the hell was shootin' an AK-47 out by my beer tree t'day? They almost done shot us rat outta dat damn tree now."

Bob, Bubba, forest, and nobody else had an answer to that, but they did have beer and a lot of it. We spent the next few hours hanging out there listening to the tall tales about blasting this and blasting that. Bill's son and I wandered aimlessly through the carnage a half-dozen times trying to pick the worst-shot animal.

Finally found one that had been hit so many times, it looked like it had been run over by a meat grinder. About another case of beer later, we all piled back in the truck and ended up back at Bill's house. As I slithered into the comfort of the cool, crisp sheets that night, I just lay there in awe of all that I had witnessed. After all, it had always been a childhood dream of mine to do a hunt like this, and it had finally come to fruition. The traditions, the customs, the logistics, skill, woodsmanship, and I didn't even puke once! My childhood dream had been fulfilled. And as I slowly drifted off that night, I made a promise to myself that I would never ever hunt like that again. That was my introduction to hunting. A cruel and bloody, liquor-filled carnival of ridiculousness, filled with an endless amount of testosterone, and, of course, endless gunfire.

The years passed, and I never did hunt again. Then in 1995 while still in the air force, I got an assignment to Alaska. Little did I know how much my life would change. Little did I know how everything would change. I had spent many years listening to people who hunted only to be disgusted by their mentality and arrogance. I mean, after all, this was the twentieth century; you can get food in the store. Why people still hunted was beyond me, and it made me regress back to that day in Florida every time.

I had shipped a car from England where I was stationed to South Carolina, so after picking it up there, I was on the road again. I figured it would take me about two weeks to get to Alaska, so with an ample supply of cassette tapes and a six-pack of Dew, I was on the road again and heading north to Alaska!

It was about day 4 into the trip, and I was somewhere in jerkwater Mississippi on some backroad when I came across a truck stopped in the middle of the road. I slowly and cautiously made my way up to the vehicle thinking this might be one of those carjacking things, when a man jumped from the front of the vehicle. I slammed on my breaks and grabbed my .45 when I noticed something on the ground in front of his truck. I got out of my vehicle, tucked the .45 in my pants, and slowly made my way toward the man who was now bent over and waving his arms in front of him.

This is weird, I thought as my right hand found the grip and trigger. Then as I peered around to where the man was looking, I realized all too well what the commotion was about. Smack-dab in the middle of the road was one of the largest eastern diamondback rattlesnakes I'd ever seen. The man had run over it with his truck, but it was still alive, and he was now trying to kill it.

I had captured one of these a long time ago and knew all too well how aggressive and deadly they could be, but I wasn't going to let this guy kill it. It was an absolute monster and probably at least a ten-footer if not more. It looked like it had just eaten a deer or something huge, for its girth was at least sixteen inches round. He had a head on him the size of a softball and a rattler as loud as thunder. He was, without a doubt, one of the largest snakes I had ever seen and an incredible representative of its species.

"Man, that there's goin' on my wall it is!" the man said in an insecure tone. "You gots a gun or somethings I can kill it wit?" he asked.

Looking at me now as if he knew I had one, I said, "No, and you're not killing anything."

To this day I don't know what came over me or what I was thinking, but like white on rice, I swooped in and grabbed the tail of that monster and with one huge pull, hacked that snake about twenty feet in the air and back into the swamp it came from.

"What in the hell was that you say?" the man now yelled. "That thar was my snake! What in the sam hill'd ya do that fo'?"

I walked purposely over to the man and stuck my finger in his face and said, "You don't deserve to have that or anything else on your walls, you good for nothing SOB!"

He was still just standing in the middle of the road the last time I looked in my rear-view mirror. I guess it wasn't until that day that did I realize what a huge impact that hunting trip so long ago had taken on me. How much it taught me about respecting our environment and the wildlife within it. And how far I'd go to enforce it, then to at least do my part in protecting it from idiots like that man who's still probably standing in the middle of that road.

I arrived in Anchorage, Alaska, without further incident in September 1995. With less than four years left to retire, I figured this would just be another tour, and then I'd go somewhere else; boy, was I wrong. Lucky me, I was assigned to a ragtag outfit responsible for keeping the snow and ice off of military aircraft in the winter, staffed solely by what seemed like some of the grumpiest civil servants in the world. After a short-lived introduction on how the military really worked, I became friends with a few of them and enemies with the rest. Like most folks up here, they were all from somewhere else and had come up with the military like me. Retired now, they held this and a few other summer jobs just to keep enough money in their pockets to hunt and fish; I mean, what else was there! To these guys, hunting and fishing was their life, and they were living it! It didn't take long for me to realize how much these guys loved this country and how much respect they had for it and everything in it. They were not just hunters and fishers, but they were also true advocates, spokespersons, teachers, and the stewards of all that is right about hunting, fishing, and living in the great outdoors.

They were the people I never knew existed and the complete opposite of what I had thought for years to be true of all hunters. Little did I know at the time but these were the people who would later teach me that there is a huge and unquestionable difference between a hunter and a killer. Aside from now being some of the best friends I've ever had, they are what I consider to be the real heroes of the stories in this book—the people who taught me all I know about what it means to be a real hunter and what hunting is all about.

On another hunt somewhere in
Prince William Sound

Since then, I have hunted and taken just about every Alaskan species there is except for a mountain goat. Having blown my knee out twice while skiing, I have yet to attempt a summit to retrieve one of these incredible animals. To my credit, however, I have taken several moose, caribou, and bear with both bow and rifle. I also had several Kodiak brown bears, one of which is number 25 in the world according to Boone and Crocket. A musk ox, foxes, and I don't even know how many black bears. In 2008 while reconning an area known for huge dall sheep, I was lucky enough to find one that felt like he needed to be added to the Boone and Crocket list.

Not to sound like I'm bragging, but also in that list are eight plains game species from South Africa to include a kudu, gemsbok, zebra, two red hartebeest, springbok, white blesbok, and of course my favorite, a warthog.

So in contrast to everything I was and had believed in all those years, after just ten short years in this great state, I had become the very person I used to despise. Unlike them though in every way, I had become and am a true hunter—not a killer. I had become and am everything I was supposed to be—a *hunter*.

Me and my trusty Blaser .338

17

THE ANNUAL

The following story is of a recent hunt with some longtime friends and a bunch of really smart black bears.

Every year for the last nine years, my good friend and hunting partner Sam have organized one of the funniest hunts in Alaska: a black bear hunt. Working off a forty-two-foot Delta in some of the roughest waters known to man, it goes without saying that every time we do this hunt, it turns out to be an adventure like no other. We call it, the Annual.

This hunt started out just like all of our other black bear hunts: endless months of anticipation followed by last-minute, panicked preparations. It was May 24 though and time to go, and as we loaded up my truck full of gear and guns, I could feel the adrenalin flowing in my blood. As usual, Sam had found two more guys at the last minute, so we would have six on the boat—a perfect combination for a two-on-two-type hunt. Not that it's impossible to get one on your own, however, having another person to back you up is always a welcomed addition.

This trip, we had two greenhorns by the names of Jesse and Devin. Jesse was your seminormal kinda guy; however, Devin was off the hook! He was, without a doubt, one of the craziest bastards I'd ever met, and I've met a few. In clinical terms, they call him "certifiable"; however, today, we just called him mate! This guy had more jokes and off-the-wall stories and tales that would keep *Guinness* book guessing. It was go time, and as we passed Potters Marsh and headed out of town, the hunt was on.

It was Thursday evening around seven, and the start of the Memorial Day weekend when we pulled into Seward. We made our way down to the slippery dock and to what would be our floating home for the next four days: the *Viking*. A forty-foot Delta with twin screws and two midget stripper poles on the table, the *Viking* was a nautical killing machine! For Sam and I, this would be our eighth voyage and between the two of us, had shed a lot of blood on it—a lot! For the FNGs (freaking new guys), though, this was new territory, and after a short briefing and a few beers, everybody started settling in. The original plan was to load up and spend the night in the harbor and motor out in the morning. Unfortunately, though, because of an impending storm, Scott decided to motor out as soon as we were done loading. No sooner than the last bag was thrown on board when Scott fired up the motors, and we were on our way once more.

As we rounded the rock wall of the harbor jetty and passed the campground, the water started getting rough. We were not even halfway out of the inlet and were already taking on four-footers. I stood next to Scott on the bridge absorbing the shock of the swells as I watched a wall of fog slowly close in around us.

As soon as we rounded the rocks off of Rugged Island, the swells were now close together and rocking the boat from all sides. Wave upon wave was washing over the bow making it impossible to see. If there were any logs or other debris in our path, we could take a hit and be in the water before we knew it. My heart was racing now as the darkness fell, and we could only see the bow of the boat. We were flying blind now, and every wave was a surprise. Just as it seemed that the water was calming down, we would drop off the edge of a swell and plummet into the next.

The hull was beckoning time after time as it slammed into wave after wave. We were about two hours out now, and it was too late to turn back. Besides, if we tried to turn the boat around now, we would be rolled over like a dingy! We had no choice except to press on and man it out. I looked back into the galley area where all I could see are the white knuckles of Jesse gripping the side of the table. Things were flying all over the cabin as we rolled around like a bobber. The swells were now becoming larger as the bow would rocket almost straight up and then fall as if the water had disappeared beneath us. Scott was forced to cut the throttles now, which meant the trip would be even longer. The wind was also picking up, making what was once four-footers into now eight-footers at even closer intervals. We were barely pushing twelve knots and bucking wave after wave as Scott pointed out the front window and mumbled something.

Between the noise of the motors and the howling wind, I had to yell over to him just feet away. "What did you say?"

He pointed out the window again at what I could now see were rocks just off our port bow. If he wouldn't have said anything, I don't think I would have seen them, which sent chills down my spine.

"Once we get around the pass, it should be a little calmer," Scott yelled back.

Finally, I thought as my fingers gripped the small wooden ledge of the bridge's console. Like he said, no sooner than we got behind the rocks of Swanson Passage, the water was flat calm. After a very short conversation about staying the night or pressing on, Scott let the anchor go, and we all called it a night. In all my days on boats, that perhaps was the worst trip I had ever taken, and as I poured myself into my bunk, it still felt as if we were moving.

The next morning, I awoke to the sound of the motors turning over and the smell of fresh-cooked eggs. Unlike myself, Jesse, or Devin, Sam was a morning person and was hot on the skillet. I crawled out of my bunk, looked over at the clock, and looked back over at Sam, who looked like he had been up since first light cooking. "Eh," I said wiping the sleep from my eyes, "where are we at?"

"Alaska," Sam said as if he was being honest. "Want some breakfast?" He scraped some eggs and bacon into a tortilla for me.

"I need coffee," I said. "Where's the coffee?"

About another half hour of trying to figure out where everybody put everything and getting some coffee going, I made my way to the bridge where, as usual, Scott was hard at the wheel.

"Morning, Scott, want some coffee?" I handed him a hot, steaming cup and went and got me another when Sam called out "Whale!"

Whales everywhere

There were a few orcas off our starboard side, but they disappeared quickly, and we never saw them again. I crawled back up the bridge and stepped up onto the seat as we motored out of Swanson Cove and headed out across Squirrel Bay. It was a cool, crisp morning, a lot colder than I was hoping it would be, but this was Alaska; prepare for the worst and hope for the best!

We got into Prince of Wales Passage around noon, and Devin immediately spotted two nice bears right down on the beach. Problem was, we hadn't even gotten the skiff off the roof or even dropped anchor yet. We would need to move fast or risk losing these bears. Sam and I were busy getting the skiff ready, while Devin and Jesse were now jumping through their asses trying to find their rifles, ammo, and everything else. We told them to be ready, but I guess they didn't think we would see something so soon. The skiff was ready, and as Sam and I turned to see where everyone was, it was perhaps the best moment of the hunt watching those guys run around as if their pants were on fire.

After what seemed like an extended panic session, they were off and heading to shore to put the hurt on some bears. Sam and I were in charge now of making sure the boat didn't run aground now that Scott was taking them in on the skiff. All we could do was wait and watch. As I took another sip of my coffee, I watched as the skiff got smaller and smaller, realizing once again how huge everything was out here. Aside from the noise that Sam and I were making, all you could hear was the sound of the water lapping at the sides of the boat, an occasional gull, or the sound of splashing water from one of many waterfalls that surrounded the bay.

As we sat there talking about this and that, we both watched as Devin and Jesse went back and forth along the beach as if looking for something they'd lost.

"What in the heck are they doing, Sam?" I asked.

"Looks like they lost something. Hmm."

We watched them for about another hour wander around the beach like they had their heads cut off; then the next thing we knew, the skiff was coming alongside the *Viking*.

"What were you guys looking for?" I asked.

"Tracks," Devin said.

It was about 1:00 p.m., and after a sandwich and another beer, I was looking to see if their bear had come back out when I spotted my bear about another mile down the beach.

"Scott, Scott, there's another one down in the honey hole!" I whispered excitedly as if the bear was going to hear me. "He's a nice one too. Let's go," I said as I just about fell into the skiff.

We had about a mile of water to cover and would need to figure out where the wind was coming from when we got closer. The bear was disappearing on and off the whole time due to the terrain, and trying to find him was becoming more difficult.

"There he is, Scott, at your one o'clock and about one hundred yards in."

Scott was used to my enthusiasm by now and just looked at me like I needed more Prozac. We got along the face of this cliff and downwind when we spotted the bear just foraging along about two hundred yards from the beach. We would need to row in and try to hide behind the walls of the cliff, or he would spot us.

Scott cut the motor and was readying the oars when the bear's head popped up.

Oh crap, I thought, *we just got busted!* His nose was straight up now trying to figure out what the new smell was when he stuck his head back into the lush, green grass. "Wow, that was close," I whispered to Sam.

We rowed in about as far as we could, but due to the way the rocks were, it was had to step into about four feet of ice-cold water. Before I even got to the shore, I could hardly feel my feet, but we were close now and needed to get up on him; I should have worn my hip waders. We made our way alongside the rocks and then up to a tree below an avalanche chute.

There he was about seventy-five yards in front of us and had no idea we were there. I even had time to range him and take a few breaths before sliding my .338 across the wet, slimy branch of the tree.

"Are you ready, Sam?" I asked.

"Ready when you are," Sam replied.

We were both watching him in our scopes now as he turned and looked straight at us. As much as I wanted to shoot in fear that he was going to run, I held off. His nose was twitching all over the place, and I was looking him dead in the eye. My finger was so close to the end of my trigger pull that I think the wind could have set it off. I was waiting for him to bolt when he turned, stuck his head back in the grass, and started eating again.

"Ready, Sam?" I asked.

"Do it," was all he said.

And after a short inhale, I let the hammer go. I heard the *whop* of my shot followed by Sam's report and out of the corner of my eye saw a black blur trying to run up the avalanche chute. I put him back in my crosshairs for just a second and squeezed off another round.

We both ran up to the base of the chute where he went in and found a lot of blood all over the ice and snow. He was hit and hit good; now we just needed to find him. Sam and I both hightailed it over the fallen trees, stumps, and roots that littered the area and were soon standing in the middle and on top of the avalanche chute.

Not the safest place, I thought as I tried to catch my breath.

Sam and I were both scouring the area looking for anything that moved when we both heard and felt a loud pop! "Oh crap" is all I remember saying as I followed Sam down and off the chute.

It was almost as if we hovered over everything we just hiked over, but before I knew it, we were back on terra firma. With nothing really left to do but to wait it out, we decided to hunker down behind a small outcropping of rocks just below the cliffs. We were downwind and in a pretty good position, so if anything came out, we'd be there to greet them. I guess we had been there for a few hours when the water on the incoming tide splashed up and over my boots waking me from a somber nap!

"Shit," I yelled as I awoke shocked to see that Sam too had nodded off!

As we made our way back to where the shore was, I looked back to find a curious seal gawking at the two dummies who almost woke up in the sea.

We made our way back to the boat a few hours later and ended up sharing stories with Devin and Jesse, who had put a stalk on another bear farther up the beach. They spotted another bear just about the time Scott had dropped us off and were off chasing through the woods. We tried telling them that this tactic didn't work, but sometimes you just have to learn the hard way. We topped off the night with the usual prime rib and red king crab legs and toasted the hunting gods repeatedly with some Pendleton and Crown.

The next morning I awoke early and made my was onto the back deck to talk to a man about a horse when something slammed the side of the boat.

Holy crap, I thought. *Did we just run up on the rocks?* My eyes still blurry, I struggled to see over the side of the boat when I caught the eye of a sea lion staring back at me. *Holy crud, you scared the bejesus out of me, you SOB.* Then as it passed by again, it was hard to stay mad, for it looked as though it just wanted to play. I reached in the bait bucket and pulled out a few herring and tossed them over, and that was all they wrote. That thing came damn near out of the water trying to get those fish. It rocketed past the bow, hung a U-turn, and had swallowed those fish before I could say you're welcome!

About that time Scott peeked his head out of the bridge door and asked what all the commotion was about. "Just a seal, go back to bed," I said. I sat there for about another half hour just watching the birds, the seals, the otters, and just listening to the silence; it was magical. It was like being in a dream. If you can imagine the most beautiful, serene place on earth and you're sitting right in the middle of it, yet really not a part of it, it is hard to describe, but everything in life seemed so irrelevant out here. The hustle and bustle of our human lives seemed so overrated. My mind was completely relaxed and drifting in and out of thought as I watched an eagle pass over.

Then Sam cracked the door open and asked, "We have any coffee?"

And that was the end of my window into a world that only a few ever get to experience.

Not sure if it was the Pendleton or the Fireballs, but the boys woke up all angry and pissed. After some griddle cakes and a few moose sausage burritos, Scott cranked the motors again, and we were off. The plan was to slowly cruise the coast until we saw something, then try to put the hurt on it.

We weren't even a mile past pulling anchor when Devin spotted a nice bear on the side of a hill. It had just crossed through an avalanche chute and was hightailing it like something had spooked it—probably us seeing that we were only about two hundred yards off the shore. Scott gave me the wheel and told me to keep it off the rocks as Devin and Jesse piled into the skiff. I whipped a U-turn and brought her about and away from the shore as Sam looked for rocks. I cut the throttles about four hundred yards out and was just drifting when we saw the skiff hit the shore. Scott dumped those guys just right of the bear, which set them up pretty good if the bear kept going in the direction last seen. Only thing left to do now was to sit and watch the show, and what a show it turned out to be.

I guess Devin was in a little better shape than Jesse because he had conquered the beach, alders, and swamp brush before Jesse was even off the shoreline. Left with nothing else to do, Jesse tried following Devin's path but was doing a really poor job of it. We all just sat there on the boat sipping on our nice, hot coffees while the show unfolded before our eyes. Those guys chased that bear for more than two hours that day, but never saw hide nor hair of it. Devin had picked up some tracks about halfway up and was doing the Daniel Boone thing trying to track the bear. Jesse was just trying to follow Devin as he busted through the bush like a freight train.

Pretty dang funny we thought as those guys later had to be helped back in the boat. They looked like they had been dragged through a war zone. There wasn't an inch on either of them that wasn't scratched, cut, or both. After a few bottles of Gatorade followed by a couple gallons of water, the story began to emerge—as so did the beers.

In the end, Sam shook his head and looked over at Devin and said, "We told you so! If you're running around in the bush, have fun cuz that's all you're doing!"

Devin and Jesse were completely spent, and as I spotted another bear on the beach just half mile up, the look on those guys' faces told me that this was all mine.

Scott and I jumped in the skiff and took off like a bat out of hell. This guy was moving fast as if he'd already been spooked. We got on step quick and were approaching the bear from the rear when I spotted a good place to put in. Scott whipped the skiff and killed the motor while I jumped at the last minute to shore. I chambered a round and dropped my pack so I could hurry up the beach to a large outcropping of rocks when I spotted the bear in front of me a few hundred yards. It had slowed down now but was still walking, so I needed to close the gap. Problem was, the rest of the beach was flat and open except for the wooded area up high. I would need to either skirt along the beach or go through the woods, but whatever I was going to do, I needed to do it like yesterday!

With the tide being low as it was, if I chose using the beach, the bear was sure to hear or see me. The woods was unfortunately my only choice now. After scaling a small cliff, I was in the timber line, which was littered with bear trails. It was like a superhighway for bears equipped with everything except lights and pull offs. I took a left and headed down a well-traveled path that was now paralleling the bear on the beach. As I scurried along the groomed two-foot-wide path, I couldn't help to think about coming across more traffic in here.

I guess I'd have to deal with that if the time came; however, I needed to stay focused on just the one for now. The trail was awesome, and as I had just about caught up with the bear, I realized that the wind had changed. It was blowing right toward it now, and as I looked back down toward the beach, I watched as the bear had turned and was standing up trying to catch my scent. I dropped to the ground and rolled in some pine needles to mask the scent the best I could. Then looking toward the bear again, he was down on all fours again but had picked up the pace.

Dammit, I thought. Now I'm really going to have to move. I was still out about two hundred yards and now upwind of the bear—not the best scenario. The only thing I could do now was to try and go high in an attempt to mask my scent and redirect it higher. I found a cutoff, and before I knew it was making my way up through the woods. As I crawled and clawed at the terrain, I couldn't help notice all of the holes beneath the maze of spruce trees. This place was a bear condo, and I was smack-dab in the middle of it. I made my way past the tree line and took another left, again skirting the beach, just higher up this time. Unlike the previous trail, this one was not so friendly, and as the sweat poured from my head, I began wondering if this was actually a good idea. I followed the path about another quarter mile and dropped back down through another maze of bear dens and then back down along some rocks on the beach. To my disappointment though, the bear was gone. I looked everywhere I could without dropping down and out on the beach but didn't see anything.

Dammit, I thought. *I missed a good bear.*

All I could think was that he had scented me and took off. I was sweating so bad that the rock I was sitting on was completely soaked. I was just starting to reach in my bag for some water when I saw something black in front of me. To my surprise, standing just yards in front of me was Mr. Bear just moseying along. Somehow I had gotten in front of him and was looking down the wrong side of the beach! My adrenalin went from "oh well" to "holy crap" in like a nanosecond. I could barely contain myself as I slithered my rifle along the top of a rock. Less than fifty yards now, I settled in for what I knew was going to be a close shot. I slowly opened the Leupold covers on the front and back of my scope while getting my footing. With the safety off, I found and put its right shoulder in my crosshairs.

Hold, hold, hold, I thought as he wandered aimlessly down the beach. I needed him to stop but was running out of room pretty quick. I could feel the veins in my head throbbing with every heartbeat as the huge bruin majestically strutted the beach. If I waited too long, I'd be upwind again, so with one last breath, I steadied the crosshairs just in front of his shoulder and let the hell rain down!

Crack! The bear spun around and tried biting at the sting as I sent the second-round downrange!

Bwop! The second round connected with its spine, dropping it dead in its tracks! I loaded another two rounds and made my way off the rocks and down to the beach to claim my prize when the next thing I know, the bear got up and started running toward the woods. Call it instinct or luck, I raised my rifle, looked down the side of the barrel, and with my straight-pull Blaser put two more in him before he could even say ow!

I made my way off the kelp-covered, slippery rocks of the beach and back up to where the bear had fallen only to be surprised again by him still kicking. I backed up while chambering another round, but he was gone. Bears are known for "being alive" well after they're dead, so I took a knee about ten yards out and gave him a little time.

As I wiped the sweat from my brow, I could see the guys on the boat trying to glass me to see what had happened. They were about two miles up the beach, so I would need the skiff. As I walked back over to the bear and gave him a muzzle poke, it was then that I realized how big this guy really was. Lying down next to him, he was about another foot longer than me, which would put him at a little over seven feet. With a beautiful coat and no rub marks, this was a beauty—a true Alaskan beauty! A beauty taken only on the best hunt in Alaska: the Annual!

Another great bear from another great hunt!

If you're reading this, then you must have liked the stories as much as I liked living and writing them. Alaska is an amazing place filled with endless beauty and outdoor adventures. My wish to all who venture here is that their Quest is realized too in this amazing place we call "The Last Frontier."

APPENDIX

To book a hunt/fish/surf trip with Scott Liska on the *Viking*, call 1-(907)-360-2375.
The following are local air services:

1. Alaska Air Cargo
   www.alaskaairlines.com
   1-800-255-2752

2. Raven Air/formerly ERA
   www.ravenair.com
   1-800-866-8394

3. Trailridge Air
   www.trailridgeair.com
   1-907-248-0838

The following are hotels around the area:

1. The Millennium
   www.millenniumhotels.com
   1-907-243-2300

2. Holiday Inn Express
   www.holidayinn.com
   1-907-248-8848

The following are local outfitters:

1. Cabela's
   155 West 104th Ave., Anchorage
   1-907-341-3400

2. Wild West Guns
   7100 Homer Dr.
   1-907-344-4500

3. Mountain View Sports
   3838 Old Seward Hwy.1-907-563-8600

4. Great Northern Guns
   4425 Wright St.
   1-907-563-3006